Shaking Up Speci

Shaking Up Special Education is an easy-to-use instructional guide to the essential things you need to know about working with students with exceptionalities.

Interactive, collaborative, and engaging, this go-to instructional resource is packed with the top instructional moves to maximize learning for all students. Featuring sample activities and instructional resources, chapters cover topics ranging from specially designed instruction, to co-teaching, to technology, to social-emotional learning and self-care.

Designed with special educators in mind, this book is also ideal for any general educator looking to increase student achievement and revitalize their practice. Shake up your teaching and learn how to build a more inclusive classroom!

Savanna Flakes, EdS is an international education consultant working with school communities to provide professional development and coaching to support leaders and teachers with effective instructional practices for students with exceptionalities. Savanna is a National Board Certified Teacher, International Standards of Technology Certified Teacher, and periodically serves as an Adjunct Professor in the American University School of Education and Health.

Shaking Up Special Education

Instructional Moves to Increase Achievement

Savanna Flakes

NEW YORK AND LONDON

First published 2021
by Routledge
52 Vanderbilt Avenue, New York, NY 10017

and by Routledge
2 Park Square, Milton Park, Abingdon, Oxon, OX14 4RN

Routledge is an imprint of the Taylor & Francis Group, an informa business

© 2021 Taylor & Francis

The right of Savanna Flakes to be identified as author of this work has been asserted by her in accordance with sections 77 and 78 of the Copyright, Designs and Patents Act 1988.

All rights reserved. No part of this book may be reprinted or reproduced or utilised in any form or by any electronic, mechanical, or other means, now known or hereafter invented, including photocopying and recording, or in any information storage or retrieval system, without permission in writing from the publishers.

Trademark notice: Product or corporate names may be trademarks or registered trademarks, and are used only for identification and explanation without intent to infringe.

Library of Congress Cataloging-in-Publication Data
A catalog record for this title has been requested

ISBN: 978-0-367-48271-8 (hbk)
ISBN: 978-0-367-47890-2 (pbk)
ISBN: 978-1-003-03894-8 (ebk)

Typeset in Palatino
by KnowledgeWorks Global Ltd.

Contents

Introduction

This book is another must-have resource for every teacher aiming to increase achievement for students with disabilities, and it is also uniquely designed to support special education teachers. The special education teacher burnout rate is high because being a special education teacher is NOT easy. Our students are more beautifully diverse than ever, and as special education teachers, we wear many instructional hats in the course of just one school day (the Case Manager with paperwork and data galore, the Co-teacher balancing reluctance and acceptance, the RTI intervention or resource-room teacher supporting executive functioning skills in Algebra 2, and many more). As an international consultant specializing in special education, inclusion, and social emotional learning, I am honored to take on this challenge of supporting our special education teachers, and ALL teachers, with the top instructional moves to maximize learning for ALL children in our school communities.

In my journey as a teacher, instructional coach, and administrator, I have met many amazing teachers, leaders, and organizations who have imparted wisdom on how to reach all students. If you've imparted wisdom, you will probably see your name somewhere in this book. I've worked hard to connect the best resources, instructional sites, and tools to support our inclusive practices. These resources have been collected in one concise book. I believe in the art of brevity; it's been said that if you truly understand something, you can explain it so a five-year-old can understand it. Chapter 1 is short and sweet, laying the foundation for a successful inclusive classroom to enrich all learners. Chapters 2–7 provide the strategies, best practices, and resources to increase academic achievement and emotional wellness of students with disabilities. The Appendix contains useful templates and instructional guides mentioned throughout the seven chapters, to constitute the finale of the book.

Any teacher (special education or general education) can read one chapter and shake up instruction tomorrow. This book is for teachers, from a teacher. I share research to support big, bold, statements, but it's less about the theoretical and more about the practical of "doing." Throughout these pages, you will find stories, lessons, and best practices that have been used with success. As you read, celebrate the practices and strategies you've already found successful and note something you can add tomorrow. Though one strategy or practice might seem small, if it matches your objective and supports a student, then the strategy is moving students in the right direction.

The practices in this book are optimized when every part of our heart, soul, and mind wholeheartedly believes that every child can be successful, especially the children who believe they are too far behind to catch up or have too many deficits listed in their IEP. Every child has gifts to give and talents to share, so our goal is to provide lots of opportunity for children to share their exceptionalities and grow upon them. Throughout this book I use "students with disabilities," "students with exceptionalities," "diverse learners," and "students with special needs" interchangeably; no matter the title, the student is first, and one thing is for sure: these students are amazing!

Our mindset and philosophy on Inclusive Practices is paramount to accelerating student growth. The instructional strategies interwoven throughout the seven chapters should be shared, discussed, and implemented across the entire school community so we can maximize and accelerate the learning of every single student we are honored to teach.

Teaching, to me, is fun and collaborative, like dancing, and so, like dancing, this book is designed to be interactive, positive, and shared. We all have that one dance that gets us excited. Grab a colleague! Let's move to our classroom dance floors, get our students dancing, and shake things up!

PART ONE

The Introductory Dance Moves

Line dances are easy-to-follow dance moves with a predictable pattern; they allow flexibility for creative innovators, and promote authentic collaboration for the group of dancers. Whether pop or country music or everything in between, line dances are a great way to get *everyone* out on the dance floor. Cotton-Eyed Joe, Chicken Dance, Hokey Pokey, Macarena, the Hustle, the Stroll, the Conga line, and the Hora are just a few of many line dances. These dance moves are paramount to getting the party started. Similarly, as teachers, our goal is for every learner to feel welcome and excited about hopping (and learning) on our dance floor. The instructional practices in Part One are necessary to build an Inclusive Classroom environment where all students can flourish. The starting place is to create a dance floor where every child feels a sense of belonging and is engaged in the learning process. Every child wants to be a part of inclusive and equitable classrooms.

Hooks to Guide Part One:

1. What concrete steps can I take to make sure ALL of my students feel welcome, included, and engaged in my classroom?
2. If I co-teach, how can my co-teacher and I co-plan instruction to ensure that every student has a voice and feels successful before our class time ends?

1

Bunny Hop

The Inclusive and Equity-Based Classroom

Everyone can participate in the Bunny Hop.

Given a dance floor, a groovy beat, and a willing leader, everyone can engage in a line dance like the Bunny Hop. The Bunny Hop is known as a social mixer dance, where people join in, hop up and down (like a bunny), and follow behind a leader as they frolic around the dance floor. There are many adaptations to and variations of the Bunny Hop, with lots of flexibility in the line dance. I don't know about you, but I've never seen someone chastised for taking a wrong step to the side or hopping off cue. For example, there's no mandate that you must touch the person in front of you; some folks prefer to join the line and leave space in front of them. If you use a wheelchair, there's always room to join the line: you choose where you want to fit in and groove, and everyone makes space. There are no assigned spots, and the unwritten/written rule is that everyone accepts everyone for what they bring to the line dance. If you are tired or get bored, just exit stage left. If you want to rejoin, more than likely the line will still be going, so pop back into it. No fuss, no muss ... a dance with no pressure and just fun.

Like the beginning of the Bunny Hop, where the leader enthusiastically smiles and invites others to join, the leader of a welcoming classroom creates an atmosphere of belonging, inviting and engaging every student to be a part of the learning experiences. The classroom is flexible, everyone feels welcome, and everyone has choices on how to navigate their learning experiences. Just as the Bunny Hop has many adaptations, allowing for various gifts of dance fever, our accommodating classroom is based on the philosophy that everyone has "something to learn, and something to contribute" to the community. This chapter outlines the instructional moves to create an equitable, inclusive, and engaging learning environment for ALL students, a classroom where every student is excited to join our dance floor.

Equity and *Inclusion* are the leaders in creating a positive dance floor in our classroom for every learner. These two mindsets complement and lead effective instructional practices for diverse and exceptional learners. These two leaders guide our thought processes on ensuring that ALL students feel welcome and get what they need, understanding that fair is not always equal, and that "good teaching" isn't every student getting the same exact thing in the same exact way. Sometimes I hear the phrase, "We are doing Inclusion." Unlike a grocery store checklist, it is nearly impossible "to *do*" inclusion. Inclusion isn't a verb. It is a mindset, an ideology, a belief, that all students can have their needs met inside our general education classroom. Equity joins inclusion as a leader in our line dance to ensure that our belief is followed with and demonstrated by our actions so every student gets access to resources and rigor at their right time.

An equitable and inclusive learning environment requires educators to strive to set high expectations for and to challenge students to reach beyond their potential. Though I long for the day when we don't say "general education classroom" or "special education classroom," and instead just say "classroom," an inclusive and equitable mindset in our general education classrooms is the first step in increasing students with disabilities' achievement. Let's move into the key dance steps of our line dance in a sequential pattern that we can all follow. As always, feel adventurous about adding some creativity along the way. After all, spontaneity makes the Bunny Hop even more spectacular for everyone involved.

Equity-Based Learning Environments

An equity-based classroom centers on relationships. As James Comer, 2015 reminds us, "no significant learning can occur without a significant relationship." Take a walk down memory lane: Who was your favorite teacher? Why was this teacher your favorite? What types of experiences did you have with this teacher? How did this teacher affect your life or experiences in education? No doubt your favorite teacher made you feel special, like they were your champion. Every student needs at least one champion in their school community. The more champions, the better, of course! Can our most reluctant learner name at least one person in their school community that they can check in with to help them refocus, feel good, and connect with?

Have you seen the viral video of Mr. Barry White, Jr., enthusiastically welcoming each one of his fifth-grade students into their classroom? Students excitedly dance their way into the classroom using a special, personalized greeting that they individually created with this teacher. This special welcome occurs before students start the "academics," and you can tell it makes a huge impact on each of the students. If you haven't had a chance to watch this minute of pure happiness, google, "Teacher creates personalized handshakes for all his students on Good Morning America." You could literally spend 30 minutes as a school team annotating and answering the question: "What do you notice from this one-minute clip?" What I find astounding is this: Mr. White provided time for each student to create their unique handshake, devoted valuable time to building this routine, and committed to memory each student's preferred special greeting into the classroom. Simultaneously, Mr. White has provided a way for students to check in, reset, and transition. Can you imagine what this simple relationship-building strategy does each morning for the student who may have had a terrible morning, or struggled just to show up? No doubt: that student instantly feels valued and seen.

No, we do not have to create a special dance with each student (though dance does connect us), but we do need to intentionally build relationships and create a supportive learning environment. In her TED talk, Rita Pierson (2013) reminds us that "[k]ids don't learn from people they don't like." Our students are intuitive: based on the amount of investment we incorporate into our daily schedule to build real relationships and a positive learning community, students determine if they like us enough to trust us enough to try hard academic stuff, even if they might fail at it the first few times. It is our privilege to show our students that no matter how they feel, we value them and believe that they can exceed their potential.

An equity-based teacher understands that successful classrooms focus on relationships *first* to create higher learning outcomes. Neuroscience tells us the brain feels safest and relaxed when we are connected to others whom we trust to treat us well. The brain responds to this sense of connection by secreting oxytocin, known as the bonding hormone. Oxytocin makes us want to build a trusting relationship with the other person we're interacting with. Trust frees up the brain for other activities such a creativity, learning, and higher-order thinking. Thus, because there is trust, the teacher can provide a degree of push or challenge without having the student experience an amydgala hijack and either withdraw or become defensive.

However … Neuroscience reminds us that trust and fear are inversely related. When the brain perceives a potential threat, based on past experience or perceived failure (without a relationship), the amygdala goes into action and hijacks the brain's other systems, throwing the body into defensive fight, flight, or freeze mode. Fear activates the amygdala and the release of cortisol. Cortisol can stop all learning for about 20 minutes and can stay in the body for up to 3 hours. Trust can deactivate the amygdala and block the release of cortisol. Building relationships supports connectivity and increases trust. Some students come to school to learn, others to be loved. Love first, and then we can teach. The following are concrete and practical strategies to build positive relationships with students:

1. Catch students doing it right more than you catch the wrong. Track the number of times that you provide a struggling student with authentic, specific, positive praise. Study after study confirms that positive reinforcement is more effective than punishment. Aim for a 3:1 ratio—three positive reinforces for every redirection or fix-up you provide a student. For many students, punishment creates resentment rather than reflection, so reverse the paradigm and provide attention for those college- and career-like behaviors we are excited to see. Try a tally sheet on a clipboard or an app like "Thing Counter," a free tool to count clicks for the times you provide positive reinforcement (like a tally counter).
2. Unconditional Positive Regard (UPR). Celebrate and get to know each student as a "human," and acknowledge them beyond academics. Ask a student their favorite color, hobby, team, food, etc., and capitalize on that interest in the classroom. Try Dr. Ross Greene (2016) "10 × 2" strategy: for 10 days, 2 minutes at a time, seek out the student and get to know them personally beyond school. Ask questions about their interest and likes.
3. Watch Your Language. The language we use creates the reality we experience. If we say things like I teach a "difficult child, an autistic child, or badly behaved child," consider rephrasing "a child with difficulties, a child with autism, a child who is misbehaving." Our language can build up a relationship or tear it down. Though bad behaviors may be learned, good behaviors can be taught. Move beyond labels and search for the child beneath. What are the child's behaviors telling us about their unmet needs for safety and connection? Change your language.
4. Connect before Content. Like dance, stories connect us. Stories make us human and are a cultural mainstay in many countries, especially Africa and Asia. Further, brain

imaging scans show that the brain of the listener can sync with the storyteller's actions when listening to a story. Tell a story about yourself as a student, your challenges, and the strategies you used to overcome obstacles. Students will see you as a human and a relatable role model for overcoming obstacles.

5. High Support-High Challenge. If you see stress-reactive behaviors, check to see if students are outside of their proximal zone of development, and either lower complexity, offer more scaffolding, or provide more structure.
6. Create Weekly Thank-You Stickers. Write a note of appreciation on a sticky note and sneakily drop it off at a student's desk as you walk by.
7. Play "Compliment Hot Seat." Invite one student up to sit in the "hot seat," and invite the whole class to write on stickies and post on the board all of the wonderful attributes of this student. The student will always spin around, read their classmates' posts, and smile superwide (or they may smile with their eyes).
8. Google and watch Ryan Speedo Green's story and reflect on his school and life trajectory. Discuss the impact of a strong teacher relationship and implications in your school with your students.

> One teacher will come to school to teach math, and one teacher will come to school to teach children. The latter teacher will have the most fun and success.

We are relationship builders. You could say that this requirement is hidden in the job description of a teacher, and not always explicitly stated. If you want high academic outcomes, strong relationships with students, parents, and community are paramount. One teacher will come to school to teach math, and one teacher will come to school to teach children. The latter will have the most fun and success. Try employing one of these eight strategies consistently, and you'll be able to build authentic relationships with your students and your classroom community will flourish.

Inclusive Practices Engage all Students

No matter how much you attempt to fight jumping into the bunny-hop line dance, as Gloria Estefan says, "The rhythm is gonna get you." In a supportive, inclusive community, all students are excited: they feel like they are valued members of a welcoming and responsive learning community. There are two big components to building an inclusive classroom community.

The first is facilitating a classroom that understands and values differentiation: "Different students are going to receive different things based on their different needs." Suppose one child is choking and needs the Heimlich maneuver. It wouldn't make sense to give every child the Heimlich maneuver, right? This is the case with differentiation. Equity means every student gets what they need to be successful and inclusion means we all have something to contribute. Students generally understand this concept of differentiation (especially after dramatizing and modeling this example of one student choking and in need of the Heimlich). Teachers are usually the ones who struggle with this idea, not the students. An essential part of differentiated instruction is helping students learn about their brains and how to foster a growth mindset when it applies to academics. We want students to internalize that at times we understand various concepts well, some skills may come easier to us, and other times we may need some more support that will look different from what other classmates get — and that is OK.

Carol Dweck, a leading researcher in the field of motivation, has shared two groups of mindsets: people with a "growth mindset" and those persons with a "fixed mindset." Those who embrace the growth mindset usually reach ever-higher levels of achievement and have a greater sense of free will, whereas those holding the fixed mindset plateau early and achieve less than their full potential. Those who hold true to the growth mindset believe intelligence is malleable, which leads to a desire to "learn from mistakes" instead of "looking smart," and a tendency to embrace challenges, use effective effort strategies, and persist in the face of obstacles. In contrast, those stuck in the fixed mindset usually avoid challenges, give up easily when facing an obstacle, and see effort as fruitless and ignore useful feedback. It's possible to have bits of both mindsets in various areas (a mixed mindset) but commit to a journey to develop growth mindset when facing obstacles, learning from mistakes, and persisting when something gets tough. However, research has shown that when children — particularly minority students, students with disabilities, and females in STEM-related fields — embrace a growth mindset they tend to excel at higher rates. The good news is that educators can teach students how to develop and utilize a growth mindset: there are four critical steps that teachers can use to support students in developing a growth mindset.

Step 1: Talk to students about their brains and the difference between growth mindset and fixed mindset.

Share with students that we all learn differently. We all have a variety of talents and areas for improvement. Create a visual poster with students on the various intelligences (musical, interpersonal, logical, naturalistic, etc.) and be sure to vary instructional approaches to incorporate various learning modalities for student success. Facilitate discussions with students to share that our brains are like a muscle that gets stronger and works better the more it is exercised. Every time you work hard, stretch yourself and learn something new, your brain forms new connections, and over time you become smarter. Class Dojo (a free, digital positive behavior system) has a series of free videos that can guide classroom discussions on growth vs. gixed mindset. Watch Mojo, a lead character, develop an understanding that intelligence is malleable and with effort he can succeed and learn concepts that are complex.

Step 2: Use specific praise focused on student behavior and effort (see Table 1.1). Utilize praise to reinforce your belief that students can achieve at high levels through hard work and effort. Focus on highlighting student effort throughout a task, not only the final product.

Step 3: Explicitly teach "effort" and what effective effort looks and sounds like for each task. The word *effort* can be quite ambiguous to students, and effort can also be ineffective (ineffective effort). Have you ever had a student say, "I tried,"

TABLE 1.1 Growth vs Fixed Mindset

Say This *Praise the effective effort a student exhibits during a task*	*Not That* *Avoid statements that suggest a student is "smart"*
I like the way you tried all kinds of strategies on that math problem until you finally got it.	Wow, you did great on that math problem — you're smart!
It was a long, hard assignment, but you stuck with it and finished it. That's great!	See, I told you that would be easy — you're smart!
For the student who gets an A without trying: "All right, that was too easy for you. Let's do something more challenging that you can learn from."	Nice job, you got an A without even trying.
For the student who works hard and doesn't do well: "I liked the effort you put in. Let's work together some more and figure out what you don't understand."	Some people are just not good at math — don't worry about it.
For the student who shuts down: "Looks like you're stuck. what strategies and resources did you use? Let's evaluate your process so we can reach your goal."	Try again, you'll get it.

when they still failed horribly at the task? Well, they may not be using "effective" effort. As teachers, we need to quantify what effective effort looks like for many learners. Specifically, two questions can support us in teaching students what effective effort is: What does effective effort look and sound like for this academic or social task? How will I know if I have employed effective strategies for this task (e.g., solving a math problem or decoding an unknown word)?

Figures 1.1 and 1.2 are examples of explicitly teaching effort. These effort checklists were created in the form of a sleekly designed bookmark. The creation of this student tool is strategic: bookmarks are easy to slip into a book or binder, or to pull out to self-monitor, and most children find them cool. I created these effort bookmarks for a sixth-grader whom I worked with in math. After assigning a challenging task, my brilliant student

EFFORT CHECKLIST

Effort Checklist	Self √	Teacher √
I read all of the directions.		
I reviewed my notes and steps before asking for help.		
I reached out and asked for help from a peer before raising my hand.		
I used alternative strategies.		
I used feedback. during my work?		
Did I push myself to continue working on the task when it got hard?		

FIGURE 1.1 Effort Checklist with Teacher Check-in

EFFORT CHECKLIST

Effort Checklist	√
Did I read all of the directions?	
Did I review my notes and steps before asking for help?	
Did I reach out and ask for help from a peer before raising my hand?	
Did I use alternative strategies or solutions to solve the problem?	
Did I get and use feedback during my work?	
Did I push myself to continue working on the task when it got hard?	

FIGURE 1.2 Effort Checklist without Teacher Check-in

with autism would quickly yell, "I tried, I can't do this, I give up." As teachers, those three words — "I give up" — never lose their sting. I knew, before addressing effective effort for problem-solving, that we had to quantify what effective "trying" looks and feels like. My goal was to help my student understand that the word "trying" entails a lot more than just saying the words, "Well, I tried." Everyone has different definitions of the words *try*, *study*, and *effort*. So, the student and I worked together to create a list of action steps on what trying and using effective effort to be successful looks like. The first bookmark was an opportunity for us both to monitor progress and talk about it, and then eventually, the student used the second bookmark to self-monitor. Within months, the student internalized the steps of trying before giving up and yelling, "I can't do this." Ultimately, the student no longer needed a bookmark and actually "tried" before giving up.

Step 4: Celebrate mistakes and the complexity of the learning process. The more we show students that learning involves mistakes and that errors are a natural part of learning something new, the more students will be willing to take risks, try harder tasks, and persist with challenges. If you have a class of students that hate being wrong, there's work to be done. I love when teachers celebrate "successful failures" on classroom bulletin boards, showcasing students who have learned something from their learning process, because that process is truly what makes a person successful. In these classrooms, students are proud of making and sharing their mistakes and working hard to fix them. "If it comes easy, it wasn't worth it," is the motto students with a growth mindset possess. The Teaching Channel has a lot of great videos on supporting students with a growth mindset. One of my favorite instructional videos on the growth mindset is entitled, "My Favorite No." In this instructional video, the teacher, Ms. Noonan, uses a warm-up routine entitled "My Favorite No" to acknowledge and build a classroom mindset that mistakes are a part of learning and growth and we need to share them so we all can get better. She collects the students' index cards, rewrites her favorite wrong answer, and has the class discusses the great work observed and how to fix the error. She uses this data to adjust instruction right in the moment.

The second component of an inclusive classroom is an effective teacher who proactively and intentionally cultivates community with and among students. Inclusion is more than just a seat in the classroom. Equitable teachers design an inclusive classroom environment that engages all students and invites all students to share their strengths and build knowledge together. A hallmark of inclusive classrooms is that a student with a disability is not always the one being taught how to do something; these students also get to teach others something. This means that, as teachers, we must deliberately plan to ensure that all students have a voice and can contribute to the learning community. *Every child can contribute.* Meaningful collaborative learning structures can support each student in bringing something to the table. Collaborative learning opportunities can teach students to be proactive learners, increase academic discourse and learning, and simultaneously provide opportunities to build a positive classroom community.

The *right* collaborative activity can invite and engage all students. Collaborative structures support teachers in providing time, space, and structures for positive interactions between students. When planned effectively, cooperative learning can encourage acts of kindness, compassion, and team building. Effective collaborative structures promote the use of positive gambits to support students in consistently coaching, encouraging, and praising each other. A few guiding questions help when we plan lessons: Is every member valuable and necessary for group success? Does each student have the opportunity to contribute their voice and knowledge? Are all students actively engaged and involved: listening, responding, or coaching? Are students working toward a team consensus, in which every member agrees with the team result?

Let's hop right to a few instructional moves to foster an inclusive learning community.

1. Stir up the Class (Kagan Cooperative Learning Strategy)

Students stand in groups of four. Assign each group member a number. Teacher poses a question. Students form a huddle and discuss their answer. When ready to share, they unhuddle. When all groups are done, call a number and ask students with that number to rotate to a new group. The group huddles again, and the new member shares the idea from the previous group. If they like the new member's ideas, they give him/her a pat on the back to show appreciation. Then students unhuddle and wait for the next question.

Ideas for Differentiation

Have students stand in groups of three for classes with a lower number of students. Provide explicit modeling of expected participation. Provide scribe/read-aloud accommodations as needed. Preset any assistive technology devices that students access with relevant answers to the topics of discussion. Be sure groups understand the "new idea" shared by the new group member when they rotate. Hand out labeled sticky notes of the group's number for a built-in support.

2. Bounce Cards

If your students struggle to get conversations started and maintain healthy communication pragmatics, try a "Total Participation Technique" called bounce cards. Bounce cards give students a purposeful way to contribute to and build a cooperative learning classroom environment.

Making it work:

Select a student with whom to practice modeling a conversation for the class to observe. Practice with that student before modeling this with the class. Model the appropriate and inappropriate ways to hold a conversation. For example, demonstrate a conversation that ends quickly once both parties have shared their response, with no back-and-forth dialogue between the two parties. Discuss the importance of conversation skills that allow ideas to "bounce" from one person to the next.

Discuss the following three approaches to responding to a peer's comments:

Bounce: Students take what their peers say and bounce an idea off it (extend the idea).
Sum it up: Students rephrase what their peers say and comment on certain parts.
Inquire: Students ask a question regarding what their peers say.

Let's go into a little more detail with some examples.

Bounce: Take what your classmate(s) said and bounce an idea off it. For example, you can start your sentences with …

"That reminds me of ..."
"I agree, because ..."
"True. Another example is when ..."
"That's a great point ..."

Sum it up: Rephrase what was just said in a shorter version. For example, you can start your sentences with ...

"I hear you saying that ..."
"So, if I understand you correctly ..."
"I like how you said ..."

Inquire: Understand what your classmates mean by asking them questions. For example, you can start your questions with ...

"Can you tell me more about that?"
"I'm not sure I understand ..."
"I see your point, but what about ..."
"Have you thought about ..."

3. Communication Gloves

Dig out those old pairs of garden gloves and put them to use in your classroom! Work gloves are the best type for this activity, but winter gloves will also suffice. This strategy is adapted from Mandy Neal (2012) conferencing gloves. On the fingers of a glove, write sentence starters for asking/responding to peers, such as "I agree with that because ...", "I agree and I want to add ...", and "What do you mean by that?" The goal is to provide supports for students who may need it to successfully contribute to a peer discussion.

Differentiate this strategy by:

- using questions only
- incorporating vocabulary by writing one or two target words on the palm for the child to use
- utilizing higher-order thinking such as "I can conclude that ..." or "I know that because ..."

They can also be content-specific, such as reading discussion gloves (retelling or summarizing a story) or math problem-solving gloves. By putting on gloves, students have an instant choice of the conversation they want to lead.

4. AEIOU

Being an equitable and inclusive teacher means that we anticipate barriers to learning and proactively plan to engage each learner, because every child can contribute. Every child has something to contribute to our classroom community. I often say we presume competence before incompetence, and this philosophy is more than just saying, "I believe every child can learn." This philosophy intentionally lives in our instructional planning and delivery of instruction. The AEIOU strategy is based on work from Discovery Education to support effective discussion on digital media that we share with students. AEIOU is a protocol in which students watch a video, observe a picture, or listen to an audio and collaborate as a team around their AEIOU:

A - Adjective List a word or two that describes something you saw or learned.
E - Emotion Describe how a specific part of the media made you feel.
I - Interesting Jot down something you found interesting about the content/topic.
O - Oh Describe something that made you say "Wow!"
U - Um Write a question about something you learned or want to learn more about.

Every learner can share their AEIOU after they engage with media. Students don't have to have a great deal of prerequisite background knowledge or be on grade level to participate and learn from each other. Most importantly, every student can enter this learning experience with success and something to contribute in discussion with peers. Students will work together and authentically build knowledge together and we can fill in gaps.

Ideas for Differentiation

Cue up a student's assistive technology device with key words for the media you will show. Add an anchor chart with examplars for criteria of success or a guided organizer as necessary. Lastly, allow students the opportunity to visually display thoughts for AEIOU by drawing any of the components.

5. List-Group-Label

List-group-label is a form of semantic mapping that aids in reading comprehension and vocabulary retention. Students can improve their vocabulary and categorization skills by categorizing listed words. Through grouping and labeling, students organize new concepts in relation to previously learned concepts.

Procedure:

1. Select a main concept in an upcoming reading selection.
2. List: Have students brainstorm all the words they think relate to the topic and visually display student responses on a board. Option—have students type their words into a shared googledoc.
3. Group: Divide the class into small heterogenous groups. Each group will work to cluster the class list of words into subcategories.
4. Label: Invite students to suggest a title or label for the groups of words they have formed. These labels should relate to their reasoning for the grouping. Provide strategic questioning to prompt removal of words and appropriate labels.

Ideas for Differentiation

Even though some students may call out words that may not reflect the main concept, through strategic teacher questioning and as students group the words in teams, groups will naturally eliminate words. As groups of words emerge, challenge and question students to explain their reasoning for placing words together or discarding them.

In Closing

Everyone gets excited when the Bunny Hop begins, everyone is included, and everyone can add their own variations, which makes the line even more fascinating to be a part of and watch! Ensuring that we have an equitable, inclusive, and positive learning community is important to laying the foundation for differentiated instruction and higher-order thinking instructional moves. If students feel invested and comfortable in a safe learning community, they will take more learning risks, which leads to discussion on higher-level content, and ultimately, higher academic achievement for our students with disabilities. Are your students excited to join your dance floor?

Top 7 Dance Moves

Which of these dance moves can you try tomorrow? Which moves can you share with your team?

1. Commit to adding one new relationship-building strategy. Collect data to track effectiveness.
2. Create an "Equity" afterschool book club. Use Zaretta Hammond (2015) book, *Culturally Responsive Teaching and the Brain*. Every chapter is amazing, but my favorite chapter to dive into is "Chapter 4: Preparing to Be a Culturally Responsive Practitioner."
3. Work with students to understand what a growth mindset is and how it can help them in life.

   Visit the free website Mindsetkit.org to provide students with a quick growth mindset self-assessment. Based on the data, pick one lesson to start the mindset journey.

   Research and the neuroscience behind
4. Make the idea of a "growth mindset" real and concrete for students. Practical steps:
   a. Watch or read Steve Jobs's Standford commencement speechfrom June 12, 2005. Discuss with students the role mindset played in Jobs's success.
   b. Watch videos of successful failures, effort, and persistence despite obstacles, such as Sesame Street's Elmo, Michael Jordan, Keanu Reeves, Bill Gates, Tyler Perry, Oprah, Lizzo, etc. (Google "successful failures" to find dozens of people in history who succeeded due to learning from their failures).

c. Analyze clips of motivational speech excerpts from the movie "The Pursuit of Happyness: (2006). For example, Will Smith and his son are playing basketball on the basketball court, and in an emotional monologue, Will Smith tells his son not to let anyone tell him he can't do something, "Protect your dream."

d. Bring former students into the classroom and interview them. Invite the students to talk about themselves as learners and the strategies they've used to be successful.

5. Form a "Mindset" collaborative learning team and subscribe to The Teaching Channel. Visit the Growth Mindset series on the Teaching Channel, which is full of articles and videos about building a growth mindset (https://learn.teachingchannel.com/growth-mindset/begin). Choose one article or video each week to begin, refine, or extend your journey on growth mindset. As a team, discuss and analyze instructional practices and goals for implementation.
6. Choose one collaborative activity to try tomorrow, or let students choose which cooperative learning structures they want to use to make meaning of content together. Differentiate instruction as necessary to support all learners.
7. Develop a staff development professional learning series on "Cooperative Learning/Student Collaboration." Introduce one collaborative activity at each monthly staff meeting.The Kagan Cooperative Learning book by Dr. Spencer Kagan and Miguel Kagan is full of ways to include every learner in teamwork structures (every student can benefit—specifically students with disabilities and English-language learners).

List your next dance steps for creating and enhancing your equitable and inclusive learning environment.

____

____

____

____

____

Accountability Partner: ____

____

Check-in Date: ____

Keep calm and hop on with equitable and inclusive practices

2

Cha Cha

Effective Collaborative and Co-Teaching Practices

Dance. Business. Marriage. Sports. You pick your co-teaching analogy ... there are many. Of course, true to the style of this book, I use the dance analogy—specifically, the "dance partnership" analogy—for co-teaching. The Cha Cha, originating in Cuba, is a dance has inspired many variations across the world. The dance has stood the test of time and has been the dominant Latin America pop rhythm for nearly 50 years. The Cha Cha dance, much like co-teaching, is characterized by intricate and intentional movements and quick spins. Co-teaching is a series of intricate and intentional movements, ongoing decisions, and actions that two teachers make to differentiate instruction based on diverse students' needs. The goal of this chapter is for us, as a co-teaching team, to consider, how we can "**R.E.V.** up: **R**evolutionize co-planning time, **E**lectrify the co-teaching models, and **V**ary co-assessment practices (see figure 2.1)." When we R.E.V. up our co-teaching practices, not only will we enhance student outcomes for our students with disabilities, but all students will benefit.

Co-teaching is often characterized as a "dance partnership" between a General Education teacher and a learning specialist (Special Education teacher, English Language teacher, and/or

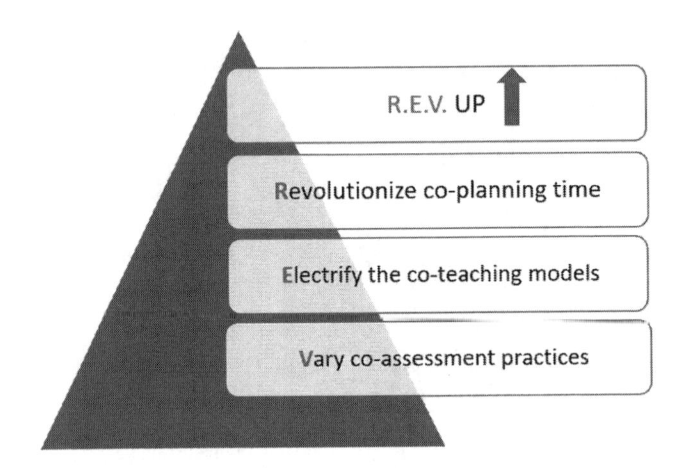

FIGURE 2.1 R.E.V. UP Co-teaching

related service provider). Co-teaching implemented with fidelity has a profound impact on a range of learners with and without disabilities from a variety of cultures (Dieker & Hines, 2013; Friend, 2013;). *Co-teaching* is "two or more educators simultaneously engaging a diverse group of students in the same space." Co-teaching involves maximizing each teacher's specialized role in the co-teaching team for planning, instruction, and evaluation for a classroom of diverse and exceptional students. Maybe this will be your first year closely collaborating with another teacher, or perhaps you have been co-teaching for 15 years … in both opportunities, our goal is to **R.E.V.** up our co-teaching practices for the benefit of our students. Perhaps you and your co-teacher are a love match, where you were able to choose to work together because you love your co-worker's teaching style. Or, more than likely, you are an in an arranged marriage or marriage of convenience: based on the schedule, we have 50 students with disabilities, blank number of General Education teachers, and this many Special Education teachers, so you two need to work together. Despite how your match was created, you both are responsible for the outcomes of ALL the students you teach in your co-taught classroom. The process of **REV**ving up your co-teaching all begins with a deep commitment to collaboration.

Commitment to Collaboration

Co-teaching is a complex art and science. It is much more than sticking two awesome teachers in a class together. If you're not excited about co-teaching, the students won't be excited about it either. The best place to start is to identify the benefits of co-teaching. The top five benefits that co-teachers report to me are: aligns with philosophy of Inclusive Practices; increases instructional opportunities for all students; two problem solvers are better than one to differentiate curriculum; fosters a cohesive and supportive environment; and expands professional expertise on instruction in the moment. Commitment to collaboration begins with an intentional understanding of what it takes to form a high-functioning team. In 1965, Bruce Tuckman, a psychological researcher, created the four stage *Forming, Storming, Norming, Performing* model. Later, in the 1970s, he added a fifth stage, *Adjourning*. The four-stage developmental process can support us, as educators, in understanding that great teams aren't formed overnight. The model can also help us understand the journey a new team will take to become a high-performing team producing high-quality results. The process begins with *forming*: valuing and reserving time in the day to intentionally invest in building a professional relationship with your team members (in this case, our co-teacher). Stage 2 is *storming:* though initially perceived as negative, storming is essential to team growth, feeling comfortable with challenging one another, ripping off instructionally sore Band-aids based on the class data (e.g., we've been teaching photosynthesis for two days and eight of our students still have no idea what it is; what will we do differently tomorrow?). It includes having honest conversations based on classroom engagement and student data to push each other to change instruction for the benefit of our diverse learners. After forming our team, feel comfortable to storm, and norming as a partnership, we eventually (drum roll, please) … start to become a high-performing team. This process takes time. It takes an investment in the co-teaching partnership to trust and learn each other's steps, with a commitment to make your partnership the best cha-cha dance ever. I've worked with teams that can "storm" and have honest conversations after one month of working together; for other teams, it may take a little longer to "form" and uproot years of same ol' instruction. One of the most dangerous statements in education is, "That's how I've always done it." Toss that statement out and rebuild together the lesson plans you didn't co-create. It's a good idea to perform regular maintenance checks using the four stages. Ask questions like, "Have we built a relationship of trust?", "Have we spent too much time in forming and it's January?", or, "Has our 'storm' gone on too long and we haven't actually changed to accommodate our exceptional learners?"

We know that it is important to build relationships and set expectations for our students at the beginning of the school year (see Chapter 1). Why would it be less important to build relationships with our co-teachers, who we will be sharing a classroom of students with? It is equally important to build relationships and set expectations between co-teachers. Co-teachers need to establish and maintain shared responsibility for efficiency, learning, and student success at the beginning of the co-teaching partnership. Whether you are working with a new co-teaching partner(s) or returning to an established partnership, dedicate time at the beginning of the year (before you both step into the classroom to teach) to discuss a shared philosophy or belief system around student achievement, pedagogy, and class climate. The foundation of successful co-planning includes time for professionals to discuss how their individual philosophies/beliefs about students, pedagogy, and classroom climate are aligned. It is essential that co-teaching teams have time to discuss these philopsophies and beliefs (Friend, 2013). Our initial conversation should cover our comforts, fears, roles, and responsibilities, including:

- Instructional strengths as a teacher, areas of growth.
- Fears around co-teaching/students with IEPs?
- Hopes for our co-teaching classroom.

- How will we evaluate success?
- What are our expectations of each other for …
  - when attendance is taken?
  - the grading of assessments and/or assignments?
  - when students are doing independent work in the classroom?
  - parent/home contact (for discipline, for praise, for concerns) for students with disabilities and students without?
  - positive discipline class-wide approaches?
  - when a student asks the same question of both teachers because they didn't like the first teacher's answer?
  - when one teacher has a substitute?

As a co-teaching team, have we shared our comforts, fears, expectations, and roles/responsibilities for our co-taught classroom?
Good News: It is not too late!

Your answers can be used to start a conversation about how you will work as a team to meet the needs of *all* your students.

One of the high-leverage practices for the special education teaching field is "effective collaboration," a set of skills for collaborating with key stakeholders to achieve student success. As special education teachers, we may have to take the lead in organizing this co-planning meeting to discuss comforts, fears, roles, and responsibilities (the CEEDAR Center and Council of Exceptional Children developed a book that outlines high-leverage practices for special education teachers: *High Leverage Practices for Special Education Teachers*, 2017).

To make the "forming" component of co-planning fun and interactive, one of my former colleagues, Haley Guglielmi, and I created a co-teaching choice board for new teams and returning co-teaching teams to use as conversation stems to structure these important conversation points for co-teachers (see figure 2.2). This choice board will support structured conversations around the essential elements in effective co-taught classrooms and provide conversation stems to start honest conversations (the Co-teaching Choice Boards are in Appendix). Your answers

"Starting" Conversations
Choice Board

Directions: With your partner, select *three* squares that would make a *tic-tac-toe* win. Next, take one minute to independently jot down your thoughts to the statements in your selected boxes. Last, take turns discussing your answers as a team.

Describe a homework policy that you've seen that is effective *Create an image that illustrates your thinking*	Take Turns: Each person take turns listing responsibilities you'd like to have in your classroom *Brainstorm your list independently. Then, each partner takes a turn sharing one item from their list*	Each person share what your philosophy is on "classroom discipline" *Take one minute each to share your philosophy. Then, create a list of three positively stated rules you both agree on*
If I was fly on the wall in your classroom, which statement would best describe what I'd usually see and hear: a.) **On task quiet:** students sitting in rows completing independent work b.) **On task noise:** students working in cooperative groupings *Explain the benefits to each type of learning*	Think of successful strategies you've witnessed for meaningfully including a student with a disability in the general education classroom *List at least two strategies and brainstorm how you can incorporate these into your classroom*	Pick the statement that best describes the type of cooperative learning seen most often in your class. a) A doubles tennis game – two players working together b) A basketball game – multiple players each with a specific role c) Three-legged race – two people working together to accomplish a common goal *Cocreate a jingle/rap/poem that incorporates your belief on cooperative learning*
Describe what your typical test/quiz looks like *Take one minute to share. Then brainstorm the answer to the following question:* *If tomorrow, paper and pencil tests were eliminated – how would you assess student learning?*	What are your strengths as an educator? *Take turns listing adjectives that describe you. Then, pick a color that best describes your teaching style and explain why you chose the color*	Using the Playdoh create a sculpture that describes an area of challenge or a pet peeve *Discuss how have you overcome this in the classroom?*

FIGURE 2.2 Co-teaching Conversation Choice Boards

can be used to start a conversation about how you will work as a team to meet the needs of all your students. As a team, choose three boxes to complete for a tic-tac-toe *win* horizontally, vertically, or diagonally. Take turns answering the questions and agree on compromises. If initially co-teachers find their beliefs are not aligned, successful teams talk it out, compromise, and plan to align their beliefs about pedagogy in order to benefit all students. Note: Chapter 4 has examples of instructional choice boards for students.

After these beginning conversations, teachers are ready to **R.E.V.** up their co-teaching practices.

R. Revolutionize Co-planning Time

Has this ever happened to you? Both co-teachers come to the planning meeting and say, "So what are we going to do tomorrow?" Month after month of approaching co-planning in this way will eventually frustrate both co-teachers, for a variety of reasons. The first is that our planning time is often limited during PLCS or creatively scheduled before or after school, and so getting one-a-day fixes only occasionally will leave us at the end of the unit stumped because a third of our class is behind in meeting the unit objective. The second is that this one-a-day approach does not utilize the unique and divergent lenses of each instructional expert in the co-teaching relationship. Not utilizing the unique lenses and strengths of each educator could result in thirds: 1/3 of our students got it, 1/3 of our students didn't get it, and 1/3 of our students knew it already. We've wasted our time and two-thirds of our students' time for that one day. The whole purpose of co-teaching is to bring two distinct educators together who will look at teaching and learning uniquely to meet a unique class set of needs.

Revolutionize your co-planning time by utilizing each other's strengths and roles of instructional expertise to differentiate instruction (see Table 2.1). Both co-teachers should view instruction and teaching through a different lens, so the goal of co-teaching is to utilize each unique educator's specialized toolkit. To facilitate effective co-planning meetings, each educator should capitalize on their area of expertise. Table 2.1 shows how each co-teaching role enhances content and provides access to rigorous instruction. These roles are not mutually exclusive; often the Learning Specialist may have some content knowledge if they've taught the same subject, and the Content

TABLE 2.1 Maximizing Each Role of Expertise Done

Learning Specialist	*Content Expert*	*Result*
Specially designed instruction (SDI)	Curriculum sequence	We are co-teaching!
Adaptation/ Modification (IEP, WIDA, etc.)	Curriculum depth (Nice to Know vs. Need to Know)	Enhanced content Access to rigorous instruction
Language acquisition	Vertical alignment (connecting concepts below and above respective grade)	Support for ALL students
Social skills/Executive functioning	Curriculum pacing	
Differentiation Guru	Rigor Investigator	
Reading Development Strategist	Relevance Finder	
Motivation and behavior strategies	Motivation and behavior strategies	
Data collection	Data collection	
Brain/Processing breaks	Brain/Processing breaks	

Expert is able to differentiate instruction for diverse learners. However, for planning purposes, if both educators come to the planning session with a specialized focus, the team ends up maximizing the limited planning time and supporting ALL students with rich instruction. Some of the roles overlap, such as motivation and behavior strategies, data collection for class objective mastery, and providing processing breaks to check for understanding.

The Learning Specialist (a/k/a Learning Strategist) has a ton of strategies to support our students with IEPs, language needs, disengaged learners, etc., and is an expert at providing best practices to engage these learners. The Learning Specialist is adept at organizing accommodations, aligning and task-analyzing standards-based IEP goals, inserting cooperative learning activities, adding specially designed instruction to help students access the content (Chapter 3 is devoted to the enhancing the Learning Specialist's SDI toolkit). The Content Expert understands the curriculum backwards and forwards, how it connects a grade below and a grade above. They are often the curriculum pacers, reminding us where we need to be at the end of each unit. The Content Expert also ensures rigor, making sure that we are providing acceleration for specific students and are challenging all learners. Together, the Learning Specialist and Content Expert co-plan to deliberately slow down for complex content and move at pace toward objective mastery.

The Content Expert (General Education Teacher) will focus on content, answering the following questions: "What content is essential for students to master?" "What is the big idea we want all students to know (nice- to-knows vs. need-to knows)?" "How can we effectively teach the content?" "What concepts do students usually struggle with?" In contrast, the Learning Specialists will focus on differentiation, answering the following questions: "What learning strategies will students need to master the content?" "How can we differentiate based on student readiness, interest, and learning profile to ensure that students are prepared for learning and objective/content mastery?" Each expert must be equipped to apply their lens of expertise. If the Learning Specialist doesn't have a ton of learning strategies to support reading complex text, or the Content Expert has no idea how the new curriculum all fits together, our co-planning meetings will take a lot longer. Each expert should seek professional development in their area of expertise to bring their 100% A+ game to the co-planning meeting.

B.A.S.E. Co-Planning

A helpful resource for moving away from the one-a-day planning conundrum is to structure the very first co-planning meeting with a guided planning protocol that develops the learning unit using the "end in mind," while we utilize the expertise of each co-teacher. One of my favorite co-planning structures to support effective co-planning time is the B.A.S.E framework developed by Becky Hawbaker and team (Hawbaker et al., 2001; BASE Co-Planning Guide Appendix). The "B" stands for big ideas, "A" for analyzing and anticipating student areas of difficulty, "S" for strategies and support co-teaching models, and "E" for evaluating data to adjust instruction and celebrate. Some teams

B.A.S.E Co-teaching Planning Guide

Big Ideas (Priority Standards, Essential Questions, Enduring Understandings, Language Objectives, Tier 2 and 3 Vocabulary)			
Week One	Week Two	Week Three	Week Four
Transfer Task and/or Summative Assessment			

⇓

Analyzing Areas of Difficulty/Anticipated Misconceptions

⇓

creating Specialized Strategies and Supports
Differentiation/ High Impact Virtual Learning Strategies/Co-teaching models

⇓

Evaluating
Assessment Data: Shines, Refines, & What are our next steps?

FIGURE 2.3 B.A.S.E Co-planning Co-teaching Planning Guide

use this protocol for every academic unit in a school year, so over time, the team accumulates go-to strategies for students in each unit of instruction, which can eventually be used and added to year after year. This, of course, reduces the co-planning work in the long term. The B.A.S.E. co-planning structure can help co-teachers maximize co-planning time at the beginning of a unit (averaging between 60 to 90 minutes to complete).

True to role expertise and to guide limited co-planning, I've adapted the BASE format (see Figure 2.3). In Figure 2.3, The team starts the B.A.S.E. process by gathering materials, such as student rosters and the curriculum maps. The Content Expert fills out the first row of "B" and sends it to the Learning Specialist before the co-teaching team meets, to allow the Learning Specialist time before the team meets to browse the big ideas, match student needs, and gather resources to provide access to the content. The Learning Specialist knows the learners in the classroom well, and already anticipates ways we need to add specially designed instruction for specific students, engaging practices to help reluctant students take in new content, behavioral adaptions, etc. The Learning Specialist has a list of specific students' special and unique needs so that when you meet as a team, after a review of the "B," the majority of your time is spent on the "A" and "S" to proactively reach student needs. As you co-plan various units, start to compile a list of go-to strategies for the "S" for each unit that you can use consistently use to support student learning. The "E," where we evaluate student progress and our teaching methods, can be debriefed at the end of each class period, each week, and subsequently the entire unit.

By using the B.A.S.E process, both co-teachers know the unit goal from the very beginning of the unit and can support each other in getting ALL of the students they share to that unit destination. Using B.A.S.E., there are no surprises as to the end goal and what students must be able to do at the end of the unit. For example, the co-teaching team knows that all students need to write a persuasive essay at the end of the unit. So, the team strategically instructs students to collect evidence in an interactive log over the three weeks so that students aren't overwhelmed with flipping through the entire novel at the end of the unit. Or perhaps all students will take a performance assessment on three objectives, so the co-teaching team intentionally provides mini-lessons during the warm-ups. B.A.S.E will save time in the long run and supports the co-teaching team with a concrete discussion on instruction for the week and day-to-day co-planning. Instead of asking what we are going to do tomorrow, we can toss out a few strategies and co-teaching models that will provide all students access to the weekly content as we move toward our unit end goal. Consider revolutionizing your co-planning "one-a-day" approach by switching to the B.A.S.E. format.

Technology Resources to Support Limited Face to Face Planning

Due to many factors and variables, face-to-face co-planning time is often limited for the weekly and day-to-day planning. After using B.A.S.E., co-teachers can build up a routine to plan 5 days of lessons in about 60 minutes (10 or so minutes per day), with time to discuss evaluation. Appendix provides an example of a weekly co-planning tool. This process of B.A.S.E. unit planning (60-90 minutes) and weekly planning (60 minutes) takes practice, timers, an agenda, and communication using technology. Some non-negotiables for co-planning should include a commitment to having flexible groups (mixed-ability groups majority of time and sometimes same-ability groups based on skill), commitment to planning on our own after tasks are assigned during the co-planning meeting (I'll create the Edpuzzle video on WW2, you create the sort on WW2), and the commitment to always be on time to our agreed-upon meeting time. While the best practice is for co-teachers to meet face to face at least once a week, I share the following technology resources that can help teachers collaborate more frequently:

- **Google Drive** Free with a gmail account; Google Drive makes sharing your files simple. In addition, Google Drive allows multiple people to edit the same file, allowing for real-time collaboration.
- Plan Book/http://planbookedu.com Basic features are free; share lesson plans; attach and print worksheets.
- Common Core/http://www.commoncurriculum.com Basic features are free; create and share lesson plans, search and link lessons to common core, and organize templates for lessons.

Last-Minute Tips for Co-Planning

By effectively co-planning and utilizing differentiated instructional strategies that promote student engagement, teachers will have a substantial impact on achievement for all learners. Top four co-planning tips:

- Schedule regular face-to-face planning meetings. Make this time and space for co-planning a "No Distraction Zone."
- Avoid "fitting it in"; set a time limit for planning. I often keep an agenda and timer so we both stay focused during our little bits of planning time.

- Focus first on planning the lesson, then set time aside for student-specific issues. We love our students, and our co-planning time can get derailed with student news ("Let me tell you what odd thing DeShaun did today..."). Plan first and then talk about specific students.
- Come to the table with ideas and guide the session with the following fundamental issues: "What are the content goals/objectives?" "Who are the learners?" "Where do we anticipate the students will struggle?" "In what areas do we anticipate the students will excel?" "How can we teach the goals/objectives most effectively?"

E: Electrify the Co-Teaching Models

The Cha Cha dance is performed in 4/4 time and requires a lot of step and hip motions. The dance is characterized by three quick steps followed by two slower beats done on the one beat and the two beat. The "cha-cha," though characterized by specific dance moves, still provides the two dancers with opportunities to specialize the dance to make it unique to the duo. Similarly, in co-teaching, there are many specific co-teaching models that two teachers can use to maximize instruction, and there's a ton of room for flexibility and creativity in how you can use the models and adapt with your own flair. Many of my respected colleagues in the co-teaching field share a variety of ways that two teachers can flexibly group students and support dynamic instruction (Friend, 2013; Beninghof, 2011; Heineman, 2013; and Fitzell, 2010). As a fan of K.I.S.S. (*Keep it Simple, Savanna*), I've shaken things up a bit, and I share four flexible co-teaching models that I've seen co-teaching teams use to yield high academic gains for all students in a co-taught classroom (Figure 2.4). I list the four models in order of amount of time needed for co-planning, starting with the least amount of time and preparation. There are planning tools and sample lesson plans for each of the four co-teaching models in Appendix.

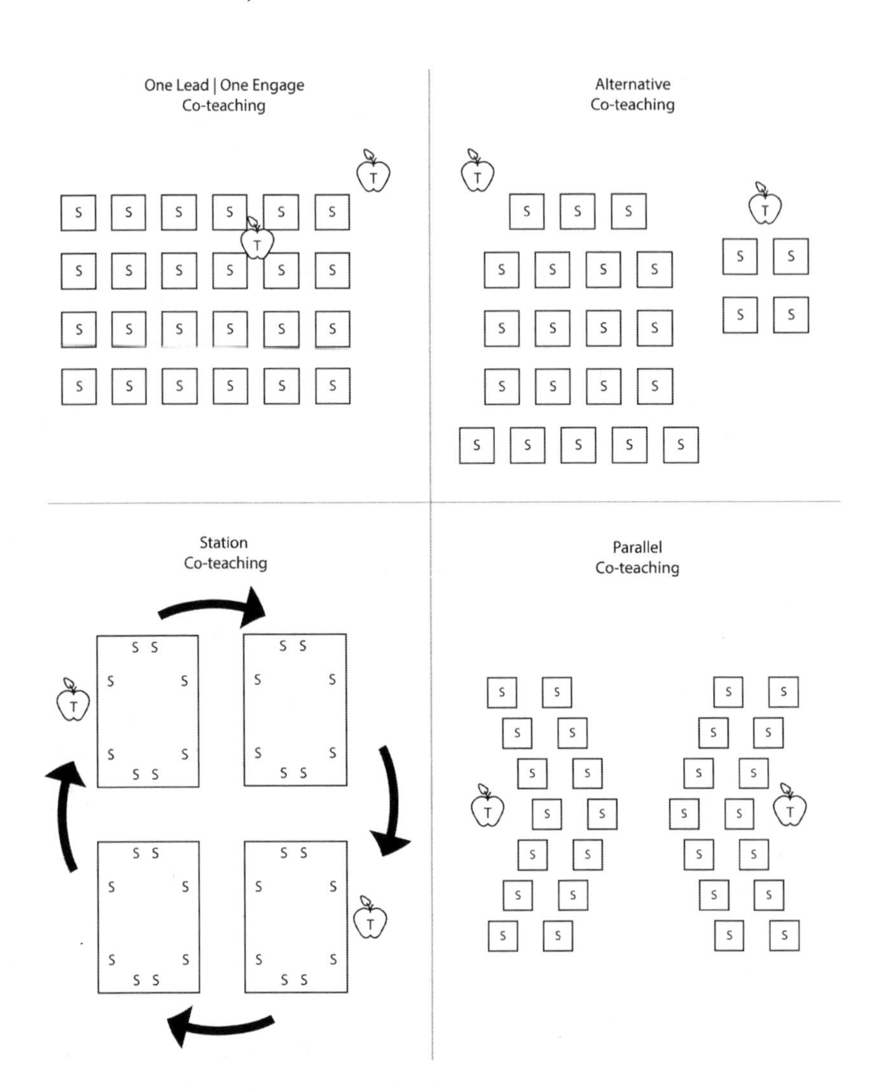

FIGURE 2.4 Co-teaching Models

One Lead and One Engage Co-Teaching

The One Lead and One Engage co-teaching model (Figure 2.5) R.E.V.s up the commonly known One-Lead/One-Support or One-Lead/One-Collect Data. The problem inherent in these other titles is that they suggest that one teacher will do most of the dancing, and the other will kinda just be there on the sideline as a spectator. Co-teaching is not two adults merely being present in a classroom at the same time. It also does not mean that the

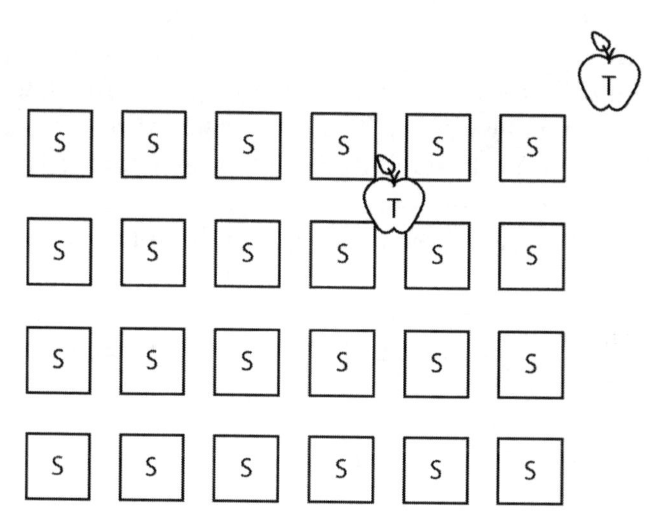

FIGURE 2.5 One Lead and One Engage Co-Teaching

General Education teacher plans and delivers all of the lessons while the Special Education teacher circulates. Co-teaching is not taking turns leading instruction to the group (i.e., one teacher leads warm-up while one teacher grades papers). Our diverse learners need both teachers to dance 100% of the time, and our students need both teachers to be engaged in the teaching and learning process for the entire class period, whether that's 35 minutes or 90 minutes.

Further, with One Lead/One Support, one teacher is often seen as superior, and one teacher is viewed as just support, hovering around one or two students with taps and redirection to focus. This approach of co-teaching is not effective: tapping a student to focus can build a sense of dependence, learned helplessness, or over-reliance that someone will always be there to remind them to pay attention, and if that person's not there, I don't need to pay attention. Also, a stigma can be attached to the support teacher: perhaps students start to think, "this other support teacher is not a "real" teacher." We don't isolate or stigmatize specific students, or peg specific teachers to work with specific students, because in our diverse classrooms, we have many ability levels, interest, and learning styles, and so both teachers are necessary for every student in our co-taught classroom. I challenge us to reframe our mindset on the possibilities of one teacher taking the lead in content and one teacher ensuring engagement for all learners. One Lead/One Engage can "R.E.V. up" the use of learning strategies to support understanding and engagement for all students throughout the class period.

Though this model requires only a little co-planning, if done well, we can ensure that we engage all students and support high levels of learning in a class period. One teacher leads, and the other teacher brings a toolkit of engagement strategies and uses them consistently throughout the class period for the benefit of all students (knowing it will support our learners with disabilities as well). Unlike One Lead/One support, we both monitor student engagement and student responses. Teachers value each role as being integral to class success and can switch roles as necessary. In this model, each co-teacher applies their lens of expertise, there is parity of voice from both teachers, and students see both teachers enhancing the class period for all students.

While one teacher is leading content instruction, our engagement teacher could be working as shown in Figure 2.6.

Making a Case for the Other Three Co-Teaching Models

The remaining three co-teaching models all involve flexible grouping. Co-teaching teams want to vary our co-teaching models based on content objectives and our learners. The goal is to use at least one of these co-teaching models a few times a week, moving a classroom from 2 teachers in front of 32 students (2:32 ratio) to possibly 2 teachers with 15 or 16 students (1:15 ratio) or four stations, and so on. When we maximize both teachers in the co-taught classroom, not only is the teacher-student ratio decreased, but we can also increase active participation, and provide quicker immediate feedback and positive reinforcement. Both teachers are flexible in the grouping arrangements to teach all groups, to avoid stigmatizing any students. This instruction

Specializing Instruction

Teaching study and organization skills with mneumonics or resources like foldables

Modeling how to take notes

Underling/circling big ideas in various colors for distinction & connections

Integrating Technology

Typing up text for a Wordle of the key points and terms

Adding visual images (pixabay) and tactile supports (concrete items) for key concepts and terms

Adding audio and/or assistive technology

Collecting Data

Monitoring engagement and reinforcing positive behavior

Using formative assessment to adjust instruction

Ensuring students are making progess on IEP data

Inserting Processing Breaks

"Stand up if...thumbs up...stomp your feet"

Stand, Turn, and Talk

Planning re-teaching or HOT extension questions based on data

Clarifying Content

Clarifying and/or explaining concept in another way

Interjecting examples or real world applications/echoing key words

Circulating, using proximity control for behavior management & praise

Visually modeling how to record notes in google doc Cornell Notes

FIGURE 2.6 One Lead/One Engage Strategies

takes place in the same physical classroom space, which sometimes requires us to be creative, using headphones, catty corners in our classrooms so our voices deflect, standing, brainstorming on the floor, and so on. To successfully build a classroom where these three co-teaching models of flexible groups can flourish, we commit to the following four practices:

1. *Ensuring equitable practices:* In chapter 1, we discussed equity. A philosophy that holds equity is an important essential. We want to ensure that students get what they need to be successful, not necessarily that every student gets the same thing. Students are all going to receive great instruction, but our materials and delivery might vary for specific learners.

2. *Fostering a growth mindset:* We use instructional time to discuss the idea of malleable intelligence, making mistakes, and needing help sometimes to be our best self. This paves the way for different students to receive different things, whether they need support or acceleration because they got it.
3. *Creating a flexible classroom ecology:* Many successful co-teaching teams follow my mantra, "ROWS GOES." At the beginning of the year, co-teaching teams create a classroom that is conducive to flexible grouping. For example, the classroom is set up to include an area in the left back for a teacher to quickly call a few students over to get some help or receive enrichment. Students are already grouped in groups of four/five so station rotations are quite easy to set up. The classrooms have standing desks or areas, multiple white boards, or chart paper so that at any given time a teacher could say, "Join me over here to look at this strategy."
4. *Building class and group norms:* Co-teachers explicitly model expectations and routines for working in groups and allow the class to create group norms for working productively as a team. Based on age range, three to six norms are adequate. Norms are not rules; rather, they're guidelines for how we should actively listen, disagree with one another, respect each other's point of view, celebrate each other, and divide work. Norms are visually posted, practiced, and reinforced continuously.

Now, let's move on to the next three co-teaching models.

Alternative Co-Teaching

Alternative teaching can be used for a variety of purposes and doesn't require tons and tons of co-planning (Figure 2.7).

Characteristics: One teacher conducts a small group that can either pre-teach, reinforce, or accelerate instruction from the large group; can occur before, during, or after large group instruction; usually last 8-10 minutes; students and

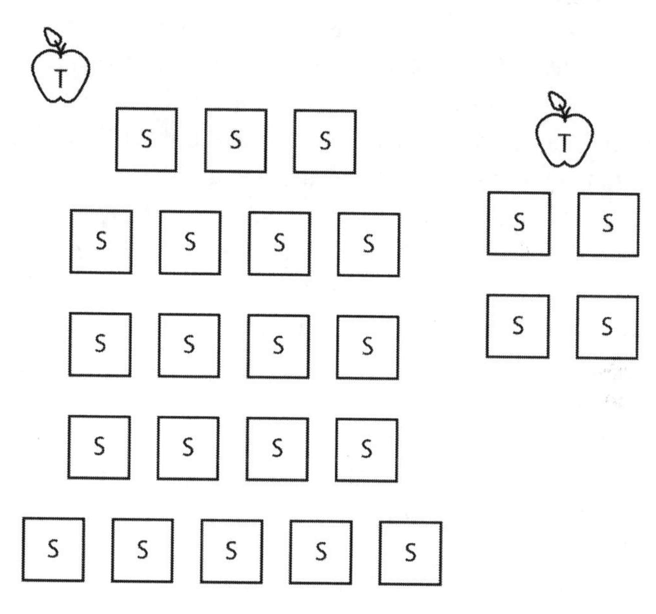

FIGURE 2.7 Alternative Co-Teaching

groupings vary; teachers use data (warm-up, exit ticket, etc.) to decide to provide something different for specific students.

Advantages: Focused attention may be given to students' unique needs; ideal for tiered lessons/tasks or other forms of differentiated instruction; can provide reinforcement or enrichment as necessary; allows for building vocabulary for one group of students or expanding the vocabulary of another group; it allows for building background knowledge before jumping into a complex text; optimal opportunity to add more specially designed instruction for specific learners.

Challenges: Teachers want to ensure students are grouped and regrouped for a variety of purpose with different teachers.

Example: Students are completing an independent activity solving math problems. Every student has a set of green and red sticky dots. As they solve their problems, if they understand and are confident of their steps to arrive at their answer, they place a green dot by their problem. If they aren't quite sure and would like some help, they place a red sticky dot by their problem. The Learning Specialist is walking around the classroom and notices that three students all have a red sticky dot by problem number 3. The Learning Specialist has a quick sidebar conversation with the Content Expert. Content Expert pulls the three students to a table in the classroom to re-teach. Learning Specialist continues to circulate and support the whole class as they work independently. Or perhaps, all students who have green dots for problem number 5 are sent to the Content Expert for acceleration or extension on that problem.

Station Co-Teaching

Station co-teaching requires moderate co-planning, in which co-teachers decide how to chunk content for learning stations, make instruction engaging, and delegate responsibilities (Figure 2.8).

Characteristics: Both teachers share teaching and divide content; effective for multiple concepts; students rotate through stations; each teacher instructs every student; instructional delivery should vary depending on student needs; requires co-planning prior to instruction.

Advantages: More individualized attention is offered; there is increased student participation and engagement; co-teachers can cover more of the curriculum and differentiate instruction when used; there is extensive opportunity for peer learning.

Challenges: Co-teachers want to ensure the independent/peer stations have engaging and challenging learning opportunities and ways for students to self-monitor success, either with a rubric or a group norm checklist.

Example: Co-teachers are planning a lesson to introduce the Great Depression. As they browse curriculum resources, they notice that there is a complex nonfiction reading article. The Learning Specialist (equipped with literacy best practices and knowledge that specific students have deficits and reading IEP goals around comprehension) decides to run a literacy station on this reading

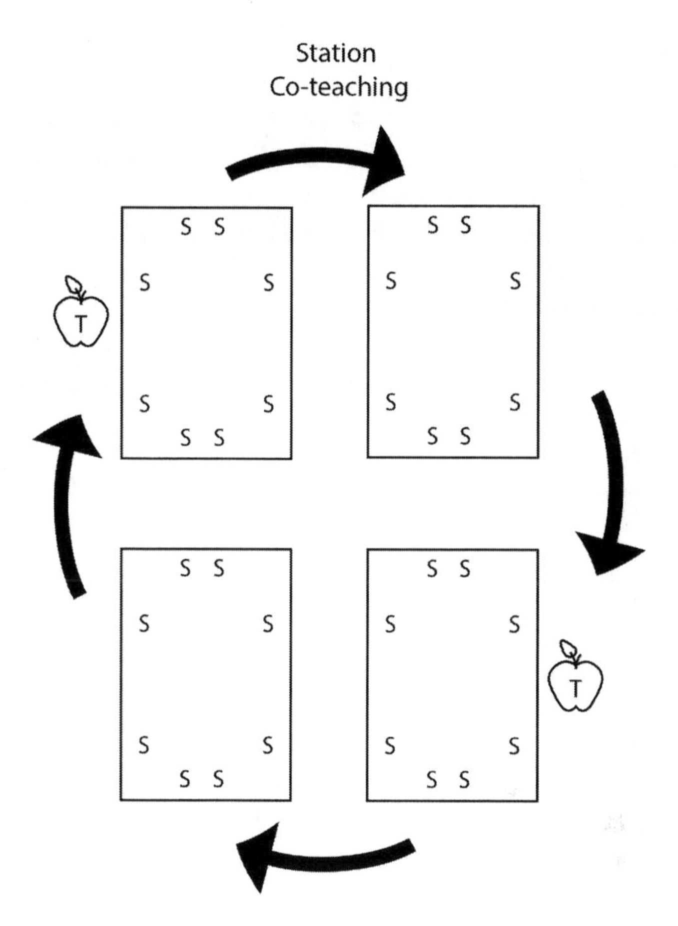

FIGURE 2.8 Station Co-Teaching

passage. In Station 1, the Learning Specialist will teach students how to annotate the nonfiction text using 1 Signpost from Kylene Beers and Robert E. Probst, *Reading Nonfiction: Notice & Note Stances, Signposts, and Strategies* (2016). The Content Expert decides to run a station providing some explicit instruction on the Great Depression and already has a great interactive slide deck using Nearpod. Station 3 will be an independent station where students watch an Edpuzzle video on the key figures of the Great Depression and answer embedded questions in the app so teachers can later evaluate the results. Station 4 will be a collaborative station where students work in teams to analyze three meaningful Great Depression political cartoons using a guided questionnaire. Students document their shared responses in their classkick.com account (teachers can view all students work and provide feedback digitally). Teachers decide the time rotations and student groupings, and delegate task and material preparation. After students transition in and complete a KWL chart, they'll locate the number of their first station and get ready to go!

Parallel Co-Teaching

Parallel co-teaching requires more co-planning, as co-teachers decide how to split content, allocate time parameters, and delegate responsibilities (Figure 2.9).

Characteristics: The goal is to reach the content objective with two student groupings or two split groups in the classroom; instructional methods on each side will vary depending on learners; can be heterogeneous groups by content or homogenous groups by skill.

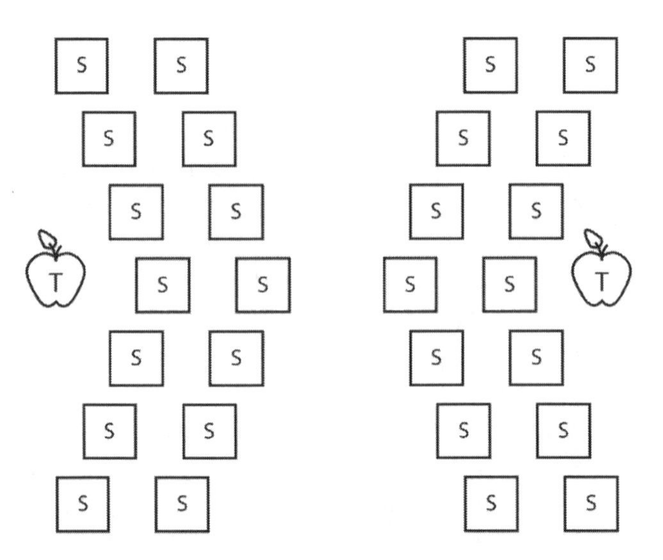

FIGURE 2.9 Parallel Co-teaching

Advantages: It decreases class size (small groups), which individualizes instruction and provides a safer environment for students to take risks; groups can swap to allow for fresh perspective; students can flip and teach other group; there is more interaction due to lower student-teacher ratio.

Challenges: Teachers should share their plans for teaching and required time parameters so teachers can work together to control the noise level. Decide placement (sitting vs. standing vs. on the floor) in the classroom to ensure that voices are deflected.

Example: There are hundreds of ways to divide content into two pieces/sides to individualize instruction and increase active participation. In science, split the class in half to debate two different issues of a controversy or look at two concepts in greater depth (mitosis vs. meiosis). In English, split the class into two groups to analyze two different characters or two different points of view in a novel. In both examples, students can swap sides and teach each other.

High-Yield Co-Teaching Models

The co-teaching models that co-teachers most want to use are those that allow for greater differentiation: Alternative, Stations, and Parallel. High-performing co-teaching teams make a commitment not to group students by labels, stick students in groups based on ability and teach them at a lower level, because if this is done all the time … when will these students ever catch up? This practice of lower standards and lower expectations widens the gap rather than bridging it. The three co-teaching models discussed here move students out of a one-size-fits-all approach and provides options for flexible groupings, smaller teacher/student ratio, increased student engagement, and higher opportunities to differentiate content, process, and product with more specially designed instruction. The goal is to flexibly group students, for a variety of reasons: students with labels should not always be taught by the Special Education teacher and students without a label by the General Education teacher, and vice versa. There are a lot of ways we can group students: of course by data, but also by interest, a variety of learning-style options, heterogenous pairs, etc. Establish a classroom environment that values differentiation, the ideology that we all are working at various paces and benefit from different avenues to learn new information. When we flexibly group students from the beginning of the year, the routine becomes authentic and transitions are quick, so ultimately students believe, "At any given time, I may need some support to learn this or I need acceleration because I got it, and my teachers are responsive and will help me either way."

High-performing co-teaching teams make a commitment not to group students by labels, stick students in groups based on ability and teach them at a low level, because if this is done all the time … when will these students ever catch up? This practice of lower standards and lower expectations widens the gap rather than bridging it.

Try shaking up the co-teaching dance floor and incorporate technology into your co-teaching partnership. For example, Edpuzzle could be used to support a pre-teaching or re-teaching for the alternative model, or could be half of the classroom for parallel co-teaching. I often say, if a student doesn't get it from me, maybe hearing it a different way can help. Edpuzzle is a phenomenal digital resource that allows teachers to differentiate instruction by individualizing videos. Teachers can select a video from YouTube, LearnZillion, and many other video-based platforms, then customize the video by editing, cropping, recording audio, and adding questions to make an engaging presentation or lesson. Teachers can also receive data on who watched the video and the score of questions answered correctly. The Edpuzzle platform is user-friendly and doesn't require a lot of time to create video lessons for students.

For station or parallel co-teaching, allow students to use Flipgrid and create a video to share their learning or engage in digital discussion. Flipgrid is a free video discussion platform that allows students to respond to teacher questions using video. Students can respond to teacher and peer questions, animate their videos, and publish their work. Flipgrid is a great technology tool because it increases student engagement by offering another product option to demonstrate mastery on an objective that moves beyond paper and pencil. Flipgrid also provides us formative data on the spot so we can differentiate instruction in the moment. If students are shy, they can create avatars and stickers to represent their voice on the video. For more lesson examples and templates to plan for the co-teaching models, see Appendix. Get creative! There is no wrong way to shake up the co-teaching models.

The following tips are the Top Ten non-negotiables in establishing an effective co-taught classroom community:

1. Use words like "our students" and "we would like." Avoid the mindset of "I" or "my students."
2. Vary roles and determine which co-teaching model could best facilitate differentiation of the lesson or task.
3. Post objectives to help both you and the students stay on course.
4. Establish consistent and shared student routines to aid in transitions or gain students' attention.
5. Create unobtrusive signals to communicate when it is time to move on, more time is needed, etc.
6. Clipboards are our friends. They help us collect formative data and adjust instruction.
7. Use sidebar conversations to discuss data and plan for adjusting instruction. The goal is 3-5 sidebars in a 60-minute block.
8. Parity is important. Be sure both teachers' names are on the door, report cards, graded papers, furniture, space, etc.
9. Group and regroup students for different purposes, in different manners, and with different teachers within the co-teaching partnership (to avoid stigmatization).

10. Apply the 10:2 rule. After 10 minutes of direct instruction, the engagement teacher can provide students with a two-minute processing or cooperative learning activity to share their learning.

Vary Your Assessment Practices

When co-teachers assess all students frequently throughout the class period, they can differentiate instruction and provide frequent feedback. Collecting data continuously throughout the class period and using the data to differentiate and flexibly group students in the moment is a hallmark of effective co-teaching. As teachers provide opportunities for student responses during instruction, there is higher active student engagement and increased achievement. When co-teachers check ALL students' levels of understanding throughout each lesson, it sets the tone and demonstrates that everyone's thinking is important and necessary, and we accelerate the learning and engagement of all. Shake up your assessment moves with this list of fun and quick brain breaks to assess all students' learning simultaneously to support differentiation

Kinesthetic

- Stand Up "If I read a statement that is true"/Sit Down
- Stand up and cross your arms if you agree *or* show on fingers.
- Stand up and use response cards (True/False *or* A, B, C).
- Touch your toes while saying two key words from today.
- Two steps forward for a correct statement and 1 step backward for an incorrect one.
- Four Corners (walk to the corner that best represents your thought; discuss with peers).
- Bean-bag toss on a board with comprehension questions with a peer or in small groups.

- In small groups, toss a cube containing various Blooms questions. Answer the question on the cube.
- Sculpture Garden: students move each other to form a position that represents a concept.

Tactile

- Use Wikki Stix to make an image that best represents the topic.
- Use modeling clay to make an image that best represents the topic.
- Draw in the air the answer to a question.
- Draw the answer in the sand pit, on sand paper, on felt, etc.
- Sort the terms on your desk into groups that make the most sense to you.

Musical

- Listen to the music while thinking about ____. When it stops, discuss the answer with the student closest to you.
- In Google Chrome Music Lab, create a 30-second song about the main character.
- Chant the main idea five times while patting your head and rubbing your tummy.
- Say the most important concept in a rap/rhythmic way.
- Have students rotate and record an answer to an essential question using iPads or recorder.

Visual

- Use a whiteboard to draw two images that relate to the topic.
- Use a cartoon to justify your answer.
- Post three images on the board from Google Images. Ask students to select the one they think best represents the concept.
- Look out the window and find an image that best relates to what we just learned.

Written

- Pick an image out of the envelope and write about how it connects to Objective/EQ.
- Write a tweet to summarize the main idea (or have students send one).
- Summarize the main idea in 10 words or less. Work with a partner until you have only 10 words. Optional: Have students write it on a sticky note and place in the text.
- Write down three main points from the lesson; highlight the one you feel is most important.
- In your own words, write two definitions for a vocabulary word: one correct definition and one incorrect definition. Quiz a partner. Their goal is to identify the correction definition.

Regarding assessment and grading, as a co-teaching team you need to agree on the following six fundamental questions:

- What counts? Participation, attendance, effort, student's individual progress
- How will we create and agree on rubrics and criteria for success?
- What varied options can students show to demonstrate mastery?
- How do we establish roles in the group for group grading (self-evaluations)?
- How will we communicate our grading policy to students? To parents?
- Who grades what? who? when?

Don't Forget to Celebrate

One of my top musical bands, Kool & The Gang, put it best, "Celebrate Good Times, Come On." To truly sustain our co-teaching momentum, we need to deliberately stop, pause, and look for areas of growth, student light-bulb flashes of understanding, and the hard work we each put into the partnership. It is easy to focus on all of the academic gaps we are filling, the flying scissors across the classroom, or the fact that a "few students still don't get it," but consider: Where would these students be without you? At the end of the day, my co-teacher and I would do a high five. We'd high-five each other and go back and forth a total of five times, each listing positive affirmations, celebrations, victories, and humorous moments until we had a total of 10 things to end our day on a celebratory high. The celebrations could be as basic as, "Mary stayed focused despite the task being hard." Then when we finished the 10 celebratory statements, we would pat each other on the back with the high-five hand and say, "Great job, Co-teacher!"

My former Special Education Director, Jane Quenneville, would often look at me and say, "You're focusing on the wrong thing, you've done some great things, now fix your face." Best advice ever! We sometimes have to remind our face to catch up! If you're happy, your students will be happy: happiness is contagious. Laugh and celebrate and be sure to look like you enjoy co-teaching. After long and crazy days, still try to smile and your body will catch up.

Overcoming Obstacles in Co-Teaching

Like perfecting the Cha Cha, co-teaching requires flexibility and an open-minded approach to new moves. The benefits of including all students, providing rigorous instruction, and collaborating with another teacher to problem-solve are worth the investment. Naturally, conflict may arise; conflict is inevitable, but it's how we handle it that makes the conflict productive or unproductive. As a co-teaching team, try a few of these tips to support conflict resolution (see Figure 2.10).

No matter where you are on the journey of Inclusive Practices, remember that we all have something to learn, we all have something to teach. As co-teachers, be willing to celebrate victories, laugh, and sometimes vent together. Together, as a team, you will enrich lives by providing ALL students access to rigorous instruction.

Co-teaching Practices: Successfully Navigating Conflict

What can cause conflict?	Strategies for Mediating Conflict
Differences in teaching styles	• Complete and revisit the Co-teaching Choice Boards to reflect and review Team progress and commitments.
Differences in philosophical approaches to teaching and learning	• Develop a mindset, "It's all about our students."
Ethics and Beliefs systems	• Anticipate possible barriers and create resolutions and potential solutions (use Collaborative Solutions Planner attached) • Consider asking someone to mediate (a colleague trusted by both parties)
The feeling of insecurity	• Hear each other out fully and without emotion
Fear of something new or change	• Focus on student data and student need • Trying saying "yes" before "no" • Agree to always compromise
Issues of trust	• Use honesty and respect in your conversations • Speak from the "I" POV vs "You" POV • Clarify roles and expectations • Focus on each other's areas of strength
The use of terms like "my students" and "your students"	• Agree to use inclusive language and build a relationship where it is safe to make mistakes
Maximizing planning time	• Use an agenda to stay on task (focus on the solution & 1-2 action steps) • Use an agreed upon lesson planner to share important lesson items and content matter with each other. • Divide responsibilities

FIGURE 2.10 Co-teaching Practices: Successfully Navigating Conflict

In Closing

Imagine that in 10 years, a student is asked, "Who was your favorite teacher?" Will you and your co-teacher be cited as a great memory from their schooling experience? It's not every day that a student can say, "I had two awesome teachers in my second-grade class." I've had students come back to my co-teacher, Alexander Duncan III, and me and say things like, "I loved having two teachers, you both had a different way of explaining concepts." Specifically, I'll never forget Taywan, one of my most challenging and intelligent students. He returned after graduation to visit the school, and shared with me, "I was afraid of getting in trouble more with two teachers in my class, four eyes always looking at me, with nowhere to hide, but together you made English 11 the best class I had. The days I didn't want to be at school or had a rough morning, I knew that I'd get a laugh from you two and feel better, and sometimes that's all I needed to turn my day around." Our students truly value the effort we put into getting this co-teaching thing right. Celebrate together every day. Co-teaching is hard work. I believe Inclusive Practices is the most rewarding investment in education today. Imagine your students coming back and saying, "I wish more of my classes had two teachers, four eyes, nowhere to hide."

Top 6 Dance Moves

Which of these moves can you try tomorrow? Which moves can you share with your team?

1. As a school community, complete the Inclusive Schools Network *Self-Assessment Survey* to guide a current review of Inclusive Practices and support your next steps in the journey. There is a digital survey and a hard-copy printout at https://inclusiveschools.org/inclusion-resources/self-assessment.
2. Dedicate co-planning time to engage in the Co-teaching Choice Board conversations to form a strong co-teaching partnership. Commit to having these important conversations, changing perspective based on student need, and creating a compromise when necessary.
3. Review the four co-teaching models. Which one could you try? Based on student data and content objectives, how could you flexibly group students more? How will you introduce the new routine and explicitly model the routine? The first time trying a new model will not be perfect and that is OK.

(*Continued*)

4. Consider adding a new assessment check to gauge student understanding. Evaluate your data collection toolbox. How are you collecting data during class as a team? Is the system working for both co-teachers? For students?
5. Try the High-Five Celebration at least once a week. Video and Tweet it out #allkids.
6. Subscribe to the Council for Exceptional Children to read journals with tons of practical and fun co-teaching strategies. My top co-teaching article is "50 Ways to Keep Your Co-Teacher: Strategies for before, during, and after Co-Teaching" by Wendy W. Murawski and Lisa Dieker (2008).
7. Leadership: Evaluate the co-teaching outcomes and student data. If necessary, revisit the school vision on Inclusive Practices, co-teacher role expectations, scheduling of co-taught classrooms to ensure heterogenous classrooms, and professional development offerings to support collaborative co-planning.

List your next dance moves for your co-teaching partnership.

____

____

____

____

____

Accountability Partner: ______________________________

____

Check-in Date: ______________________________________

____

Optimism (n)

> *"Someone that knows that taking a step backward after taking a step forward is not a disaster, it's a Cha Cha."*
>
> *—Robert Brault*

PART TWO
Spicing Up the Rhythm

Part One was dedicated to the foundations necessary to create and enhance inclusive classroom communities with equitable and collaborative learning practices. Co-teachers are thoughtfully considering how to move from a one-size-fits-all classroom community to more flexible groupings, where students receive different things, at different times, based on their different needs. Part Two points up opportunities to add layers of specialized instruction, proactive choice, and novel assessment practices to engage learners with exceptionalities. Chapter Three is uniquely designed for special education teachers, discussing specific practices that enrich our craft and support us in providing evidence-based instruction based on a student's area of disability impact. Chapter Four uses the engagement principle of Universal Design for Learning (UDL) to share instructional strategies to differentiate instruction and motivate students. Chapter Four initially appears to be just about "choice," but the instructional practices shared there target literacy and math instruction. Chapter Five explores dozens of assessment strategies that move beyond boring and allows students to share their smarts in numerous ways, in addition to the traditional paper and pencil. Part Two will transform learning and teaching for students with disabilities and spice up the rhythm on your dance floor.

Hooks to Guide Part Two:

Chapter Three: By the end of a class period, how many times have I added more "special" in addition to "good teaching" for specific students based on their Individual Education Programs?

Chapter Four: When I proactively plan instruction, do I include choice, recruit student interest, and use a variety of learning modalities to support concept acquisition?

Chapter Five: If our school copier was destroyed, how many worksheets could I get rid of? How could I engage and assess student learning?

3

Jitterbug

The 'Special' in Special Education Teacher

If you're looking for a social dance that will increase your energy every time you do it, try learning some jitterbug dance steps.

The Jitterbug is a type of swing dance that is very energetic and is characterized by lots of acrobatic feats. The Jitterbug was made famous by jazz singer Cab Calloway and Blues musician Muddy Waters. To say that the jitterbug swing rhythm is complex would be an understatement. At the basic level, it includes the single rhythm, which is one weighted step for every two beats of music; then there's the single delayed rhythm, double rhythm, and triple rhythm. All that to say…it's a beautifully complex dance.

I've YouTubed dozens of variations of the Jitterbug, and I'm convinced that this is one of those dances that takes much more than "watch, step, and repeat." The Jitterbug requires meticulous observations of skilled swing dancers and tons of practice with feedback on fidelity of movements. There are many parallels between the nuances of Jitterbug dancing and being a special education teacher. The biggest parallel is this: dancing the Jitterbug requires a lot of soul, passion, and a commitment to learning the strategic moves (in this case, the moves are the triple step, underarm turn, the inside turn, the cuddle step, and so on). Being a special education teacher likewise requires soul, passion, and a commitment to learning the strategic moves: in this case, creating quality Individual Education Plans, staying current on specially designed instruction, and collecting and monitoring data to support instructional and behavioral practices for children. Being a special education teacher is really, really hard work. In working to provide access to grade-level curriculum, we often must solve two questions: "Based on where this student currently performs, how can I bridge the gap and provide the student with access to this grade level content?" How can we remove learning barriers to meaningfully include this student that has a specific area of impact (reading, writing, math, behavioral)?" Answering these two questions to provide specially designed instruction is like solving a hard puzzle with pieces that don't easily match while balancing on a physio ball. It's not always linear, because each student will need something different, and it requires innovative, outside-the-box thinking.

This chapter is organized to fortify special education teachers with the "Special" that is necessary to accelerate the learning of our students with exceptionalities.

What Is Specially Designed Instruction?

General Education teachers often ask me, "What is Specially Designed Instruction?" In the least amount of words, I respond, "Specially Designed Instruction (SDI) is evidence-based teacher actions necessary to provide students with disabilities access to core content. SDI is a layer of specialized instruction above and beyond, in addition to good, effective instruction."

This answer then leads to a follow-up question, "Well, what is good, effective instruction?" Carol Ann Tomlinson would probably answer, "Good, effective instruction is Differentiated Instruction." Differentiated Instruction is what great teachers do every single day. Does anyone have a classroom in which every student is alike? Of course not! Thus, great teachers proactively and purposefully plan to account for different academic readiness levels and various learning styles. Great teachers provide students various ways to engage with new content and offer choice in ways that students can demonstrate learning. Differentiating the learning process, content, and product is good, effective instruction. However, for many of our students with disabilities, "good, effective instruction" is not enough to fill in big gaps, so we must add an additional layer of "special" evidence-based approaches according to a student's disability area of impact (writing, reading, mathematics, executive functioning, behavioral, etc.) to bridge their gap to reach grade-level content. This extra and additional layer of specially designed instruction is aligned throughout a student's Individual Education Program/Plan (IEP): it aligns to the student's annual IEP goals and is necessary to provide access to the curriculum. The top two reasons we provide SDI are: 1. Meets the unique needs of students with disabilities based on their IEP. 2. Provides *access* to the general education curriculum.

> Good, effective teaching can be compared to a sweet cupcake. The various flavors of icing and types of toppings we add on top of the basic cupcake is the specially designed instruction. Everyone's preferred toppings will be different.

The legal definition of Specially Designed Instruction is "adapting [differentiating], as appropriate to the needs of an eligible child, the content, methodology or delivery of instruction to address the unique needs of the child that result from the child's disability; and to ensure [meaningful] ACCESS to the general education curriculum so that the child can meet the educational standards that apply to all children" (Section 300.39, Code of Federal Regulations; IDEA 2014). SDI is not just beneficial, it is legally required. Students who require special education services will still receive great instruction like personalized learning, universal design for learning, project-based learning, etc., but they will *also* receive specially designed instruction in addition. SDI is the teaching that helps us bridge the academic gap between where a student is and the curriculum objectives we are trying to reach. I often remind teachers that there is no special education McDonald's, special HVAC school, or special education college. SDI helps us take a student who might be grade levels behind, or lack self-regulation, or hate writing—and facilitate skill-based teaching to provide that student with access to and means of mastery of grade-level core content.

It is important to note that accommodations, modifications, and specially designed instructional strategies all serve different roles in providing a student access to the curriculum. Accommodations don't change the content; they are supports or services that help a student fully access the general education curriculum. Modifications change the content or what a student is expected to learn and/or demonstrate. Specialized Instructional Strategies (SDI) are methods that are used to deliver a variety of content objectives. Instructional strategies determine the approach a teacher may take to achieve learning objectives. Look at Table 3.1, which has examples of each of these three approaches to providing access to the curriculum. Any surprises? Sure, one could make an argument, that there's crossover between some accommodations and modifications and specially designed instructional strategies based on teacher action and intention behind it, but it's important to note that SDI ensures that the curriculum is not watered down, expectations are not reduced, and classroom instruction represents what students will see on end-of-year assessments. For example, students will not see simpler language or reduced options on an end-of-year assessment needed to graduate high school with a diploma, right?

The examples for each category are debatable, but consider the frequency and duration of the accommodations and modifications you use to support a student. Our end goal is to get our students to the BIG cheese: the standard HS diploma indicating readiness for 21st-century college and/or career success. That's why it's so important to increase strategic use of specially designed instructional strategies and decrease modifications.

Use the Figure 3.1 for an overview of what Specially Designed Instruction is and is not. This figure highlights the "Big 5" distinctions of SDI (see Figure 3.1)

To unpack what Specially Designed Instruction looks and sounds like, let's take a quick, low-stakes quiz. Working in a team or with a partner to discuss the following three scenarios

TABLE 3.1 Access to the General Education Curriculum

	Accommodations *Don't change the content, but are supports or services that help a student fully access the general education curriculum*	**Modifications** *Change the content or what a student is expected to learn and/or demonstrate*	**Specialized Instructional Strategies** *Methods that are used to deliver a variety of content objectives. Instructional strategies determine the approach a teacher may take to achieve learning objectives*
Examples	Extra time for processing information/ taking test Use of timers and pacers	Decrease expectations on course mastery by focusing on BIG ideas and objectives only	Learning Strategy Instruction such as mnemonics for reading comprehension, solving word problems, etc.
	Large-print textbooks	Word bank of choices for answers to test questions	Peer-assisted learning structures (think-pair-share, high/low pairings, etc.)
	Graph paper to assist in organizing and lining up math problems	An outline in place of essay for major project	Graphic organizers or graphics containing titles, words, labels, pictures, and acronyms
	Tape-record lectures/audio accessibility	Film or video supplements in place of text	Breaking tasks and processes into manageable parts with a step-by-step checklist
	Guided or cloze notes or ability to use computer for writing	Picture Communication Symbols (PCS) choices on tests	Formula triangles representing relationships between concepts and mathematical operations
	Pre-teach vocabulary	Questions re worded using simpler language	Specialized writing techniques Specialized math techniques Specialized reading techniques
	Token reinforcement systems for behavior support	Projects substituted for written reports	Executive functioning/behavior support: organizational contracts, social skills stories and peer buddies

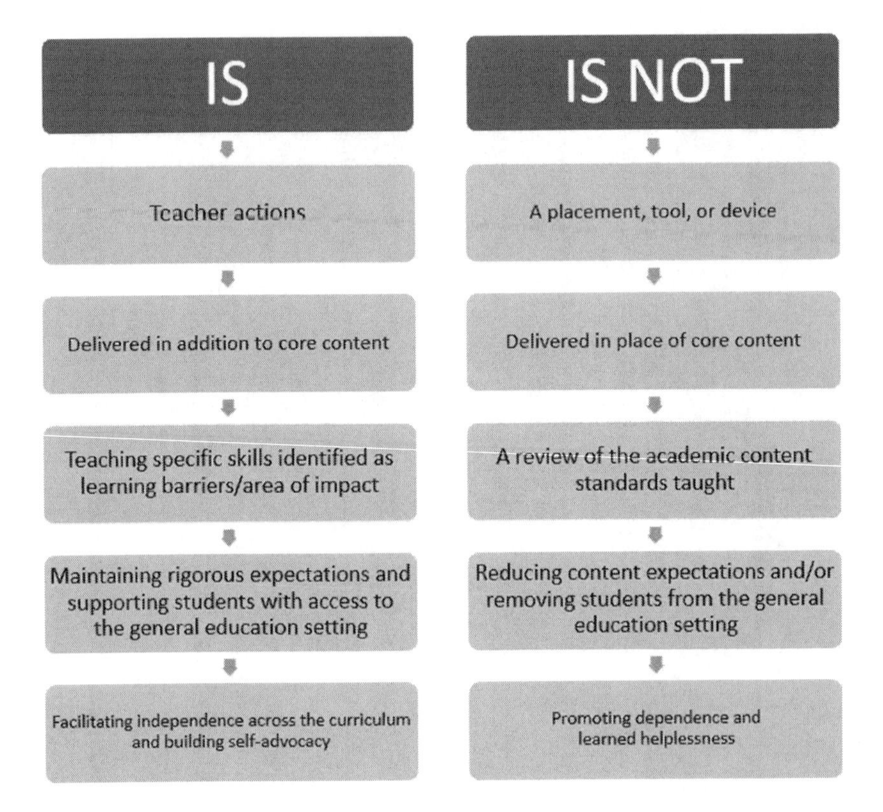

FIGURE 3.1 Specially Designed Instruction

will lead to rich discussion and reflection. There will be three situations to discuss. As a team, decide if **A**. Yes, it's SDI **B**. No, it's not SDI or **C.** It depends. Justify and share your rationale for each answer. After discussion, turn to the next page to find the thinking on Specially Designed Instruction.

1. Highlighting tape (think of a highlighter that is actually strips of colorful restickable tape that students can write on)
   a. Yes, it's SDI
   b. No, it's not SDI
   c. It depends

2. Explicit Instruction
   a. Yes, it's SDI
   b. No, it's not SDI
   c. It depends.
3. An electronic device (Chromebook, laptop, iPad)
   a. Yes, it's SDI
   b. No, it's not SDI
   c. It depends.

Next Page

1. Highlighting tape is a great tool to have in our teacher toolkit! Highlighting tape comes in various colors and widths and is restickable, a great substitute when students can't write in a school textbook. Students can write on the highlighting tape or use it to code specific elements. Highlighting tape can be purchased at most office supply stores, or on Amazon. Specially Designed Instruction is not a tool. Providing a student with a highlighter or highlighting tape by itself does not provide access to the content. Perhaps you've experienced this: After giving a student a highlighter and asking them to highlight the main idea, without instruction, they highlight the entire paragraph. SDI is teacher action steps. What teacher action could support a student in using highlighters or highlighting tape effectively? One of the best examples is to have the student use highlighting tape to strategically annotate text. For example, in the *"Flag Your Strategy"* approach, a teacher models and provides the student with a process to make meaning of a text using five colors of highlighting tape. Throughout their reading, they are to metacognitively think about the strategies good readers use and flag their text using the corresponding highlighting tape. This is very effective for books that students can't write in.

Blue Highlighting Tape = Connect: Flag where a character, plot event, or setting reminds you of something in your life, another text, or a prediction.

Green Highlighting Tape = Question: Flag points where you have a question.
Yellow Highlighting Tape = Infer/Predict: Flag where you've used the author's clues to figure something out or stopped to confirm or refine a prediction.
Orange Highlighting Tape = Monitor for Meaning: Flag where you have stopped to clarify words or meaning.
Pink Highlighting Tape = Synthesize: Stop every three minutes and create a gist of what you've read about. Share an opinion, something interesting, or surprising.

If we teach a metacognitive process like "Flag Your Strategy" to decode text, the student can practice, internalize, and independently apply this strategy across the entire curriculum. Eventually the student will no longer need highlighting tape and will naturally use this strategy to make meaning of any text they pick up or any text they read online. That's the power of SDI. We create expert learners who can advocate for themselves and self-select strategies for success. We could list tons of other tools here, like a graphic organizer or a ruler, but the point is this: by itself a tool is not SDI, it's just a tool that every other student has. Specifically, providing a student with a graphic organizer does nothing: it is just a tool. But we can teach students how to create cognitive maps based on their purpose for reading or how to choose specific organizers based on the writing prompt. Always ask: What are the teacher actions that enhance the student's usage of a specific tool?

2. Explicit Instruction. Explicit Instruction probably created lots of rich debate. Afterall, Explicit Instruction involves teacher action. Let's start with the definition of Explicit Instruction. Fisher and Frey (2006) define Explicit Instruction using a four-step guided release of responsibility framework, moving from teacher responsibility to student responsibility. Explicit Instruction is not be confused with a boring lecture (it is the opposite of *Ferris Bueller's Day Off*). The process begins with "I Do (Explicit Instruction), We Do (Guided Instruction),

You Do (Collaboratively), and You Do (independently). Is Explicit Instruction good, effective teaching? Yes. Will every student, in general, receive Explicit Instruction? Yes. Do our General Education teachers generally provide good Explicit Instruction? Yes. Specially Designed Instruction is an extra layer added on top of what a General Education teacher might provide. Explicit Instruction, by itself, is not enough for many of our students with disabilities. In fact, providing the same Explicit Instruction over and over again could fall into that definition of *insanity:* repeating the same thing over and over again in the same way and expecting a different result … for instance, wondering why Bob still doesn't understand the steps in solving a multistep equation after we retaught the concept the same way, slower, or louder.

To start with the concept of Explicit Instruction, ask, "How can I add something special that is evidence-based that will target my students' area of disability impact with a much more unique approach beyond gradual release of responsibility?" For example, it is quite common for many of our students to have areas of need around memory and processing. Thus, if we don't add a layer of "special" to concept and vocabulary acquisition, students may forget the terms quite quickly. Not every student will need this layer of "special," but based on disability area of impact, specific students might. If this is the case for a student who often forgets key vocabulary terms, I might add to Explicit Instruction a vocabulary acquisition strategy such as LINCS.

LINCs Vocabulary is part of a larger framework of a Strategic Instructional Model (SIM) developed at University of Kansas Center for Research on Learning, based on 25 years of research. LINCs is an auditory memory device and a visual memory device that helps students learn and remember the meaning of complex terms and key vocabulary. Learners need strategic approaches to transform and remember information in a variety of ways (visual imagery, mnemonic devices, relating to prior knowledge, etc.). Students complete the following five steps:

1. List the parts
2. Identify a reminding word
3. Note a LINCing story
4. Create a LINCing picture
5. Self-test

Each step in the process is intended to cue focus on the critical aspects of a vocabulary word, and then to use the keyword mnemonic devices, mnemonic stories, visual imagery, associations with prior knowledge, and self-evaluation to enhance memory of meaning. After we provide explicit instruction on the LINCS routine, students are empowered to make their own connections and contextualize their concepts and terms in ways that they will remember. Students can cut out their LINCS tables and store them in actual envelopes or digitally in a folder; afterward they can quiz each other and use the tables as a self-test study guide. This process teaches students how to independently manipulate vocabulary terms in every subject, for SATs, and so on. Ultimately, students begin to feel a sense of control over their learning and use this strategy to support their own learning and study skills across the curriculum. That's the power of SDI.

For example, after explicit teacher modeling, a young student might begin to contextualize the word "aloof" in this way: The definition of aloof is "reserved or *distant*." A reminding word that reminds me of aloof is "*roof*." A LINCing story linking the definition of the term and my reminding word is, "My brother is so distant from us, it's like he's far away on the *roof*." The LINCing picture that I'll draw is my brother on a *roof*, and we are eating dinner at the table in the dining room, and he is *aloof* because he is not here with us (see Figure 3.2). Self-test: what does *aloof* mean? My brother is so distant, he is on the tall *roof* away from the family, it might mean that he is far away. Is this student's contextualization of the term perfect? Not necessarily, it's not completely perfect, but this is their

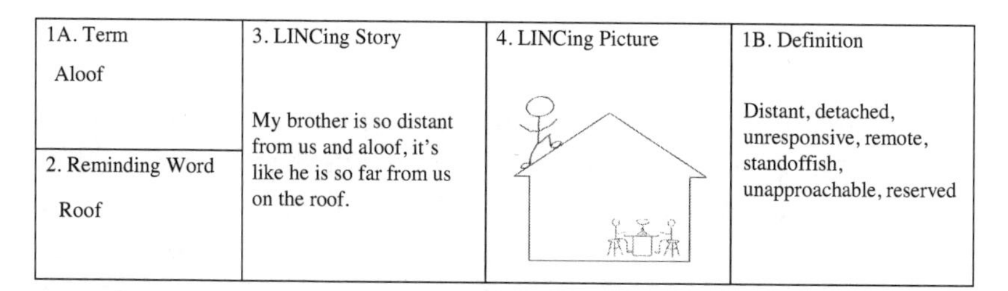

1A. Term	3. LINCing Story	4. LINCing Picture	1B. Definition
Aloof	My brother is so distant from us and aloof, it's like he is so far from us on the roof.		Distant, detached, unresponsive, remote, standoffish, unapproachable, reserved
2. Reminding Word			
Roof			

FIGURE 3.2 Example LINCS Table

connection with the term and ultimately when they see this word, they will remember it. With practice and teacher reinforcement, students get stronger at the LINCS routine.

3. A device is just a device is just a device. If I had a penny for every time a student was awarded with an iPad for "good" behavior or received a worksheet on a Chromebook instead of a worksheet paper, I would have more pennies in my piggybank than I want. Methods like this are "twinkie" SDI that offer very little long-term substance. Though technology will never replace a good teacher, a good teacher knows that there are many ways to effectively use a device to level the playing field for a student with an exceptionality. Technology can be a powerful tool to assist students with learning exceptionalities and provide access to the curriculum. For example: *Word Prediction* software can reduce the number of keystrokes needed to write a word; *Text to Speech* software reads text aloud; *Speech to Text* (speech/voice recognition) turns spoken words into printed text; and handwriting recognition turns written text into digital text. Accessibility features like Microsoft's Learning Tools- Immersive Reader, Textcompactor.com, and Rewordify.com can all support students in manipulating complex text.

> For most of us, technology makes things easier. For a person with a disability, it makes things possible.
> Judy Heumann, American Disability Rights Activist

The Chrome web browser allows students to install a wide variety of web extensions that provide tools that can help all learners, regardless of ability level. Start by downloading the Google Chrome browser for free; this

> gives students access to the many accessibility extensions on the Chrome Webstore for free. The Chrome Webstore is like my Amazon Prime, in that I spend quite a bit of time looking up things. The big difference is these items can be "purchased" for free! A person can type in any area of specific need and find free apps and extensions that can be added to the Google Chrome browser to enhance accessibility. For example, if student has dyslexia, there are tons of accessibility tools that can support this student as they engage with text digitally. Specifically, type in "dyslexia" into the omni search box in the Chrome Webstore and tons of free extensions like *Helperbird* pop up. Helperbird can change fonts, color blind features, add a dyslexic ruler, change colors, overlay, and much more.

For a student who has difficulty getting their great ideas onto paper or a student who has motor limitations, teachers can search "speech to text" and find tons of extensions similar to GoogleDoc's "voice typing" tools, such as *Read and Write for Google Chrome*. This extension can be added to a student's computer to remove barriers to writing. With any of these extensions, students can verbally share their words, sentences, and paragraphs and their words will be typed for them. Specifically, *Read and Write for Google Chrome* is what many of us call the "Swiss Army Knife" of extensions, with tools including word prediction, dictionary, picture dictionary, text to speech, screenshot reader, speech maker, screen mask, translator, highlighters, voice note, and more. It works on webpages, PDFs, Google Docs, and Google Slides. Basic features are free and educators can get the paid version for a year at no cost by filling out the form at https://www.texthelp.com. *Co:Writer Universal* is another great extension that includes word prediction, vocabulary builder, and highlighting tools.

Text-to-speech instruction also helps students with writing and reading. The combination of seeing and hearing text when reading:

- improves word recognition,
- increases the ability to pay attention and remember information while reading, which can then support the writing process,

TABLE 3.2 Chrome Extensions and Apps

Readability: BeeLine Reader	*Reading Comprehension: Google Dictionary*
Provides a variety of color gradients to text to help read faster and more accurately to improve comprehension.	Double-click on any word to get a pop-up definition, as well as spoken pronunciation for many words.
Reading Comprehension: Summary Summary tool gives you a pop-up window with a short bullet list of the main sentences from the page.	Reading Comprehension: TLDR: Summarize Anything The user can decide between three levels of summarization: short, medium, and long.
Reading Comprehension: Resoomer Summary tool that captures the main points and ideas of a text; you can refine as necessary.	Reading Comprehension: Auto Highlight This extension automatically highlights the important content on article pages.
Reading Comprehension: Internet Abridged This summarization extension can summarize the current tab and/or selected content.	Focus: Move It This extension can be set to provide various break periods during work time. Excellent for "work first and then ___ minute learning breaks."

- allows students to focus on comprehension instead of sounding out words, and
- increases kids' stamina (sustained attention) for reading.

By listening to the audio, students can recognize and fix errors in their own writing.

Some of my favorite free text-to-speech extensions are *Select and Speak*, *Read Aloud*, *Voice Instead*, and *Announcify*. See Table 3.2 for more free extensions and apps to support access to text.

Examples of Specially Designed Instruction in Action

Mathematics: Concrete Representational Abstract

Some of our students with learning disabilities have trouble with abstract reasoning. As such, they may have difficulty verbalizing what they have learned or observed, and difficulty making the connection with symbolic representations and/or understanding the math concept that is being explained or shown. The concrete-representational-abstract (CRA) approach is a framework that research suggests can enhance math understanding and performance for students with learning disabilities. CRA is a three-part instructional strategy, with each component building on the previous instruction to promote student learning, retention of concepts and conceptual understanding. Numerous studies have found using direct and explicit instruction like the CRA approach for students with learning disabilities in mathematics to have strong effect sizes (Baker, Gersten & Lee, 2002; Gersten, Chard, Jayanthi, Baker, Morphy & Flojo, 2009; Flynn, Zheng & Swanson, 2012)

The three stages

Concrete (The "doing" stage): During the concrete stage of instruction, the teacher models and students use three-dimensional objects to build conceptional understanding of the math objective. The use of manipulatives (red and yellow chips, cubes, base ten blocks, pattern blocks, fraction bars, and geometric figures) increases the number of sensory inputs a student uses while learning the new concept, which improves the chances for a student to remember the procedural steps needed to solve the problem (Witzel, 2005).

Representational (The "seeing" stage): In the representational stage of instruction, teacher transforms concrete into a representational level. Students are taught to use pictorial representations (drawings using circles, dots, tallies; or stamps to imprint pictures for counting).

Abstract (The "symbolic" stage). At this stage, the teacher models the mathematics concept at a symbolic level, using only numbers, notation, and mathematical symbols to represent the number of circles or groups of circles. The students are taught how to translate the two-dimensional drawings.

Conduct a CRA assessment (see Figure 3.3) to differentiate instruction for various learners. Not every student with

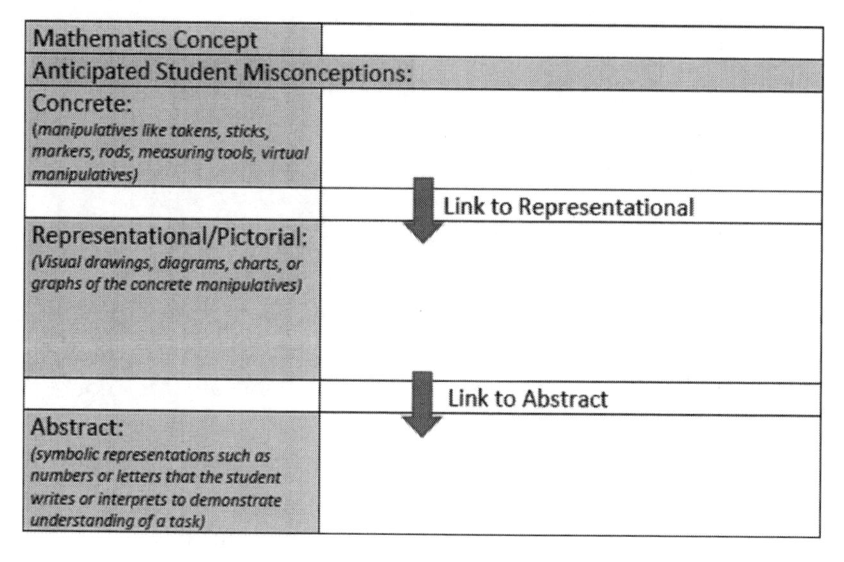

Concrete-Representational-Abstract
Planning Sheet

Mathematics Concept	
Anticipated Student Misconceptions:	
Concrete: *(manipulatives like tokens, sticks, markers, rods, measuring tools, virtual manipulatives)*	
	Link to Representational
Representational/Pictorial: *(Visual drawings, diagrams, charts, or graphs of the concrete manipulatives)*	
	Link to Abstract
Abstract: *(symbolic representations such as numbers or letters that the student writes or interprets to demonstrate understanding of a task)*	

FIGURE 3.3 Concrete-Representational-Abstract Planning Form

a disability area of impact in math will need this, but some students do. Here's how it works: Start by posting the problem/equation that the student needs to solve. The problems must go in reverse order of CRA (abstract-representational-concrete) because the end goal is for students to successfully solve an abstract problem. Show the student one problem at a time to solve.

For example:

1. Abstract: 90 – 12 = ____ Ask the student to solve the problem the abstract way (just ask them to solve it and note the strategy).
2. Representational: 40 – 15 = ______ Ask the student to solve the problem using a representational tool provided (e.g., number line, 100 chart, grid paper, etc.).
3. Concrete: 20 – 9 = _____ Ask the student to solve the problem using manipulatives provided (e.g., two-colored counters, base 10 blocks, fraction bars, etc.).

The student must solve all three problems regardless of how he/she performs on each problem. Note on a data sheet if the student demonstrated:

Mastery (highly proficient with the skill/prerequisites)
Instructional (some knowledge of skills/prerequisites)
Frustration (little/no knowledge of the skills/prerequisites)

After the assessment, analyze the data trends. The data will help you determine which students need more support with the foundational concept/prerequisite skills using manipulatives, which need support with the representational concept using pictures/diagrams, and which need support with the abstract concept using numbers only. Appendix provides a CRA planning flow chart to help plan instruction from concrete to presentation to abstract for students, to ensure that explicit connections between lessons and stages occur to support the student in learning the targeted material. Practice is key. Provide students ample opportunities to practice after each stage. Be sure to create routines and an organizational system for manipulatives so students can always use them as needed.

Virtual Manipulative Resources for CRA

Virtual manipulatives can also be used to support CRA, The following is a list of websites with free manipulatives.

Videos of CRA in action: Digital Promise, The Learner Variability Project, Concrete-Representational-Abstract (CRA) https://lvp.digitalpromiseglobal.org
Sample scripted CRA lessons with manipulatives: Hand2Mind.com
Didax Free Manipulatives Library: http://www.didax.com/virtual-manipulatives-for-math
National Library of Virtual Manipulatives: http://nlvm.usu.edu
National Council of Teachers of Mathematics Illuminations: http://illuminations.nctm.org

Explore Learning Gizmos: https://www.explorelearning.com/free
Geogebra: https://www.geogebra.org
Math Learning Center: https://www.mathlearningcenter.org/resources/apps
Mathies Interactive Electronic supports- https://www.mathies.ca/#gsc.tab=0
Mathigon Polypad - https://mathigon.org/polypad
Toy Theatre- https://toytheater.com/category/teacher-tools/virtual-manipulatives/

Writing: Compare Diagnose Operate

The C-D-O (Compare, Diagnose, Operate) strategy from La Paz, Swanson, & Graham encourages struggling writers to spend extra time in the revision and editing process. The C-D-O strategy has students compare the differences between what they wrote and what they meant to say, diagnose the reason for the discrepancy, and operate by fixing the problem and then evaluating how successful the change was. Students examine each sentence and each paragraph in a prescriptive manner using their set of C-D-O cards that you create based on each student's writing development level.

Students follow these three steps in three cycles:

THE FIRST CYCLE has the student follow C-D-O to examine their work sentence by sentence.

Compare

First Cycle: Ask myself, "Does my sentence match what I really wanted to say?"

Diagnose

First Cycle: Pick a diagnostic card (e.g., words are too vague, forgot some words, sentence lacks detail, sentence is too long or short, words are in the wrong order)

Operate

First Cycle: Make the change and evaluate the impact by asking, "Was the change effective?"

THE SECOND CYCLE has students follow C-D-O to examine each paragraph.

Compare

Second Cycle: Ask myself, "Does my paragraph match the main idea I wanted to express?"

Diagnose

Second Cycle: Pick a diagnostic card (e.g., forgot a topic or main idea sentence, lacks a transition, paragraph is too long or short, sentences are in the wrong order, need more details about the main idea)

Operate

Second Cycle: Make the change and evaluate the impact by asking, "Was the change effective?"

THE THIRD CYCLE focuses on the whole text (this cycle is optional depending on students' need).

Adaptations: Teachers can target a student's specific writing skills by adapting and changing the CDO cards to meet each student's diagnostic writing needs. For example, some students need support with punctuation and others are working on subject-verb agreement. Students' individual cards should match their writing level. Teachers should still confer with students about their writing consistently through the writing process. To print off sample C-D-O diagnostic flashcards, visit Johns Hopkins University Secondary Support Initiative (JHUSSI) C-D-O Strategy.

Learning heuristics

Teaching students learning strategies such as how to create and use mnemonics to support understanding and retention of key concepts and processes is essential. *Mnemonics* are memory devices that help learners recall large and important pieces of information. Mnemonics connect learning experiences, encourage independent learning, and engage all learners. Teachers and students should create their own mnemonics to match content and learning needs. Researchers such as Marilyn Friend recommend using six steps to help with strategy acquisition of a mnemonic device.

Steps for teaching learning strategies:

1. Assess student's current strategy use, including the need for strategy instruction.

2. Clarify expectations so that the student understands the purpose of the strategy.
3. Demonstrate the strategy and when it might be useful.
4. Assist students in memorizing the strategy steps (massed practice and repetition).
5. Provide guided and independent practice in using the strategy. Be sure to provide immediate feedback.
6. Administer a post-test to determine whether the strategy has been mastered.

Here are a few mnemonic strategies (See Tables 3.3 and 3.4):

Reading

TABLE 3.3 Reading Mnemonic Devices

POSSE (for Reading Comprehension)	*CAPS (Self-Questioning for Reading Comprehension—Young Children)*	*SCROL (Reading Comprehension)*
Englert, 2009 **P** Predict ideas **O** Organize the ideas **S** Search for structure **S** Summarize the main ideas **E** Evaluate your understanding	Leinhardt & Zigmond, 1988 **C** Who are the characters? **A** What is the aim of the story? **P** What problem happens? **S** How is the problem solved?	Grant, 1993 **S** Survey the headings **C** Connect the headings to one another **R** Read the text **O** Outline major ideas with supporting details **L** Look back to check the accuracy of what's written

Math

TABLE 3.4 Math Mnemonic Devices

PIES (Problem Solving)	*STAR (Problem-Solving)*	*CUBE (Problem Solving)*
Picture—draw a simple picture showing the situation **Information**—find important facts (information) and list them next to the picture **Equation**—find an equation that matches the information on the picture **Solve**—insert information from picture into equation and solve algebraically	**S**earch the word problem **T**ranslate the words into an equation in picture form **A**nswer the problem **R**eview the solution	CUBE is an acronym that stands for the following word problem-solving steps: ♦ Circle the numbers. ♦ Underline important words. ♦ Box the question. ♦ Eliminate unnecessary information.

I like to add even more "special" by teaching students how to create and use their own mnemonic devices. Teaching students how to create buzz words that will help cue them to a process to remember key content is so valuable. I often tell students to find one good mnemonic for this concept, share it, and stick with it. The goal is always for our students to develop lifelong strategies that can help them remember key information, and a mnemonic device is a great, long-lasting learning heuristic. This is the power of SDI.

A large percentage of our students with disabilities are tactile and kinesthetic. So, consider getting students' full body involved or having students create something with their hands around a mnemonic, process, or step framework. For example, for kinesthetic additions, students could jump on each letter of the *Order of Operations* mnemonic device sequentially, like hopscotch, or jump on a shower curtain that has a keyboard imprinted on it to spell their sight words. One of the best tactile resources is a foldable: students can create a foldable to support skill acquisition and retention. Dinah Zike, one of the creators of foldables, shares dozens of ways students can take one or two sheets of paper and create a study resource to support concept retention. A foldable is also known as *cognitive origami*. This tactile study resource can be referred to as a study aid, act as a reference tool during assessments, and be easily inserted into an interactive notebook to collect concepts. My 11th-grade students would often get excited about creating foldables; they'd often ask, "Can we create something to support us with writing a literacy analysis or distinguishing between tone and mood for the *Scarlet Letter*?" My answer was always, "Yes." Try googling "Dinah Zike Foldables" and lots of free booklets with foldables for math and literacy will pop up!

Thinking outside the box

Anne M. Benhinghof, an internationally recognized consultant and trainer, who also works with teachers to incorporate specially

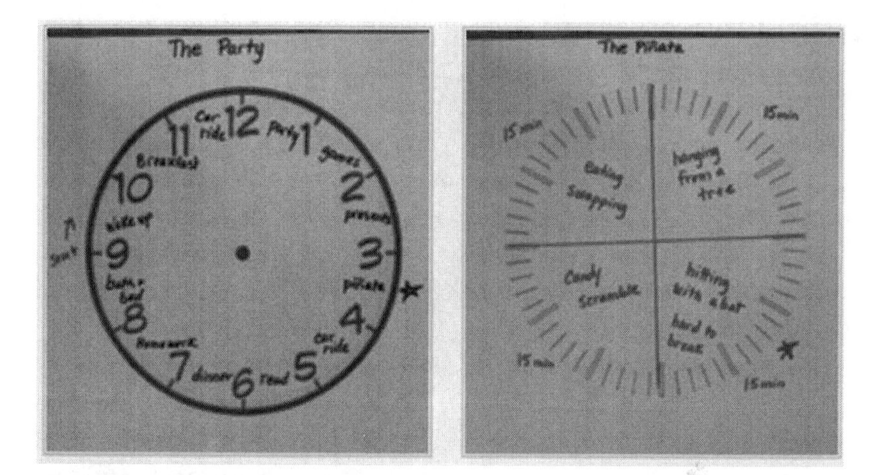

FIGURE 3.4 Anne M.Benhinghof, SDI Writing Example

designed instruction, recently taught an amazing lesson packed with specially designed instruction.

Personal narratives are best when they capture a moment in time and help the reader to experience each detail fully. The challenge is helping students to narrow their topic and give lots of detail to support big ideas.

After students chose a day they wanted to write about, the teachers used a clock face as a planning tool for specific learners that would benefit from an additional approach to support their narrative writing (see Figure 3.4). Students broke the day into 12 one-hour segments. Then students flagged one of the hours that was the most interesting. Using another clock face, they broke the hour into four 15-minute segments, and again flagged one segment that was most interesting.

Next, the teachers taught a "slow motion writing strategy" to slow down even a short amount of time. For example, we had each student write down, "They threw the ball." Using the iPad app SloPro, the teachers videotaped students throwing a ball, then viewed it in slow motion. Students were asked to rewrite the original sentence, adding more detail based on what they saw in slow motion. One student wrote, "He quickly glanced at the catcher, cocked his arm back, aimed with precision and let the ball fly off his fingertips."

Finally, the teachers had students think of a simple action they might include in their personal narrative, such as "I hit the piñata." Then students practiced envisioning it in slow motion and rewriting it with greater descriptive detail on each of the minute or second increments, etc. "I gripped the bat tightly, threw my hips into it and swung at that stubborn piñata with all my might.

Using the time continuum (12 hours to 1 hour to 15 minutes to 1 slow-motion minute) really made sense to the students and helped them to write a focused and rich personal narrative. What a great example of adding "special" to support students with exceptionalities! It required creativity and outside-the-box thinking and supported bridging the gap for students. Although, all students didn't necessarily need this strategy for writing, it definitely supported some of our learners with disabilities. Of course, you could add even more SDI for specific students. Visit Anne's Ideas For Educators blog for even more ideas at http://www.ideasforeducators.com.

Putting It All Together

The following charts (Tables 3.5 and 3.6) combine SDI and accommodations/modifications for various disability areas of impact in literacy and math. Table 3.5 will provide examples for literacy and Table 3.6 will provide examples for mathematics. The Communication and Vocational Charts are in Appendix. These charts are not an exclusive list, but rather a combination of best practices observed, and a starting place for your special education department to clarify, provide specific examples, and add on to.

> Three guiding questions support our justification for the SDI selected: "How does this student's instructional day look different than any other student's?" "How is instruction specialized in addition to what all other students receive?" and "Is the SDI for this student bridging the gap to provide access to the content?"

Literacy

TABLE 3.5 Literacy Supports

Area of Impact	*Specially Designed Instruction (SDI)* *What the "teacher does" through instructional practices*	*Accommodations and/or Modifications* *What the student will use to access curriculum and make significant progress*
Basic Reading	-Grapho-Phonic strategies (visual/auditory) including letter/sound knowledge, phonemic awareness, decoding -Visual strategies including word recognition and visual memory for words -Auditory strategies including language structure at the word, sentence, and text level -Fluency strategies -Direct Braille code instruction -Direct instruction in functions and use of portable note-taking device (BrailleNote, VoiceNote, Braille 'n Speak, etc.) -Meaning strategies, including word meanings and associations and precision in word usage -Instruction in identifying and pronouncing words and reading fluently orally includes: • using content clues; • visual word recognition strategies including environmental print; • word analysis strategies such as prefixes, suffixes, compound words, and word derivations; • text management strategies such as rereading/reading ahead, deep reading, skimming/scanning; • decoding strategies such as identifying word families, chunking, point & slide, looking for known words inside words;	-Graphic organizers -Prompting and cueing -Recorded materials -Alternate electronic/digitized materials -Oral/visual presentation of materials above independent reading level -Extended time -Large print (specified font size) -Highlighted material -Colored overlays for reading/glare reduction (specified color) -Instructional technologies -Direct/indirect lighting -Photocopied materials on preferred colored paper -Tracking guides -Braille, Braille 'n Speak, Refreshable Braille, Type 'n Speak -Manipulatives (letter tiles, flash cards, etc.) -Access to technology (computer, software, voice-to-text software, etc.) -Limit visual clutter/stimuli -Screen enlargement software or magnifier -Spelling dictionary or electronic spelling aid with speech capabilities -Peer editing or teacher assistance in the revision process -Chance to correct identified spelling and grammar errors -Audio books

(*Continued*)

TABLE 3.5 Literacy Supports (*Continued*)

Area of Impact	*Specially Designed Instruction (SDI)* *What the "teacher does" through instructional practices*	*Accommodations and/or Modifications* *What the student will use to access curriculum and make significant progress*
General Reading	• cross-checking across systems (does the word make sense, sound like language, do the letters match the sounds) or ask another reader. -Direct instruction on functions and use of low-vision devices (assistive technology for near and distance viewing) -Direct instruction in accessing alternate formats and associated technology	-Assistive devices that translate text to speech: —reading pen, Read, Write, Gold, Kurzwiel reader, scanner with character recognition software -Videotapes or movies that present the same information -Interactive CDs or computer-assisted training with auditory and visual cues rather than written descriptions. *Students who are blind or visually impaired may need:* • Books-on-tape or large-print versions of text • speaking computers with books on disk • books and instructional materials in Braille • class handouts and materials in an embossed format • Special tilt-top desk or book stand to hold materials for easier reading • Specialized equipment—optical enhancer, magnifier, tape recorder • Directions and test items read aloud or on audiotape • Repetition or paraphrasing of the directions • Important words in the directions underlined or highlighted • Text-to-speech technology to communicate directions

(*Continued*)

TABLE 3.5 Literacy Supports (*Continued*)

Area of Impact	*Specially Designed Instruction (SDI)* *What the "teacher does" through instructional practices*	*Accommodations and/or Modifications* *What the student will use to access curriculum and make significant progress*
Reading Comprehension	-Explicit Instruction in how to use graphic organizers -Modeling using self-regulated strategy development (SRSD) -Instruction in cloze procedures -Mnemonic strategies -Instruction using advance organizers -Instruction using visual prompts -Pre-teaching concepts/vocabulary -Strategy Instruction; for example, • LEARN strategy • **L**ist what you know • **E**xplore what you want to know • **A**ccess information • **R**eflect on what you're learning • **N**ow make connections KWL Strategy • List what you **k**now • Tell what you **w**ant to know • Tell what you **l**earned -Instruction in verbal summarization -Instruction using open-ended stories -QAR (question, answer, response) strategy -Instruction using choral reading, paired reading, echo reading, visual imagery, and story mapping -Direct instruction in: monitoring for meaning, determining importance, creating mental images, synthesizing, relating new to known, questioning, inferring	-Recorded books with appropriate pacing • Recorded materials • Electronic/digitized materials • Highlighting -Large-print materials/textbooks (specified font size) -Standard text to accompany large print text for colored illustrations/maps • Braille • Refreshable Braille • Braille 'n Speak • Type 'n Speak • Reader • Paraphrasing -Oral/visual presentation of materials above independent reading level • Manipulatives (i.e., story strips, etc.) • Advance organizers • Tactual graphics • Visual prompts -Frequent rest breaks to reduce eye fatigue and strain • Slant board/stand • Note-taking guides • Study guides • Highlighted study guides -Audio books or assistive technology to support audio version -Sticky notes or highlighter to mark key points in the textbook or manual -List of important vocabulary with definitions -Demonstration of steps and procedures

(*Continued*)

TABLE 3.5 Literacy Supports (*Continued*)

Area of Impact	*Specially Designed Instruction (SDI)* *What the "teacher does" through instructional practices*	*Accommodations and/or Modifications* *What the student will use to access curriculum and make significant progress*
Reading Comprehension	-Direct instruction and support for specialized software and equipment -Applying Braille reading (or use of low-vision devices for literacy tasks) in authentic contexts -Instruction in hand/finger skills, tactile discrimination/perception skills -Integrated use of visual skills (e.g., scanning for information, reading charts, graphs, maps) -Direct Braille code instruction -Direct instruction in functions and use of portable note-taking device (BrailleNote, VoiceNote, Braille 'n Speak) -Direct instruction on functions and use of low-vision devices (assistive technology for near and distance viewing)	-Guided questions to follow for independent reading -Complex information divided into chunks or sections -Hands-on activities, visual aids, pictures, or diagrams to provide alternate ways of learning abstract concepts or complex information
Written Expression	-Explicit instruction in graphic organizers -Modeling using self-regulated strategy development (SRSD) -Modeling tactile kinesthetic tracing -Guided practice through repetition -Explicit Instruction using advance organizers -Visual and physical prompts and cues -Small-group instruction in writing process -Explicit structured approach to sentence writing -Explicit Instruction in the writing process, including prewriting activities, writing, revising, editing, and publishing	-Assistive technology -Advance organizers -Cue cards (definitions, examples, story starters, picture prompts, etc.) -Journals, logs, notebooks -Rubrics/scoring guides to guide -Editing checklists -Production of written pieces -Mnemonic strategies -Error monitoring, self-monitoring -Webs, diagrams, or charts and outlines to plan and respond to open-ended or essay questions -Highlighting and color-coded direction words -Manipulatives (sentence strips, word cards, personal and classroom word banks, etc.)

(*Continued*)

TABLE 3.5 Literacy Supports (*Continued*)

Area of Impact	*Specially Designed Instruction (SDI)* *What the "teacher does" through instructional practices*	*Accommodations and/or Modifications* *What the student will use to access curriculum and make significant progress*
Written Expression	-Direct instruction in idea development, structural patterns, sequencing, organization, standards of correctness, awareness of audience and purpose -Direct instruction in open-response writing, writing-on-demand, transactive writing, personal writing, literary writing, reflective writing, and writing-to-learn (graphic organizers, journals, note-taking) -Direct instruction in mechanics and usage of slate/stylus -Direct instruction in mechanics and use of Braillewriter/note-taking device -Direct instruction in functions and use of magnification systems -Direct instruction for keyboarding/computer skills	-Apps like Dragon Dictation and Google Drive Microphone to talk into and write from -Specialized writing utensils (Pencil Grips, 20/20 pens, #1 Lead pencil, bold marker, slate/stylus, etc.) -Specialized writing materials (Braillewriter, portable note-taking device, signature/letter guide, typoscope, computer with screen reader/magnification software) -Limit visual clutter/stimuli -Access to technology (computer, software, tape recorder, voice-to-text software) -Bold line, raised line, Braille paper -Alternate demonstrations of knowledge and skills

Math

TABLE 3.6 Math Supports

Area of Impact	*Specially Designed Instruction (SDI)* *What the "teacher does" through instructional practices*	*Accommodations and/or Modifications* *What the student will use to access curriculum and make significant progress*
Math Calculation and Reasoning	-Multisensory teaching strategies, K-symbols using full body movements, and math chants/rhymes -Use of manipulatives using the Concrete-Representational-Abstract framework -Modeling with guided checklist and references -Direct instruction in computation and reasoning strategies, word problem strategies -Direct instruction in functions and use of abacus	♦ Mnemonic strategies ♦ Cue cards with problem-solving strategies, definitions, examples, models, flow chart, process steps ♦ Small-group instruction ♦ Visual, nonverbal, verbal, physical, picture, and written prompts and cues ♦ Repetitive practice ♦ Advanced organizers

(*Continued*)

TABLE 3.6 Math Supports (*Continued*)

Area of Impact	*Specially Designed Instruction (SDI)* *What the "teacher does" through instructional practices*	*Accommodations and/or Modifications* *What the student will use to access curriculum and make significant progress*
Math Calculation and Reasoning	-Direct instruction in functions and use of accessible graphing calculator software -Direct instruction in functions and use of portable note-taking device (BrailleNote, VoiceNote, Braille 'n Speak, etc.) -Direct instruction on functions and use of low-vision devices (assistive technology for near and distance viewing) -Guided practice mnemonic strategies and problem-solving strategies -Guided practice through chunking, self-questioning, and skills -Pre-teaching and re-teaching of key vocabulary and processes (of the initial learning of difficult skills and supervised practice to prevent misconceptions) -Guided practice of subskills explicitly related to the performance of the whole task and what the student has already learned -Additional independent practice until fluent responses are possible -Direct instruction of specialized vocabulary and mathematical symbols -Modeling of abstract math concepts through concrete materials and manipulatives or computer-based models -Explicit Instruction for use of flowcharts to plan strategies for problem solving	♦ Extended time with word problems ♦ Graph paper/vertical lined paper ♦ Manipulatives/xoncrete representations ♦ Tactile graphs/graphics ♦ Calculator (large display/talking/graphing/audible graphing calculator software) ♦ Low-vision devices (near and distant) ♦ Additional hands-on resources: Abacus, Magnifier ♦ Colored overlay ♦ Number line ♦ Study guides and reference formulas ♦ Peer buddy/peer tutoring ♦ Oral presentation of materials/assessments ♦ Assistive technology ♦ Calculator for computation tasks ♦ Talking calculator or on-screen computer calculator ♦ Flowcharts to plan strategies for problem solving ♦ Additional examples and explanations ♦ Use of graph paper or color coding to organize answers to math problems

Next Steps

There is no federally mandated list of SDI examples, but we have guidelines and useful resources to support our work with SDI. Thus, we need to be able to justify why we choose the specific approach to support each student. Three guiding questions support our justification for the SDI selected: "How does this student's instructional day look different than any other student's?" "How is instruction specialized in addition to what all other students receive?" and "Is the SDI for this student bridging the gap to provide meaningful access to the core content?" This Brainstorming Form (inspired by members of my Inclusion Specialist team), titled Specially Designed Instruction Planning Form "" can support teachers with matching area of impact, specially designed instruction, and teacher actions (see Table 3.7). Table 3.7 is a guided organizer and is intended to be

TABLE 3.7 Specially Designed Instruction Planning Form

Description of Area of Need and/or Impact of Disability	*Required Service and Goal*	*Specially Designed Instruction Teacher Actions during Service Delivery*	*Amount of service time required to address the area of need*	*Data Collection*
	Required Service: Goal:			
	Required Service: Goal:			

used as a planning guide to assist in the determination of specially designed instruction, services to support SDI based on students' impact of disability, and intentional data collection to support IEP goal mastery. (Appendix).

Step 1: Identify area of need/impact of disability.
Step 2: Describe the required service and goal area.
Step 3: Task-analyze the annual goal area and align specially designed instructional approaches that would help the student reach their goal area.
Step 4: Consider how much time it would take for the teacher on average to provide the specially designed instructional approaches. Describe the "looks like" and "sounds like" of the SDI approaches' required amount of service time.
Step 5: Explain how you will collect data to progress monitor the effects of the SDI approach.

In Closing

Adding the "special" is *necessary* to accelerate the achievement of students with disabilities. It requires going above and beyond "good, effective instruction." SDI is complex work and takes time to create and analyze, but it's worth the time to reach the highest outcomes for our students. Celebrate the victories in this dance as we monitor progress for effectiveness and growth. Collaborate with related service providers, the student, and the family to ensure that the specially designed instruction used is incorporated in every setting for the highest outcomes. Be creative, innovate, and think outside the box. Consider learning barriers that students have around core content, remove the learning barriers, and create access for students using specially designed instruction. Specially designed instruction will prepare our students to navigate college and career life successfully. Ultimately, our students will be able to use the skills, tools, and strategies we teach them forever. They will become the best dancers.

Top 7 Dance Moves

Which of these moves can you try tomorrow? Which moves can you share with your team?

1. Create a team book study on Explicit Instruction using the book, *Explicit Instruction: Effective and Efficient Teaching: What Works for Special Needs Learners*, by Anita L. Archer and Charles A Hughes. Visit Archer and Hughes's explicitinstruction.org website to watch videos of Explicit Instruction and analyze instructional moves as a team.
2. Visit the Google Chrome browser's Webstore and search for accessibility apps and extensions that could support a specific student. Some of my favorite extensions are Text to Speech, Highlighters, Visual Dictionaries, and Summarizing Tools.
3. Evaluate one of your struggling students with a disability. Is SDI interwoven throughout the present level of performance and support reaching the student's goals and objectives? Does the selected approach of SDI help the student reach their IEP objective and provide access to the content? Have we tried some outside-the-box approaches? If another educator picked up the IEP, would they have an idea of how to provide SDI for this student? Use the Brainstorming Form – Starting Point for Discussions on Specially Designed Instruction to analyze the approach and alignment of SDI.
4. Add an evidence-based approach to supporting vocabulary acquisition such as LINCS, or check out the University of Kansas Center for Research on Learning website (https://kucrl.ku.edu) to pick up a few more strategic learning structures.

(*Continued*)

5. Consider adding more kinesthetic or tactile opportunities. Pinterest or google "foldables" for your specific objective. Provide time to model and create a foldable to support retention and study skills.
6. Create a Go-To toolbox of specially designed instruction examples based on various areas of disability impact areas for your team (academics and behavioral). Utilize InterventionCentral.org and National Center on Intensive Intervention at IntensiveIntervention.org to compile a bank of specially designed instruction approaches that are evidence-based and can be used with intensity for specific learners.
7. Take a free Iris Center Learning Module and earn a free continuing education certificate on "Learning Strategies" for students with disabilities at https://iris.peabody.vanderbilt.edu.

List your next dance steps for adding more "special" for students with disabilities.

____

____

____

____

____

Accountability Partner: ________________________

____

Check-in Date: ______________________________

____

Whether you stick with the most basic steps or you become very adept at the fanciest turns, jitterbug dancing is a whole lot of fun to learn, and even more fun to do! So just go for it and add some more "special."

4

Kathak

Choice and Multiple Learning Modalities

Kathak is one of the eight forms of Indian classical dance. The origins of the dance are largely attributed to the traveling poets of ancient northern India known as *kathakas* or storytellers. The term *Kathak* is rooted in the Vedic term *Katha* (Sanskrit: कथा), which means "story, conversation, traditional tale." Dancers say that there is no classical dance style that is as free in its presentation as Kathak. Every Kathak dancer starts their performance in their own way and arranges the many different dance pieces however they choose. Choice and interest are huge motivators, and allow a person to create something beautifully unique. Who doesn't love choice? Even adults prefer choice. Teachers enjoy choice in class schedules, staff book studies, and professional development. Aerospace scientist and the eleventh president of India, Dr. A.P.J. Abdul Kalam, provides context for adding choice, using a variety of learning modalities, and recruiting interest with our students: "Without your involvement you can't succeed. With your involvement you can't fail." Teaching with a one-size-fits-all approach will inevitably exclude many students, most likely students with disabilities, whose very involvement and investment are dependent on flexibility and a variety of learning approaches and resources. It may feel unfair to provide some students and not others with multiple chances or flexibility, but that is what's necessary to ensure that all of our students receive access to the curriculum.

Teaching with a *one-size-fits-all* approach will inevitably exclude many students, most likely students with disabilities, whose very involvement and investment depend on us providing a variety of learning approaches and resources.

Ever hear a student say, "I can't do school?" I have. It is never easy to hear and stomach. Consider reflecting, "What do I need to change so a student feels like 'school' is relevant and achievable." In my TED talk, "Inclusion and Fast Food: Designing a Meaningful Learning Experience," I advocate that learning experiences at school should be so delicious that the thought of "school" is right up there with our favorite food memories. School should be a place that *all* children are excited to wake up and go to, and not just for social reasons. As innovators in education, we have lessons to learn from companies like Taco Bell that seek to create spectacular, mouthwatering, memorable experiences for their consumers.

Some opponents of providing choice might say, "The standardized test is a one-size assessment, multiple choice, right or wrong, there's no space for creativity." While this may be true, we have eight or so months to not be standardized, drill-and-kill teachers. Avoiding "drill and kill" doesn't mean cutting preparation for students; it means avoiding hundreds of worksheets. I refer to this phenomenon of lots of white paper as "Death by Worksheet." Students still need practice and an opportunity to take timed practice tests to figure out an approach that works for them, but there's tons of time to *not* "drill and kill." As I write, the world is undergoing a pandemic in which schools have been shuttered, and the fact is that no student will ever remember something that they did on a worksheet during highly challenging experiences or under stress to pass a test in school. We have the gift of eight months in which we can provide choice, options for creativity, and project-based learning, infuse student interest into lessons, integrate high levels of thinking, and use various learning modalities to involve, engage, and excite all students.

"Drill and kill" test prep can be thought of like a candy bar. Consider the wise words from Ryan McCarty with the Teaching

Channel: "Test prep worksheets are the educational equivalent of a Snickers bar. They're a bad habit from before we knew better, in a nice, ready-to-go package, with the illusion of nutritional value. Both may temporarily soothe us and make us feel like everything is going to be okay, but in the long run they are empty calories. Once the sugar rush wears off, we're in worse shape than before: Unhealthy, feeling guilty, lacking the energy for real change." This is an accurate metaphor, as research reveals mixed results on the benefits of "drill and kill" before a test—and after the test is over many students don't remember much.

This chapter is centered on the power of choice and infusing student interest, and for each choice strategy discussed I also share a variety of teaching methods that can remove barriers to concept acquisition. For me, Universal Design for Learning (UDL) is the process of purposefully and proactively planning to account for learner variance and removing barriers in the learning experience to stimulate ALL learners. Universal Design for Learning isn't a "SPED thing," it's an "every teacher, for every student thing." By planning with the three Universal Design for Learning guidelines (Engagement, Representation, and Action and Expression), we can remove educational barriers to content mastery and provide access for every learner. One of the three UDL guidelines is "Engagement," which entails motivating students and providing students with multiple ways to engage with content beyond teacher lecture. If we start with engagement, the other two guidelines will naturally fall into place. Our goal is to create independent and strategic learners, and choice will get all students involved, so it simultaneously creates self-regulated and motivated learners (that's kinda the whole point of education, right?).

Student Interest

The goal is to recruit student interest and motivate students; this increases the engagement of all learners. In the movie *Field of Dreams*, there is a catchy quote, "If you build it; he will come." Changing a few words around for our purpose, "If you ask, they will engage." The first element of providing various options for choice is to learn the different ways students like to learn. We're not trying to trap students into a specific learning style track by finding out these preferences; rather, by garnering student feedback, we can provide lots of different learning modalities in daily instruction. Students can have some autonomy to choose and we can challenge others to try something new that's out of their comfort zone. Teachers can collect student interest data in a large number and variety of ways. For example, at the bottom of an assessment, ask students one or two questions, such as "Do you like watching videos about content? What's your favorite way to show me you understand?" Do you like hands-on experiences? Would you prefer to talk your process over aloud with a peer?" The second way teachers can obtain student interest data is have students take a 15-minute learning styles/interest survey that they can score and reflect on themselves as learners. There are lots of free interest surveys: some are pictorial for elementary learners, others have guiding questions for secondary learners. Teachers Pay Teachers has tons of multiple intelligence surveys, and some are even free, like Laura Candler's MI Survey for Kids. These surveys don't take too long, and they give students an opportunity to build self-awareness about themselves as learners. As a bonus, we can use the data to inform our instruction, motivate diverse learners, and incorporate a variety of learning modality opportunities.

Choice with Learning Menus

Students benefit greatly from being provided with choices, whether it's choice in how to learn something new, choice in how to navigate their learning pathway, or choice in sharing their learning. Providing students with choice doesn't have to take a lot of extra prep time. In fact, once the routines for choice are established, students' levels of working independently or with partners effectively increase.

Learning menus offer students a way to make decisions about content. A menu could be designed for 10 minutes, a single lesson, a week-long lesson, or even a month-long period of study. The teacher decides what the essential understandings and/or skills are, and then creates a menu of meaningful choices. Though there are many different formats of learning menus, choice boards are a great place to start and shake things up a bit. Choice boards can help teachers differentiate learning paths, remove barriers, and engage all students.

Choice Boards

Choice boards provide instructional activities that address a variety of student characteristics and support a range of student abilities in order to promote student achievement. They come in a grid format of typically three, six, or nine boxes. This allows greater individualization in a class and helps target instruction as the teacher can navigate around the room to support student learning. Choice boards allow students to make decisions about how they will process learning and/or demonstrate their learning.

Teachers should first analyze a unit's big ideas. Next, choose the content, topic, and/or desired learning for the choice board. Then identify the most important elements of the lesson/unit/what you want the student to know and be able to explain. Lastly, create a variety of activities that your students can choose from to navigate learning or show their understanding of the topic.

Vocabulary Choice Board

Look over this vocabulary choice board (see Figure 4.1). Students will complete a tic-tac-toe "win" horizontally, vertically, or diagonally. What do you notice about this choice board?

Create a Crossword Puzzle Use Discover Education's Puzzle Maker to create a crossword puzzle using all of your words.	Make a Cartoon Use Toony Tool to create a cartoon using 2 of your words.	Use a Quizlet Create a set of study cards for terms and play one of the games with your cards.
Record It Use Vocaroo to record yourself using 3 of your vocabulary words in a sentence or rap.	Discuss It Visit our Flipgrid link and record yourself acting out 3 of the vocabulary words. Answer at least one of your classmate's responses.	Movie Cards Pick one of the Movie cards and pretend you're the main character in the movie. Use the vocabulary terms as the main character would in the movie.
Create a Meme Create a meme about 1 of your words using Addtext.com. Use copyright-free images from Pixabay or our class photos.	Map It! Using the vocabulary maps on our class Google slides, map out 3 of your vocabulary terms.	Draw it Using Google drawing to illustrate 2 of your vocabulary terms.

FIGURE 4.1 Vocabulary Choice Board

This vocabulary choice board provides students with a variety of ways to engage with their terms or concepts. There are a lot of different learning modality options and the various opportunities can engage diverse students' interest. Some students may like the technology options, other students who love to draw might choose the "Draw It" option, and others who like music might choose to create a rap or poem. There's something in this vocabulary choice board for every learner. Such a choice board can be used to support vocabulary for a variety of subjects and grades. Our social studies and science teachers have tons and tons of vocabulary terms that they need students to remember, as concepts build on other concepts. Why not let students have some fun with their terms, possibly for the first 10 minutes of class as a warm-up? This choice board gets all students involved in reviewing content vocabulary right away at the beginning of class, whereas homework review can quickly exclude students (those who have completed it correctly and those who didn't do it) and create disengagement. The lack of student involvement right at the beginning of class can set a downhill tone for the rest of the class period. Good instruction requires great behavior management. This choice board can be used repeatedly throughout a unit as students obtain new terms and concepts.

Allowing students the opportunity to play with and use their terms in a variety of ways can support long-term acquisition of those words. Many of our adolescents with disabilities experience low motivation to read (Legault, Green-Demers, & Pelletier, 2006). We want students to love written language and get excited about learning new words! Vocabulary practice doesn't have to be boring or a practice of rote memorization with lots of worksheets. In fact, route memorization doesn't work—try asking a group of ninth-graders what "mitosis" is! Can they tell you? Students excel in literacy instruction when teachers follow Robert Marzano's six steps of vocabulary acquisition to engage students in understanding and using vocabulary (*Building Background Knowledge for Academic Achievement: Research on What Works in Schools*, 2004).

Step 1: Introduce the new term by providing a description, explanation or example of it. Students should not copy words out of a dictionary (they will not remember the terms, and this is drudgery). Provide a context for the term, tell a story that integrates the term, use video or computer images as the stimulus for understanding information, or use current events to connect the term to something familiar. Some of my favorite tools to add visual support to terms are visuwords.com and visualthesaurus.com. Subscribe to *Flocabulary* on YouTube for a library of educational hip-hop songs and videos on key concepts and vocabulary terms to give students context.

Step 2: Ask students to restate the description, explanation or example in their own words and monitor and correct understanding. This must be student's original ideas, not parroting the teacher. Have students discuss with a partner or community circle. Students should record their definition in a running vocabulary log (interactive notebook or digital journal). There are tons of vocabulary organizers from a Frayer's model to a K.I.M. chart (Key word, Information, Memory cue). Choose one vocabulary organizer that works for you and your students.

Step 3: Ask students to construct a picture, symbol or graphic representing the word. Provide examples of students' drawings (and your own) that are rough but represent the ideas. Paste a picture of the term or find a picture on the Internet of the term. Specifically, have students create infographics on how the terms connect or are different. Piktochart.com is a perfect way for students to create infographics on key terms and concepts learned.

Step 4: Engage students in discussion activities that help them add to their knowledge of the terms and word analysis in their vocabulary notebooks. Some examples are: highlight prefixes, suffixes and root words that will help them remember the meaning of the term, sort or classify words, identify synonyms and antonyms for the term, translate the term into another language or point out cognates for second language students. Interactive word walls are great visuals to manipulate and elicit discussion on new terms. A great way for students to make meaning of key vocabulary words is for them to create comics using the key terms. Check out these free story creation resources: storyboardthat.com, makebeliefscomix.com, and pixton.com.

Step 5: Ask students to discuss the terms with one another. Think-pair-share is a great way to let students discuss terms. Students can compare their descriptions and pictures of the term. Students can explain to each other any new information they have learned about the terms. Try using autodraw.com or awwapp.com, interactive whiteboards to remove the barrier of some students feeling like they can't draw.

Step 6: It is easy to stop at step 5 and forget about step 6, but don't skip any steps in this process. Following all six steps helps students with long term vocabulary and concept retrieval. In the last step, we aim to involve students periodically in games that allow them to play with terms. The games don't have to be long or every week. A few oldies but goodies are Pictionary, charades, or jeopardy. Quizlet allows students to create and play games with their vocabulary term flashcards for free. Students can add images, sentences, etc., to match their vocabulary terms. Students can download the app on their phone and manipulate the virtual cards in any setting.

Fun Vocabulary Games

Vocabulary loop cards

Loop cards enable a vocabulary game where each student has a card on which there is both a question and an answer (see Figure 4.2). As a question is called out, each child looks for the answer; if the vocabulary term is on their card, they call it out and read the question at the bottom of their card. This continues and works its way around a group or the classroom until all children have participated and it loops back to the *Start* person.

Why use Loop cards? This card game is a fun way to acquire and practice vocabulary knowledge (or solve math problems); enhance children's listening and concentration skills; and provide an opportunity for students to work collaboratively to enrich their academic vocabulary and language (all subjects). The Loop cards can target academic vocabulary, core content review, and mathematics facts and problems, among others.

A: I have ______________________

Q: Who has __________________?

Example

A: I have Mitochondria

Q: Who has, "Suicide sacks that contain digestive enzymes?"

FIGURE 4.2 Vocabulary Loop Card Game

There are different types of Loop cards with different names—for example, "I have…who has" cards, "Who am I?" cards, "Follow me" cards—but all generally involve a loop of some sort so that students can self-monitor and self-evaluate the answers throughout the loop to ensure that their loop has been completed correctly. The last card's answer should always loop back to the start person's answer card. When all students have completed the game and it loops back to Pupil No. 1, that student calls the answer and says "FINISH."

Differentiation: The Loop card game could be played as a whole class, in small teams, or solo on the table, akin to dominoes, where the child would link up the card containing the answer to follow the question card. A loop card game takes no longer than five minutes. If it is a version new to the class, stop every so often to make a whole-class activity of working out the solution or explaining the particular word. Students love to time how long it takes to loop around the class and to beat their previous time.

Management: Students remember who speaks before them, because, in some cases, the only link being formed in their head is between the previous person's question and their own answer to it; that is, they do not listen to the other questions. This can be avoided by getting students to switch cards occasionally and write down specific answers. The teacher will also need to keep an at-a-glance answer sheet handy, which may be needed in the event a loop breaks down or a card gets lost.

Create the Loop:

1. Fill in questions (Q) and answers (A) on the cards. Then copy all the cards and give each player one or more.
2. Start with the first card. One student starts reading the Q on their card. The pupil who has the correct A answers, and then reads his or her Q, and so on. If you do it correctly, the last A will be on the first card, and you will have made a complete loop!

Tea party

Tea Party is a great vocabulary/concept strategy that also serves as a pre-reading strategy because it prepares students to pull out key terms and read challenging text. The teacher reads the upcoming text and writes key words, quotes, pictures, and phrases that will support understanding of the text little slips of paper. As students come into class, the teacher hands each student a slip of paper with their item. Students mingle around the classroom and partner up with various peers to share their term, phrase, or picture. After they share their item, they make predictions together on what the upcoming text will be about. As they read the text, the teacher stops them periodically so students can refine or confirm their predictions. Students are building background knowledge together and activating their cognitive schemas as they become actively engaged in the text; all of these skills support reading comprehension. The Silent Tea Party strategy can be seen in action on the Teaching Channel under pre-reading strategies (https://learn.teachingchannel.com/video/pre-reading-strategies).

Swat game

1. Buy a few fly swatters from the dollar store.
2. Cut out vocabulary terms and lay them on the floor or write all of the terms on the board.

3. Split the class into two relay teams.
4. Read a definition out loud.
5. Students identify the correct vocabulary term that matches the definition and swat the word with the fly swatter. (Adaptation for students who need more processing time: tell them the definitions ahead of time based on their turn in the relay).
6. Rotate to the next set of students.
7. Repeat new definition with a new term.

Vocabulary dice

1. Buy a few dice from the dollar store or Amazon (or make a dice template by cutting out a paper cube or use google's virtual dice).
2. Choose the specific tasks that you want students to engage in using their vocabulary.
3. Print off the board and laminate it so it can be used multiple times for vocabulary review.
4. Students work in teams and take turns rolling the dice.
5. Based on their roll, they match the number with the vocabulary task and respond.

There are many variations of a dice board, Figure 4.3 is one example.

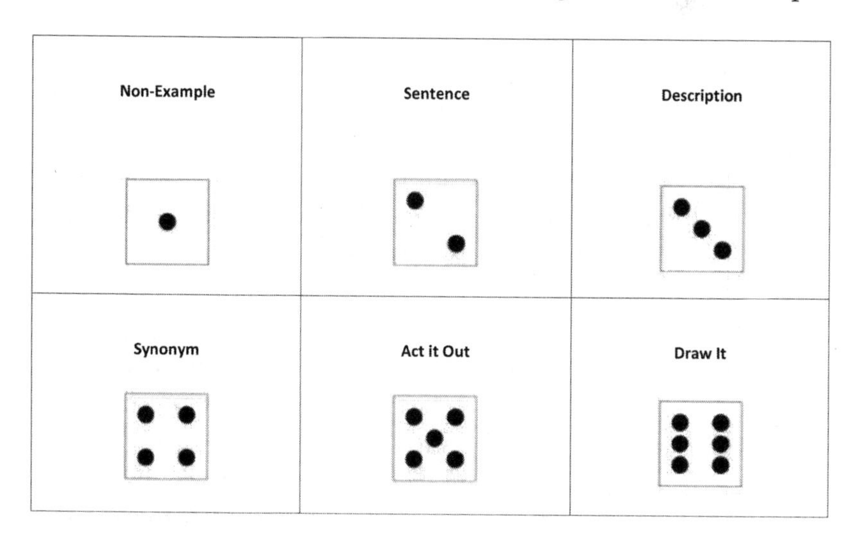

FIGURE 4.3 Vocabulary Dice Board

The vocabulary dice board is very similar to the differentiation strategy *Think Dots,* in which we differentiate instruction by providing multiple points of entry. The vocabulary dice board can have a variety of different types of activities that correspond to the numbers on the die. Some of the vocabulary activities can be hands-on, infuse technology, or include art (acting out/singing). This board can work for groups of two, three, or four (small group or stand-alone center). The board can also be adapted to increase levels of thinking on a concept, or to support students in discussing text or solving problems. For example, with reading comprehension, the six tasks could be arranged to support effective reading strategies, so that as students chunk text and stop to discuss, based on their role, they respond to the prompt. Example task: Create a "GIST," predict (refine or confirm), create a visual representation of the scene, cause and effect, etc. In mathematics, as students are completing multistep problems, the various math tasks for the dice rolls could involve important components such as "Graph It," "Explain the process using academic vocabulary," "Write the equation in slope intercept form, ""Share a strategy to solve the problem," and the like.

When we say "vocabulary time" we don't want students to sigh and think, "painstaking task of copying a long list of words, look them up in the dictionary, and I still won't know what the word means." Instead, our goal is to shake up our vocabulary instruction with evidence-based practices and fun, so students think, "Yeah, I want to learn more words." Providing students with choice on how they manipulate and make sense of their new terms is much more meaningful. Vocabulary time should be a fun learning experience because it is a precursor to building comprehension across every content area.

Reading comprehension choice board

A reading comprehension choice board can help support reading comprehension (see Figure 4.4). Students will choose one box from each row. What do you notice about this choice board on reading comprehension?

In our inclusive classrooms, we have readers at every stage of reading development: readers who are above grade level,

CHOICE BOARD

DIRECTIONS: Complete a TIC-TAC-TOE pattern to win! Circle your **three** choices.

MAKE AN INFERENCE: Make a guess on what is happening in the passage or why a character did something that the author didn't tell you, based on your prior knowledge.	**VOCABULARY:** Create a comic strip using at least five vocabulary words.	**COMPARE/CONTRAST:** Make a diagram about what is similar or different in this passage compared to another text, passage, or character.
QUESTIONING: Write three higher-level Blooms questions about the passage.	**CHARACTERIZATION:** Write a song or rap about your favorite character/person. Be sure to include at least five facts and details.	**SUMMARIZE:** Write a tweet to Beyonce summarizing the order of events in the story.
SUMMARIZE: Write a GIST about what happened in the passage (beginning, middle, and end).	**VISUALIZING**: Draw a picture of what is happening in the beginning, middle, and end of the passage. Annotate your picture.	**MAKING CONNECTIONS:** What do you have in common? *Text to self *Text to text *Text to world *Text to media

FIGURE 4.4 Reading Comprehension Choice Board

below grade level, reluctant readers, and readers who have failed so much that they despise the act of reading. About 80% of students with learning disabilities have a reading disability, and on average such students read three to five years behind grade-level peers. Other students struggle with word reading and fluency, and still other students demonstrate low vocabulary and content knowledge (Levine & Wagner Biancarosa & Snow, 2004; Fuchs, Fuchs, & Compton, 2010; Vaughn et al., 2013). Motivation matters and plays a role in increasing reading comprehension (Hwang & Duke, 2020). For this choice board, the choices are strategically created and placed in each row to provide every student access to build comprehension of a text. Even if students are just asking questions as they read, they are building their reading muscle, and teachers can layers of strategic instruction based on the questions they create.

The goal is to provide ALL students access to complex text and get students excited about jumping into text. Kylene Beers says it best, "If we teach a child the skill of reading without encouraging the love of reading, we will have created a literate illiterate." This issue of providing all students an opportunity to engage in challenging text is one of the biggest topics of equity in our time (next to the digital divide). Students who are denied access to grade-level complex text are at a disadvantage, lacking opportunity to be ready for 21st-century literacy demands in college and or career. Teachers hold the power to ensure that all students are ready to engage in informational text when they graduate, whether it's for freshman-year philosophy or an HVAC manual. Among the top skills for tomorrow's jobs, many employers would say reading comprehension is essential. Every student should have opportunities to engage meaningfully with rich, authentic, complex text. Literacy unlocks the door to opportunity beyond high school.

Complex Text

Complex text is text that is worthy of repeated readings over multiple instructional periods, to allows readers to re-read, investigate, and deeply analyze the text for language and meaning, and ultimately make connections to the author and the world. Student should be able to answer the three following questions after reading: Why is this important? What can I learn about me from this text? How does this text inspire me to be a change agent in the world? If they can't, why spend time re-reading it? In short, if a text doesn't allow students to grapple with these questions, it's not worthy of repeated readings, so let's spend more time analyzing a more pertinent and relevant text.

Though background knowledge and vocabulary are often underdeveloped among secondary students with disabilities (Shanahan & Shanahan, 2008), teachers can build the necessary background knowledge students need to access complex text. Daily, effective literacy work around background knowledge and vocabulary can provide students with meaningful access to grade-level text, help them develop language and critical thinking skills, and improve their ability to engage in academic discourse. In fact, there is a strong evidence base showing that the most important factor in comprehension is how much knowledge a reader has of the topic. Specifically, a widely replicated experiment from Recht and Leslie (1988), known as the Baseball Experiment, sheds light on the importance of background knowledge. The experimenters found that students who scored poorly on a reading test but knew a lot about baseball outperformed "good readers" who knew little about baseball — when the reading passage was about baseball. Knowledge counts a lot in understanding text. We don't deny access to complex and grade-level text; rather, we create access by building students' background knowledge before students start to read a challenging text.

How can we build background knowledge for challenging text and create access for students with disabilities? First, teachers analyze the complexity of a text before students begin the close-reading journey so that they can anticipate difficulties, target necessary background knowledge, and add important scaffolds. The first step in analyzing the complexity of a text is developing an understanding of what makes a text challenging at each grade level. By answering the question, "What are the text complexity factors that students will struggle with as they engage with this text?," teachers can identify important scaffolds to add.

Three text factors should be taken into consideration for the analysis: quantitative features, qualitative features, and the reader and task. The quantitative features are the quantitative measures, such as Lexile level. Quantitative measures can be determined by computer measurement of things such as the number of words, the length of sentences, and the difficulty of words. Go online to lexile.com and google the title of your text with the words "lexile level"; sometimes the Lexile level is on the back of the book itself. Caution: Don't use the lexile level alone to determine the complexity of a book or text students are about to read. For example, students at the ninth to tenth grade level average a 1050-1335 Lexile level. Students generally read *The Grapes of Wrath* by John Steinbeck in grade 9 or 10. The Lexile level for *The Grapes of Wrath* is around 680, equivalent to a third- or fourth-grade level. However, we know that this book's metaphors, language, themes of hard work, self-determination, and reasoned dissent are substantially deeper concepts. A third-grader probably wouldn't enjoy or understand this book ... right? This leads us to the qualitative measures of a text.

A qualitative evaluation of the text involves:

1. the structure of the text, which includes aspects such as organization, graphics, and text features.
2. the language features of the text, which includes language conventionality, vocabulary, and sentence structure.
3. The meaning or purpose of the text, which includes levels of meaning, theme, whether is it theoretical/abstract or concrete/explicit.
4. knowledge demands, that is, what type of prior knowledge must the reader have to be able to comprehend the text?

The final aspect of text complexity is "reader and task" considerations. Teachers should consider variables specific to specific readers (such as motivation, knowledge, and experiences) and to particular tasks (such as the purpose and the complexity of the task assigned, and the questions posed).

The second step in the process of providing struggling readers access to complex text is to decide what supports you will put in place to build background knowledge. How about a semantic or concept map so students can make connections between concepts? Or perhaps, based on the analysis of these three factors, the teacher could create an "Expert Pack" on the text for students.

Expert Pack

An "Expert Pack" is a literal collection of resources for building a student's background knowledge on a text (historical figures, key people, specific places, things, time periods, events, vocabulary, etc.). Expert Packs can help students gain background knowledge on topics in both fiction and non-fiction text. This strategy is a great scaffold for learners with exceptionalities. Expert Packs contain a variety of resources: a collection of leveled text, videos, graphics, virtual tours, and websites. Specifically, Expert Packs should have at least three to four different types of media: leveled articles, visuals, videos, art, virtual tours, etc. We create an Expert Pack by analyzing the text complexity, anticipating gaps in student background knowledge, and organizing a variety of different resources on the topic(s). The leveled text options provide students the opportunity to read at their instructional or independent levels. Thus, if students choose to read in order to build knowledge, they won't struggle to understand the text by themselves. Graphics/images/videos are visuals and video supports we may find on the topic in the text that will stimulate understanding and inquiry. Enter the opportunity for *choice:* after collecting and organizing the resources, students choose one to three resources from the Expert Pack they want to explore. It's OK if students only choose the videos or visuals. They will remember their learning a lot longer as they take their concept knowledge into the reading of the grade level's challenging text. Lastly, students share the knowledge they gained from their selected resources with a small group, a peer, or the teacher. Top free resources to put in our Expert Packs:

Leveled Text

A. Newsela.com (3-12): At the click of a button, tier a non-fiction passage. Students can access comprehension quizzes and highlighting text features.
B. ReadWorks.org (K-12): A full collection of nonfiction and literary articles along with lessons on reading comprehension and vocabulary, assessments, and instructions for educators. The curriculum offered is cognitive and science-based, and includes questions, vocabulary, paired texts, daily articles, StepReads, audio options, and more.

C. ReadWriteThink.org (K-12): Online resource that contains lessons, interactive activities, printables, and an app to help kids improve their reading and writing skills.
D. New York Times (K-12): The Learning Network: A weekly collection of lesson plans, articles, paired passages, digital media, art, writing prompts, and activities to support background knowledge.
E. Scholastic Learn At Home (K-12): Digital magazines and articles with vocabulary supports, speech to text, and videos embedded in the articles arranged around thematic clusters in science and social studies.
F. DoGo News (primarily elementary): Hundreds of articles, with audio options, improving accessibility. Many articles have related video clips to increase engagement and domain knowledge of a topic.

Graphics/Images/Videos

A. Google Arts and Culture: Provides great virtual tours for places around the world, time periods, and historical events. Students can explore collections, pictures, videos, and stories of people, historical events, and time periods from more than 1,200 museums, galleries, and institutions around the world.
B. Google Lit Trips: Lit Trips are downloadable files that mark the journeys of characters from famous literature on the surface of Google Earth.
C. Library of Congress Teacher Portal: The Library of Congress offers classroom materials and fabulous primary resources for hundreds of topics.
D. National Geographic Geo Stories: GeoStories are interactive slideshows that combine dynamic maps, pictures, video, and captions to take viewers on tours of places and topics.
E. The Literacy Shed: Home to a wealth of quality short films and animations for various thematic people, events, and ideas. A great video resource hub to support students in building background knowledge.

Intentional planning to provide students with rich literacy experiences should include strategies to activate and construct background knowledge of a text before reading. Are you thinking: "This will take a lot of time, why don't we just jump into the reading passage or text?" Consider the investment and return on this time in the long run. Over the course of a year, as the class continues to read complex text, students will accumulate more background content and concepts, and eventually when students read, they won't stop every other line confused because they don't know who Gandhi is or can't visualize Jupiter. Imagine if we did this when students were in elementary school! We'd possibly close the vocabulary and content gaps by the time students reached middle school. As a result of providing time to build background and vocabulary knowledge before jumping into a challenging text, students' fluency, reading comprehension, and motivation increase.

Mathematics choice board

Figure 4.5 shows a choice board given to third-graders at the end of their math unit. What do you notice about this mathematics choice board (see figure 4.5)?

In our math classrooms, students are moving at a variety of paces, with various math gaps, and are acquiring skills at different rates—and this is OK. To truly create a flexible classroom where all students can be involved and grow as mathematicians, we

Catch Up	**Choice Board Procedures**	**Review or Acceleration**
Independent Practice: Google Classroom Login Math A: 2345 Math B: 4343 Math C: 4656 Math D: 6453	Complete the activities in any order. Your goal is to complete all activities by Wednesday. Keep track of your progress by keeping all assignments in your math folder.	Visit Edpuzzle.com and complete the 8-minute video you need to practice. Enter code 44336 for review or EF3549 for acceleration.
With Me	**Prodigy**	**With a Partner**
Stop by the group table so we can conference on your progress on 2.1.	Set timer for 15 minutes and log in to Prodigy. Use code 34899 to link to me.	Choose a fluency practice game. Be sure to record your and your partner's scores.

FIGURE 4.5 Math Choice Board Example

must provide variability in how students improve or extend their learning. Using choice boards in our inclusive classrooms provides the teacher(s) with time to differentiate instruction as necessary. Based on students' choices, we can provide small-group instruction or work one-on-one with students as other students continue their learning journeys. This math choice board is a great example of providing differentiation based on readiness level, so students can navigate their own learning journey based on where they need/want to start. Perhaps they need catch-up, or perhaps they want to work with the teacher first. There are no bells or timers in this learning experience, so students can move fluidly at their ownpace and the teacher is not tied down to just one area.

Did you know that many students prefer visual and tactile math learning? When we add various learning pathways in math, students are more motivated and can work at their own pace, allowing the teacher to remediate or accelerate the students' learning. This technique moves the teacher from using a one-size-fits-all approach to individualizing and allowing students to facilitate their own learning and grapple with the content in other meaningful ways beyond "direct instruction." The following are the top free video and game-based platforms that can be easily incorporated into a learning menu to add another avenue to engage with math content:

A. Learnzillion, like Khan Academy, has tons of videos that contain tutorials mixed with independent problems for students to solve.
B. Edpuzzle.com allows teachers to use pre-existing videos or create their own and add checks for understanding. The student's responses are stored for teachers to use and analyze.
C. Scholastic's Studyjams has interactive videos and lessons where students solve various concepts with fun tunes and pop cultural characters.
D. Game-based platforms: Math Playground, Greg Tang Math, Cool Math Games and Math Game Time, Minecraft.net

Choice boards are a great way to provide different opportunities around content for different students at different times. In classrooms infused with choice, multiple learning modalities, and student interest, every student is involved, engaged, and flourishing as a self-directed and motivated learner.

Additional Web-Based Resources

Consider shaking up the choice board and adding a few of the web-based educational sites listed in Table 4.1 to support literacy (from phonics to reading comprehension), math (fluency and problem-solving), science (inquiry), and social studies (critical thinking) standards. Many of the resources are free, others have school subscription opportunities (See Table 4.1 Choice Board Learning Opportunities).

TABLE 4.1 Choice Board Learning Opportunities

Literacy	*Mathematics*	*Science*	*Social Studies*
Scholastic Learn-at-Home	PBS Math	Mystery Science	Crash Course
StarFall	Math Playground	Mystery Doug	Brainpop.com
Skybrary	Greg Tang Math	Science Mom and Math Dad	Wonderopolis.org
Khan Academy Kids	Cool Math Games	NASA	Kidsdiscover
NewsELA	Math Game Time	Breakoutedu	iCivics
Audible.com	YouCubed - Tasks	Educational Podcast	KidCitizen
Storyline Online	Summative	Discovery Mind Blown	Virtual Museum Tours
Adapted Mind	ABCya	Disney Nature Movies	Cnn10.com
ReadWorks	IXL	How Stuff Works	Time for Kids
Oxford Owl	Reflex Math	Farm Food 360	Actively Learn
HippoCampus	K5learning	Mysteryscience.com	Smithsonian for Kids
Seussville	Khan Academy	Khan Academy	Oregon Trail
Arcademics	Cool Math 4 Kids	National Geographic Kids	National Women's History Museum Online Exhibits
PBS Reading	Starfall	Ted Talk for Kids	One Globe Kids
StoryCorps	Dreambox	Skype a Scientist	
	Zearn	Stop Motion Studio	
	Scratch.mit.edu		
	Code.org		

Choice for Homework

Homework is a touchy subject with lots of controversy. In *The Homework Myth* (2006), Alfie Kohn states that there is no reason to believe that children would be at any disadvantage in terms of their academic learning or life skills if they had much less homework, or even none at all. Lots of school districts are banishing homework and some are rethinking homework policies and grading. Do you know how much homework European countries' schools, such as Finland's, give to students? Little to none or none at all. The negative effects of poorly chosen homework assignments are many. Poorly thought out homework creates a split in the classroom, among those who got the content quickly in 45 minutes, those with no adults to do the assignments for them, and those who don't go to a "home" when the school day ends. A surefire way to exclude, disengage, and widen the opportunity gap further is to assign lots of unnecessary practice. I pose a suggestion: Use choice for homework. Choice can be a practical way to support students with practice and help them become expert learners on content (call it "practice makes better work" instead of homework).

Look at this self-assessment pyramid for homework (See Figure 4.6). What do you notice?

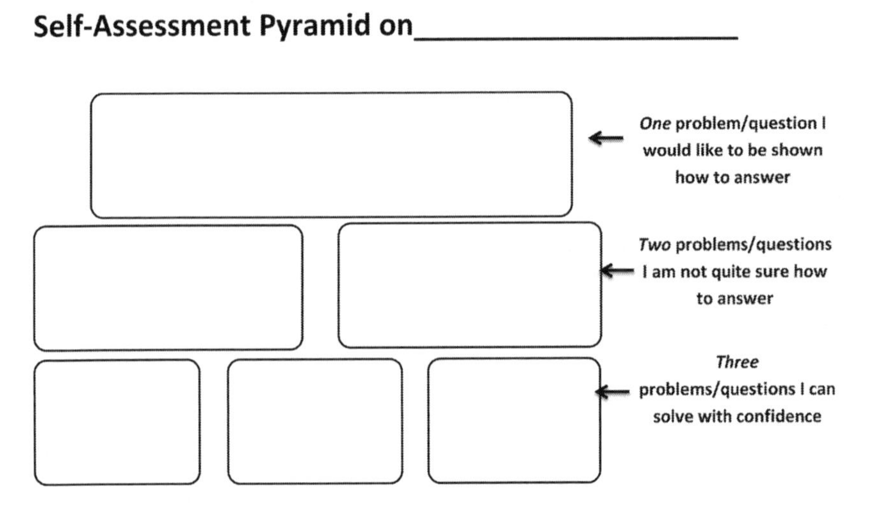

FIGURE 4.6 HW 3 Tier Self-assessment Pyramid

The pyramid approach offers students the choice of looking at the assigned task and self-evaluating their readiness for completion and success. The bottom row is, "three problems I can solve with confidence." The second row asks students to answer, "Two problems or questions that I am attempting but not quite sure how to answer." The top row is, "One problem/question that I need to be shown how to answer." This template is in HW – 3 Tier Self-Assessment.

There are many ways to challenge and support students with this tiered pyramid approach. For example, for students who need acceleration, say "based on of these 10 problems, focus your choices on the last six problems." This pyramid is based on the principle "less is more." Students can demonstrate mastery in a few problems rather than 20. For students who understand the homework, it's just a repetitious, mundane 20 problems. Students who struggle may shut down with 20 problems and do none. The tiered cake allows every learner to be successful and feel valued wherever their entry point is. This approach also provides the teacher with necessary data: Which problem should we work out as a class based on consensus of the top box? How many student(s) need re-teaching? How can we heterogeneously pair up students for peer-based teaching and learning?

The self-assessment pyramid can be used to support reading assignments as well. Instead of giving students a long list of comprehension questions, let students create their own questions from the text: "Write a test for the book. Include 3 questions. Create an answer key for your questions." Give students space to write down unknown words or confusing parts of the story; after all, good readers are always stopping to think about what they read, reread parts that were confusing, and use fix-up strategies to monitor comprehension. The top box could be, "Identify a quote or line you would like the class to discuss."

Some teachers work together with students' parents to create personalized weekly choice boards for their children while they are at home. The homework choice board in Figure 4.7 is an excellent example of teacher-parent partnerships. This choice board

Read a book. Draw your favorite character or redesign the cover.	Go outside and find pieces of nature to make into art.	Learn a new skill to share with your friends (juggling, instrument, etc.)
Look at this famous piece of art. Try to recreate it using materials from home. Be creative!	Free Space	Learn about one of the Sustainable Development Goals and write a comic about it using makebeliefscomix.
Research a different country and create a book about it using bookcreator.com.	Learn how to cook/bake something. Measure all quantities. Film yourself making it.	Take photos of things that look like the alphabet.

FIGURE 4.7 HW Choice Board: Student & Parent Partnership

allows the student to practice necessary skills from the entire curriculum, includes non-tech and tech, gets the student outside for fun, and invites others into the student's learning process (see Figure 4.7).

Choice, Interest, and Multiple Modalities

A helpful resource to guide purposeful planning for diverse learners is the following Differentiation Planning Guide (see Figure 4.8 and bigger template is in Appendix). Start the lesson planning process by considering three questions. First: Is the content accessible to all students? What barriers might exist? Where will students struggle? What difficulties do students have every year with this content? Will all of my learners engage, and if not, what can I add? Second: Is the instruction presented in multiple ways? Have I moved beyond teacher talk to infuse tactile, kinesthetic, and multimedia modalities? Could my choice board enhance different learning styles by offering multiple ways to navigate content? Third: "Is learning assessed in multiple ways?" If we use a choice board, we can provide all learners with different ways to share their smarts beyond just paper and pencil. With differentiated instruction we move from "How smart are you?" to "Share with me your smarts." Don't worry, we dance our way into lots of assessment ideas in Chapter 5!

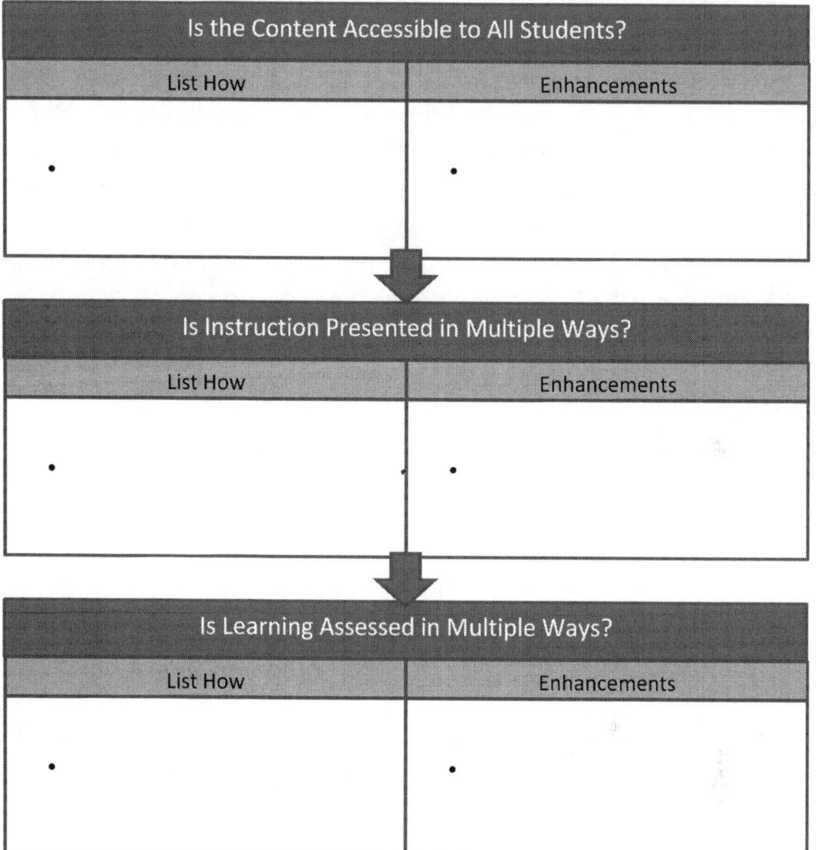

FIGURE 4.8 Differentiated Instruction Planning Guide

In Closing

There is no wrong way to create a learning menu. The choice boards shared throughout this chapter are a starting place, and you can always add more rigor, higher-order tasks, and real-world connections. Choice boards are a great way for students to actively explore new topics, practice skills, and extend their learning. No, providing students with choice won't solve every academic problem, but it will motivate ALL students by providing a successful entry point into objective mastery. Ultimately, choice boards provide a flexible classroom environment so that teachers can differentiate instruction: different mini-lessons to students based on their choices, enrichment for a student or two, review for a student who is stuck, or remediation to small groups. Differentiation is a journey: start small and trust the process. Perhaps introduce just three or six meaningful options in a choice board. Be sure to set norms as a class, model the routine for independent or partner work, and practice and provide immediate positive feedback as students complete their choices. Incorporating choice, student interest, and multiple modalities allows us and our students opportunities to create multiple masterpieces.

Top 6 Dance Moves

Which of these moves can you try tomorrow? Which moves can you share with your team?

1. Add one new learning opportunity to support vocabulary acquisition. Consider: Are students excited about vocabulary time? Do your students have a consistent log or journal where they record and collect their terms? Could you add some mini-lessons on morphology around the terms so students can learn how words connect? Are interactive word walls posted and changed out for each unit/group of terms? Is there a 10-minute time period where you can add a vocabulary game or intentional discussion around terms? Can students create a product using their vocabulary terms (comic strip, poem, etc.)?
2. Invest planning time to create a learning menu for an upcoming lesson. Start with the objective. Consider infusing student interest and provide a few choices for engaging with new content or sharing knowledge on an objective. Infuse multiple learning styles to navigate learning or show mastery. Bonus: Include a free space and let students decide and get teacher approval.

3. Invest the time to analyze a text and build background knowledge before entering a challenging reading selection. With a colleague, visit The Teaching Channel and watch "The Silent Tea Party: Pre-reading for Challenging Text." As a team, discuss, "How does this strategy help students prepare for a challenging text?"
4. Differentiate math instruction. Can you add a visual, tactile, kinesthetic, or video-based opportunity beyond lecture to support math content? Maybe you could provide a wild space and let students decide how to share their learning on the objective.
5. Evaluate your homework systems and policies. How can you incorporate more choice, self-monitoring, and access so all students can practice skills successfully?
6. Create a UDL professional learning team and explore the three UDL guidelines. CAST's http://udlguidelines.cast.org provides examples and checkpoints for each of the three guidelines.

List your next dance steps for adding more choice, recruiting student interest, and using multiple modality learning opportunities.

____

____

____

____

____

Accountability Partner: ______________________________

____

Check-in Date: ______________________________________

____

"Dance to inspire, dance to freedom, life is about experiences so dance and let yourself become free."

—*Shah Asad Rizvi*

5

Hip Hop

Assessment Practices That Work for All

Hip Hop is the umbrella term for various street dance styles like breakdancing, freestyle, the Harlem Shake, or the recent Flossing that many of our students love (that dance where they twist their arms back and forth). Hip hop culture is responsible for some of the most viral dance moves ever. Nothing makes me smile more than visiting the Ron Clark Academy on Twitter and seeing our star director and his students dancing down the hallway, celebrating success by bopping up and down on tables, and cheering their classmates on with modern hip-hop dance moves down a hallway.

The freestyle is one specific form of hip-hop dance that many find pure happiness in. There is no choreography or exemplar in freestyle dancing: you just move the body spontaneously. Because freestyle dancing is about your own original voice, there is no wrong way to do it. Just go! Similarly, there is no wrong way to "move beyond paper and pencil": just go. By using a variety of assessment strategies, we can provide students the opportunity to share their voice and make sense of the content in lots of different ways. I am urging an important paradigm shift from "Show Me if You Are Smart" to "Show Me How You are Smart." If I had a dollar for every student who knew the answer but couldn't write it down on a worksheet (including students with mobility or speech-related impairments), I'd have a lot of dollars. In the real world, students will not take a multiple-choice assessment once a week or spout memorized facts on pieces of paper, so consider making the assessment process more *freestyle* to stimulate creativity and promote higher-order thinking and application of academic skills. Allow students to share their smarts and apply knowledge learned using a variety of assessment products. Following the ideals of the freestyle hip-hop movement, there are a lot of ways students can show up and show off.

This chapter is not about the theory of assessment or research on the importance of formative assessment. We are teachers. We know that ongoing evaluation, student reflection, and meaningful feedback are high-impact strategies. On John Hattie's 2018 updated list of factors related to student achievement, evaluation, student reflection, and feedback are all strongly correlated with higher academic outcomes. All three of these factors yield a 0.70 effect size and higher (scores of 0.40 can have a significant positive effect on student achievement, increasing student growth within one school year). If implemented effectively, evaluation, student reflection, and meaningful feedback will prove extremely important and can increase student learning dramatically in as little as one school year. This chapter is about the practical: examples of assessing student learning beyond paper and pencil, assessment strategies that build higher-level thinking, and technology tools that students can use to share their learning.

Moving Beyond Paper and Pencil: Reading Comprehension

> *"If they can do the worksheet, they don't need it. If they can't, it won't help them."*
>
> —*Marilyn Adams*

Nothing makes reading a challenging text duller then having to fill out a long, tedious worksheet with lots of "check your understanding" questions. The research is clear that reading comprehension is increased when students discuss their reading strategies with a peer, share their connections to the text, and debate how the reading applies to a larger context. Consider the following reading strategies that increase student discussion and comprehension, develop effective teamwork skills, and simultaneously provide us with valuable assessment data on students' reading progress.

Reciprocal Teaching

Reciprocal teaching is a highly effective reading structure to support meaningful conversations about a text. Reciprocal teaching has a John Hattie impact effect size of .74, which means it can increase student learning dramatically in as little as one school year if implemented effectively. Specifically, the National Institute for Literacy (2007), found that as students with disabilities encounter increasingly complex content in the middle grades and beyond, their deficits in reading hinder their ability to successfully comprehend content area texts when used in general education content area classrooms. A strategy such as reciprocal teaching is an effective comprehension-building strategy for students with disabilities. Students learn how to use four integral comprehension skills: predicting, questioning, clarifying, and summarizing (see Figure 5.1). The purpose of this structure is to bring meaning to the text by practicing four reading strategies that successful readers consistently use as they read. It promotes team effort and dialogue among teacher and students. Reciprocal teaching can be used with both younger and older students and adapted for use in every subject across the curriculum.

Differentiation

If your students could benefit from a guided organizer to jot down each group member's contributions, visit ReadingRockets.org, ReadWriteThink.org, Readworks.org, Pinterest, and Teachers Pay Teachers for a variety of reciprocal teaching organizers. Some students will benefit from role cards that provide sentence stems to support role success for the four reading strategy roles. For younger students, consider providing students with props and hats to cue their various roles. For example, the Predictor

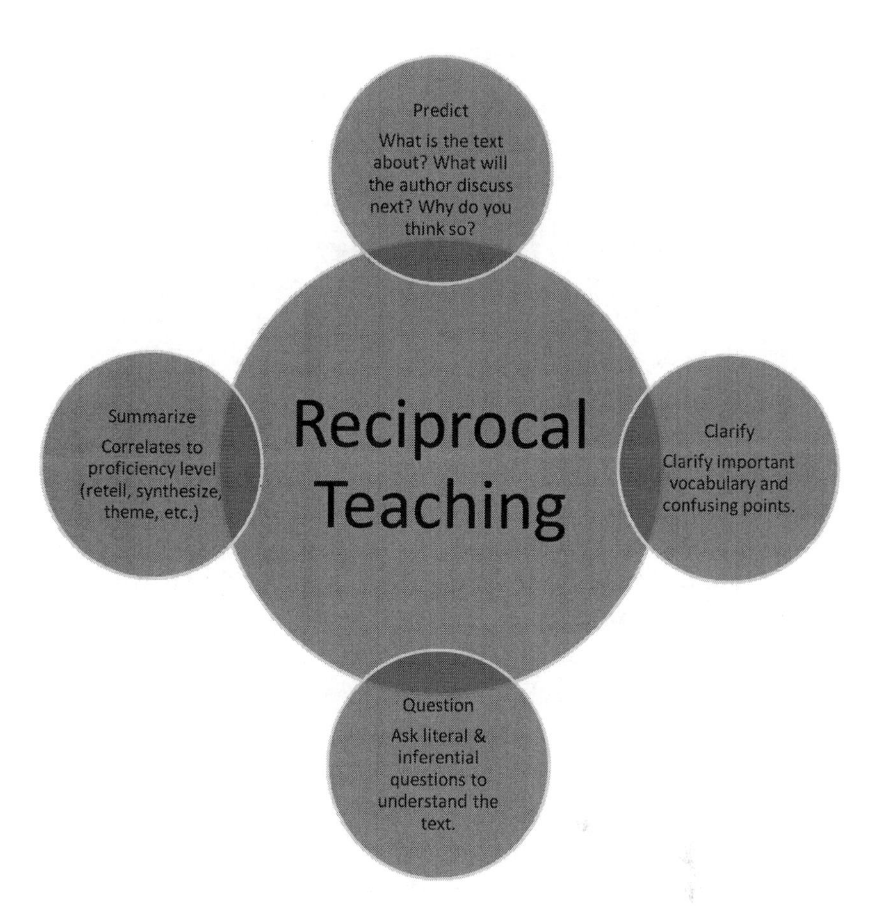

FIGURE 5.1 Reciprocal Teaching

Teaching process

Part One – Modeling and guided practice

1. Start the process by discussing the differences between just reading the words on the page and being active readers in order to comprehend the meaning of the words one reads (passive vs. active reading). Ask students to give examples of the difference and why it is important to be active readers (metacognition improves understanding, fix-up, and overall enjoyment of a text).

(*Continued*)

2. Introduce the process of reciprocal teaching to students. Discuss the four skills used by successful readers to engage in a reading and comprehend the text. Provide concrete examples of what Summarizing, Questioning, Clarifying, and Predicting look and sound like in an instructional text.
3. Explicitly model and think aloud the appropriate use of each of these four skills after reading a short selection. For example, to demonstrate summarizing, first model the skill: After you read a short selection to the class, share a one- or two-sentence summary of the text. Then read the next selection, this time asking students to summarize the text. Students can discuss their summaries with their partners before responding. Provide positive reinforcement and fix up.
4. Re-read the selection and repeat this process for Questioning, Clarifying, and Predicting.

Part Two – Independent practice

Divide the class into teams of four students. The first time the strategy is used, consider pre-assigning roles based on reading data. Differentiate reading instruction by selecting specific students for each role. After students have practiced, allow choice. Ask students in each group to choose to be the Predictor, Summarizer, Questioner, or Clarifier for the first reading. As they read the passage, ask them to stop after a few paragraphs, discuss, and add on to each other's reading roles.

could have a wizard hat with a magic wand stick. The Clarifier could have a detective hat andith a magnifying glass, and so on. Be sure to circulate and collect data from student discussions on text comprehension and challenge learners to think deeply about various features of the text with higher-order questions.

Variations

Literature circles or group reading roles can also ensure that heterogenous groups of students challenge and support each other as they work to increase comprehension of a text. Based on your students' developmental level, level of reading, and the type of text, teachers could use the following reading roles in student groupings.

Tour Guide: Your mission is to guide the conversation about the text. You will write prompts and use them to help your group have a successful discussion about the text.

1. "__________, can you share what __________ just said?"
2. "What do you __________ about what __________ just said?"
3. "Do you __________ or __________ with what __________ just said? Why?"
4. __________________ can you share your role?

Discussion Detective: As the Detective, your job is to be curious. This means you have to record your questions and thoughts as you read the text. You will write discussion questions that your group will respond to in order to discuss the text.

1. Why do you think the author had ____________________ happen in the story?
2. How would the story have been changed if the author had not let ____________________________ happen?
3. How is ____________________ alike/different from ______________________?
4. Now come up with three more discussion questions of your own! You will need to use one word from the following list within each question you create (create, opinion, change, develop, recommend, decide, imagine, evaluate, defend, elaborate, determine).

Reporter: Your job is to dig up and find two sections of the text to share and discuss with your group. Choose a paragraph or sentences from the chapter. The purpose is to help your group by spotlighting something interesting, powerful, funny, puzzling, or important from the text. You are looking for sections (paragraphs or one to two pages) that are full of meaning and/or description.

Text Find #1

Page _____ Paragraph ____

I chose this section to share and discuss because…

1. Direct each of your peers to turn to your selected page.
2. Read your selected passage aloud and share your reasons for selecting this passage.
3. Ask your peers what they think: do they see the importance and meaning in the passages you chose?
4. Your goal is to have a focused discussion based directly on the text!

Illustrator: Design and create a picture to help your group reflect on the chapter. Share your picture and use labels. Be sure to create a picture based on evidence from the text.

Book Title:______________ Today's Reading:______________

Here's what I pictured (drawing below):

1. Direct each of your peers to turn to your selected page.
2. Read your prediction and share your reasons for selecting this passage.
3. Ask your peers what they think—what were their predictions?
4. Your goal is to have a focused discussion based directly on the text!

Literary Luminary: You job is to make three predictions based on the text. As you read, you may find information that is different from what you expected. Then you will need to revisit your prediction. Ask yourself "Was I correct, incorrect, or partially correct?" Explain your reasoning.

Book Title:____________ Today's Reading:_______________

Prediction #1

Page _____ Paragraph ____

Note clues or evidence that support your prediction. as your prediction correct, or did you revise your prediction? Explain.

1. Direct each of your peers to turn to your selected page.
2. Read your prediction and share your reasons for selecting this passage.
3. Ask your peers what they think: what were their predictions?
4. Your goal is to have a focused discussion based directly on the text!

Connector: As the Connector, it is your job to help your group connect the text to our unit. Review the reading to build connections to share with your reading group and inspire your discussion.

Book Title:____________ Today's Reading:_______________

This is a connection between the book and the reader:

1. Explain the connection you have made with the text.
2. Ask your peers what they think: can they make a similar connection with the text?
3. Ask your peers to make connections: can they share the connections they made with the text as they were reading?
4. Your goal is to have a focused discussion based directly on the text!

Product Engineer: Your job is to design and create a product to help a character/person in your book. Share your creation with your group and explain how your product would help the character.

I think ____________ needs ______________________________.

- (character) (product)
- Here's what the product looks like:
- This is what the product does:
- This character needs this product because ____________.
- If this character had this product, then ________________.

1. Explain the product you have designed and created, and why it would help the character.
2. Ask your peers what they think: do they think the product would work? Why or why not? What would they change about the product to make it better?
3. Ask your peers to be creative: what would they design to help the character?
4. Your goal is to have a focused discussion based directly on the text!

Having a variety of roles (from Visualizer to Word Collector) ensures that every single student can participate and actively build comprehension of a text. Could a struggling reader or student with a disability participate as the Illustrator? Absolutely. Listening comprehension is higher and they'll build knowledge through connecting visuals with the text. We can strategically preassign roles, with the goal of eventually providing choice and letting students switch and practice different comprehension roles. Did you notice, in each role, that the end outcome

conversation card

Excuse me…

I'd like to add…

I disagree because…

I agree because …

I'm not sure what you mean...

I'm confused about...

According to page…

Can you share more about…?

I like how you …

was "group discussion"? Students may need an organizer to jot down notes or sentence starters to frame the conversation. Model success for each role and ensure that students have a visual anchor chart, role tents with their job, and conversation cards. On the conversation card, provide support for students with accountable and productive conversation stems such as "Excuse me," "I'd like to add," "I disagree because," "I agree because," "I'm not sure what you mean by," "I'm confused about," "According to page," "Can you share more about," etc. Through practice, our students will excitedly dig deep into text and have rich discussions about it.

Patterned Partner Reading

The Patterned Partner reading approach differs from traditional partner reading because it involves structured patterns to help both students stay focused on the reading, whether they are reading or listening. I came across this reading approach while reading Maureen McLaughlin's "Read Alouds and Recreational Reading Always, Round Robin Reading Never" in the July 2013 *Reading Today* magazine. The article highlighted many reasons that round robin reading does more harm than good, from students subvocalizing incorrectly to stage fright to such hyperfocus on reading every word correctly that comprehension gets lost. In place of round robin reading, Patterned Partner Reading was shared as an alternative. This structure is a valuable way to engage students who read at various levels. Listening comprehension is usually higher for struggling learners, so it's easy to differentiate who reads first and supply additional reading scaffolds as necessary. There are three cycles in Pattered Partner Reading (see Figure 5.2). After we explicitly model each cycle, we let students pair up with a partner and choose which pattern cycle(s) they want to use to make meaning of a reading selection.

Question Answer Relationship (QAR)

Question Answer Relationship is yet another powerful reading and assessment strategy that can improve reading comprehension for students with disabilities. By helping students

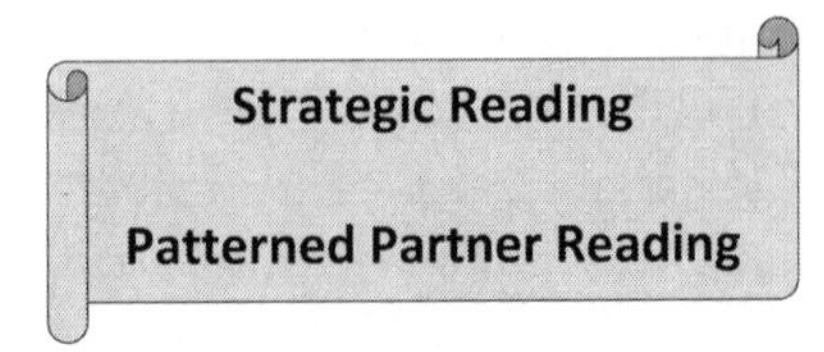

This reading approach differs from the traditional partner reading in that it involves structured patterns to help both students stay focused on the reading, whether they are reading or listening.

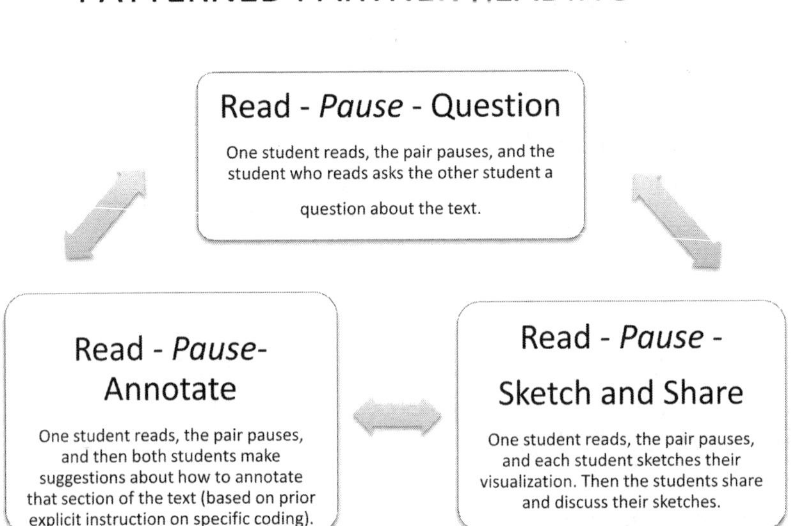

FIGURE 5.2 Patterned Partner Reading

understand the different types of questions, student learn that answers to some questions are "Right There" in the text, that some answers require a reader to "Think and Search," and that some answers can only be answered "On My Own." Through this process, students recognize that they must first consider the question before developing an answer. This method allows teachers to model higher-order questions, which leads to higher-order thinking and answers. We can assess students' reading comprehension merely by the questions they ask (themselves and peers) and answer. This process should move beyond paper and pencil, and the questions should be shared and answered orally between partners or groups of students.

Description:

Explain to students that they will encounter **four** types of questions. Define each type of question and give an example.

Four types of questions are examined in the QAR (see Figure 5.3). Figure 5.3 provides the definitions of the four types of questions and an example question to model for students.

- **Right There Questions**: Literal questions whose answers can be found in the text. Often the words used in the question are the same words found in the text.

QAR **Q**uestion **A**nswer **R**elationship	
In the Book	
Right There The answer is in one place in the text. • Reread • Scan • Look for key words *How old was Amelia when she became the youngest person ever to ski to the South Pole?*	**Think and Search Questions** The answer is in several places in the text. • Skim • Reread • Summarize *What are the different conditions Amelia faced that made her journey challenging?*
In My Head	
Author and You The answer is not directly in the text. • Reread • Predict • Think critically about what the author says *How would you adapt to traveling through Antarctica?*	**On My Own** The answer is not in the text. • Think about what you already know • Think about what you read before • Make connections *What is the coldest temperature ever recorded in Antarctica?*

FIGURE 5.3 Question Answer Relationship (QAR)

- **Think and Search Questions**: Answers are gathered from several parts of the text and put together to make meaning.
- **Author and You**: These questions are based on information provided in the text, but students are required to relate it to their own experience. Although the answer does not lie directly in the text, the student must have read the text in order to answer the question (this question may require additional prompts or scaffolds).
- **On My Own**: These questions do not require students to have read the passage, but they must use their background or prior knowledge to answer the question.

1. Find and read a short passage aloud to your students.
2. Create predetermined stopping points and questions you will ask after you stop reading. When you have finished reading, read the questions aloud to students and model how you decide which type of question you have been asked to answer.
3. Show students how to find information to answer the question (i.e., in the text, from your own experiences, etc.).
4. After practice, students partner up and ask each other their questions. Students should respond with textual evidence to support their answers. Students go back and forth asking their questions.

Moving Beyond Just Paper and Pencil: Math

Students can sit at a desk and complete a worksheet of 20 math problems independently, but why? Research on math achievement shows that when students discuss their thinking, their strategies, and the resources they used to solve a problem, their retention of the process is far stronger. Teachers will be able to add higher-order applications more quickly when students remember the process and skills learned. We want to hear students discuss their process of solving the problem, their conceptual understanding around real-world connections, and use rich math academic language. Edgar Dale's *Cone of Learning* confirms that when students can teach a concept to another student, they will retain understanding a lot longer. Engage students with structured approaches to facilitate student discussion and support team problem-solving skills.

A Team of 2: "I'm the Teacher"

This cooperative learning protocol builds academic vocabulary, supports language acquisition, and allows both students the opportunity to play the teacher. Each student assumes the role of the teacher and teaches the other student how to successfully solve the problem. The students alternate roles, but share one pen and one piece of paper to jot down notes.

Step 1: Student A coaches and teaches problem #1 to Student B. Student B writes down the process. The team agrees on the answer. Student A praises student B.
Step 2: Student B repeat this process with Partner A for problem #2.
Step 3: Students repeat with a set of 5–10 problems as a team.

A Team of 4: Team Consensus Using a Placemat Organizer

This collaborative learning strategy holds each student accountable for their learning, provides processing time, elicits responses from every student, and supports effective team discussion. With processing time and this placemat organizer (see Figure 5.4), every student's thinking is made visible to the teacher before students chat and share.

Step 1: Divide students into heterogenous groups of three or four.
Step 2: Number each student.
Step 3: Pose a question or problem to the class.
Step 4: Students in the groups record their responses in their designated box.
Step 5: After students have responded to the question individually in their respective box, students gather as a team and come to an agreement; the recorder writes their collective

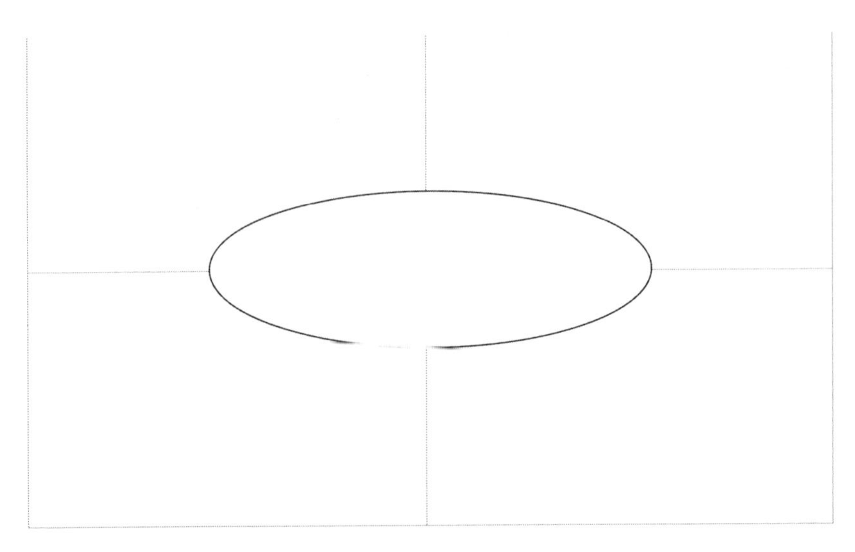

FIGURE 5.4 Team Consensus Placemat Organizer

response in the center circle. Have students discuss the answer, making sure everyone in the group can share their written answer. Once all students in the group have shared their response and come to a team consensus, they stand up and await the teacher.

Step 6: The teacher calls out a random number (1 through 4) and the corresponding student shares the team's consensus. Teachers can choose to call on individual students who are standing or ask for a choral response from the team. Be sure to establish team norms for productive conversations and reinforce positive gambits you hear students using with their peers. There are many variations to this strategy, such as Numbered Heads Together (Kagan Cooperative Learning), Heads Together, and Butts Up (The Teaching Channel).

Outside-the-Box Assessment Strategies

When teachers use outside-the-box assessment strategies and shake up how students share their learning, we can move our students up the Bloom's or Webb's depth-of-knowledge scale toward higher-order thinking. Often, I hear students exclaim,

"If I see another exit ticket again, I am going to scream." Just think about it: wouldn't you get bored from six hours, six class periods, day after day, with the same exit ticket, "What did you learn?" These nontraditional assessments promote higher order thinking and often result in deeper discussion and lasting connections with the content.

Six Thinking Hats

The Six Thinking Hats Method was developed in the 1980s by Dr. Edward Debono, an expert in creative thinking. Originally, this protocol was used to support business decisions by helping teams look at decisions from several different and important perspectives. However, this strategy can be used to discuss theme, justify character actions, and support students in brainstorming for persuasive essays or controversial issues. It is a framework for guiding effective discussion because it challenges each student to assume a role and move outside their habitual thinking style. It helps them to get a more rounded view of a situation, a text, or a perspective.

Description: The six thinking hats

Yellow Hat: Explores the positives and probes for value and benefit of actions taken by the key figure, character, solutions to an answer. Sentence stems for this optimistic hat are, "This is valuable because …" "This is an important lesson because …".

White Hat: Calls for information, data, trends known or needed: "the facts, just the facts." The sentence starters for this hat are, "The important facts or details in the story are…" "The evidence is…" "Based on…".

Green Hat: Focuses on the possibilities, alternatives, and new ideas. Expresses new concepts and new perceptions. Looks for solutions. The sentence starters for this hat are, "A great idea for [the character] would be …" "It is possible that this math strategy …".

Red Hat: Signifies feelings, hunches, and intuition. When using this hat, you can express emotions and feelings and share fears, likes, dislikes, loves, and hates. Sentence starters for this hat are, "I believe …" "I feel that …" "I think that…".

Blue Hat: Is used to manage the thinking process. It's the control mechanism that ensures the Six Thinking Hats guidelines are observed. Invites all team members to speak and have a turn. Sentence starters for this hat are, "Overall, we learned …" "To conclude, …" "To sum up …".

Black/Purple Hat: This role discusses why something may not work. This hat spots the difficulties and dangers, where things might go wrong. Sentence starters for this cautious hat are, "The consequences of this decision or action could be …" "The difficulties could be …" "That might not work because…"

Example

Strategically decide which students would best fit each role and provide each student a cone-shaped hat with their designated perspective (the cheesier, the better). Based on learners and content objective, students can engage in sharing their viewpoint on a range of topics, real-world solutions, text analysis. For instance, students have read a text in which the main character (Bob) has made a big decision to buy an expensive sports car. Based on students' specific discussion perspectives, responses could look like this:

Yellow Hat –"Bob will look cool," "work hard, play hard, right?"

White Hat – Cost analysis: gas prices and monthly payments could be expensive

Green Hat – What about a Corvette? Looks similar but costs less

Red Hat – I feel like he may not be able to pay his mortgage, or may have to work overtime… my intuition is…

Blue Hat – Let's consider all perspectives: his mom is working two jobs … what about?

Purple Hat – There are potential risks, like Bob may drive faster, get pulled over by the police, more consequences = more tickets = danger = accidents = lose money.

The Six Thinking Hats promotes team effort and dialogue among teacher and students.

Brown Bag Assessment

A Brown Bag assessment uses found objects and images to help students activate prior knowledge, or creates an assessment framework for students to express their understanding. Think of all the random items in a junk drawer—paper clips, pen, rock, tape, etc.—that could be placed in a student's brown bag or envelope. Students work individually and in collaboration to create concrete connections between the concept and surprise Brown Bag items. Unlike traditional assessment, the Brown Bag exam is a joyful experience, an assessment filled with conversation, idea exchange, laughter, and learning.

A typical Brown Bag exam follows five steps:

Step One:

Open your bag (or envelope)!

Step Two:

List all possible connections between your item(s) and the novel. Items may (or may not) fall into the following categories: plot, character, theme, setting, symbol, event, or something else entirely.

The item(s)in your bag might not even be in the novel. Start swimming on the surface, then take a breath and go deeper... Be open to thinking both literally and metaphorically. Use the first box to make a bulleted list of all the connections you see.

Step Three:

Get into triads.

Each person shares connections and then asks group members for the connections they see.

List all additional connections in the second box.

Step Four:

Find at least two passages from the text connected to your brown bag item(s).

Copy those passages into the third box (ellipses are encouraged). Provide enough of the passage so that you (and others) can find it. Please be sure to include page numbers!

Step Five:

Choose one idea you'd like to share with the class about your brown bag item(s). (This could be a bit about your discussion, connections, passages, initial reaction, or surprises.). Note this idea in the final box and prepare to share with the entire group.

Sample brown bag items can include cotton Balls, sticks, batteries, balls, paper clips, and anything. Get ready to be struck by the depth and enthusiasm with which students talk about ideas and items, ideas and insights that we unlikely to learn from a traditional test, essay, or even a whole class discussion!

A scaffolded version is to simply have students make a connection between the item and the concepts they learned in class period. Provide a few key terms and have them use any of the terms as they write a few sentences or draw a labeled image/diagram to describe the connection. An even easier prep version is to have students work in a team of four, pull out a total of four items from their bookbags/pockets/purses, and make a connection between the items and the objective or tell a story about how the four items relate to content they learned.

Tap-Back Assessment

The Tap-Back Assessment is used to randomly assess student learning during a lesson. Teachers can utilize the Tap-Back Assessment to assess the entire class or a small representative group. This assessment requires that teachers familiarize students with the routines of tapping students on the shoulder/back. Students learn that when they are tapped on the shoulder they should report to the teacher.

A typical Tap-Back Assessment follows five steps:

Step One:

Determine a question to ask students that is related to the essential question and/or objectives.

Step Two:

Select a student by tapping that person on the shoulder.

Step Three:

Ask the student you have selected the predetermined question. Record the response on a data sheet. You may choose to record the entire response or simply categorize students by those who have mastered the objective and those who still need additional support.

Step Four:

Ask the student to select a peer by tapping them on the shoulder.

Step Five:

The newly selected student will report to the teacher. Repeat the steps with the new student.

The Mannequin Assessment

The Mannequin Assessment (very similar to Tableau) provides students with a kinesthetic opportunity to share their learning. Students use their bodies to "strike a pose" that represents their thinking on a concept. Vary the strategy by having more than one student interact to form symbols or abstract representations. Encourage students to be creative and provide processing time for a quick write or quick draw before having students stand to construct a "pose" on the targeted objective. Assess learning by having students share their poses for the content.

A Mannequin Assessment follows five steps:

Step One:

Choose a topic, question, or connection to an essential question that can be represented with kinesthetic movement.

Step Two:

Model exemplar poses and have the whole class practice appropriate representations.

Step Three:

Provide a summarizing question or prompt.

Step Four:

Give students processing time for a quick write or quick draw before having them stand. Be sure to visually post how much time students will have to create their pose.

Step Five:

After students have created a pose, ask students to guess each other's connection to the prompt and have students explain their poses.

Which One Doesn't Belong (WODB)

Within each lesson, the goal is to move students toward higher-order thinking skills, and therefore teachers need to plan for higher-order tasks. Consider switching up the regular warm-up routine where students answer three review questions to a more engaging and higher-order thinking activator that involves analyzing and justifying. Putting a fun spin on the lesson starter is a great way to stimulate thinking and problem-solving by all students. A bonus to Which One Doesn't Belong is that is a low-stakes, high-interest starter that can also evoke interesting discussions on math in the real world. Which One Doesn't Belong is an assessment strategy based on error analysis, inviting students to evaluate which item doesn't belong in the set (shape, equation, graph, etc). Begin by analyzing the mathematics objective and set of standards. Next, visit the "Which One Doesn't Belong" website at https://wodb.ca to find a variety of sets for mathematics objectives from K-12 grades. Post one of the problems and let students discuss which of the four objects doesn't belong (for an even more complex task, students could discuss why each one of the four objects doesn't belong).

For example, a first-grade objective is that students will use mathematical language to compare and contrast shapes and

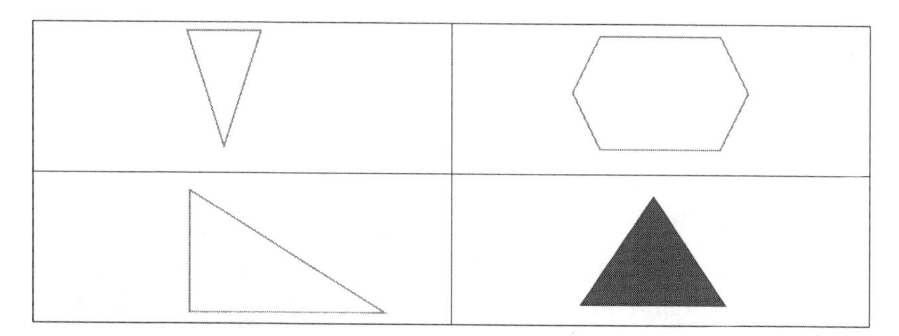

FIGURE 5.5 Which One Doesn't Belong

their properties. Next, we post the picture from Figure 5.5 and ask students which shape does not belong. Provide processing time, instruct students to buddy up (each partner has 20 seconds uninterrupted to share), elicit whole-class different responses, and post key vocabulary and terms as they are discussed on the board. Figure 5.5 is just one example of many conversation starts on shapes and their properties.

Mathematics is at its most powerful when the knowledge and understanding that have been developed are used to solve problems like the WODB activator. The follow-up task could be to have students identify where the shape is found in the classroom and the school, tell why your shape is used in the places it is, create an item that includes all or part of your shape, and so on.

Checks for Understanding

Think back to your lesson today. On average, how many times did you check for student understanding? How many of those times did you elicit *full* class responses (rather than one or two students responding singularly by raising their hands)? Giving ALL students lots of opportunities to respond during a lesson has many benefits and can help teachers quickly clear up misconceptions and adjust instruction. If instruction is truly interactive and students consistently share their learning, attention, on-task behavior, and learning increase and behavioral issues decrease. Engaging instruction is good classroom management. More importantly, in the act of responding, students are retrieving, rehearsing, and practicing the information, concepts, and skills or strategies being taught, thereby increasing the probability of retention. Students with disabilities soar with lots of repetition. Through monitoring of student responses, teachers can check the clarity of their teaching and differentiate the lesson as needed. Preview this list to add a new assessment strategy to your dance floor.

- $2 Summaries: With each word worth 10 cents, write a $2 summary of the learning from the lesson. This can be scaffolded by giving students specific words related to the learning that they must include in their summaries.
- Squares, Triangles, Circle: List four things that "square with my thinking;" three "angles" I disagree with (or three details to support _____, three things for which I need more information, three different way to look at the idea, etc.), and one question "circling" in my head.
- 6-Word Memoir: In six words, tell your peer what you learned. This is a variation of the Smith Magazine writing contest. See http:www.smithmag.net/sixwords
- 5-3-1 (alone, pair, group): Pose a question/topic. Students brainstorm five answers. Then they work in a pair to come up with the three best. Then the pair joins with another pair to come up with the one most important.
- Clothesline: Students move to a place in a human line that most closely matches their level of understanding. The line is a continuum, with the beginning of the line indicating no understanding of a concept and the opposite end of the line indicating a high level of understanding.
- Fist of Five: Students response to a whole-class question by showing the number of fingers that corresponds to their level of understanding (one being the lowest, five the highest)
- Four Corners: Students move to a corner of the room that most closely matches their level or understanding or viewpoint on a question posed by the teachers.

- Individual response boards (use plastic plates or clear pocket protectors): Students will use sheet protectors or white boards to respond to a question posed by the teacher. The students hold up their answers for the teacher to check, or the teacher can circulate around the classroom to check individual responses.
- Signal Response Cards: Students use a card to indicate their level of understanding of a concept. Cards may be labeled as
  - Red, Yellow, and Green
  - Yes/NO
  - A, B, C, D
- Speedometer: Students think of a speedometer going from 0-100 miles per hour. They then lay one arm on top of the other with hands touching elbows. Students should raise the arm that is on top, stopping at a point between 0-100 mph to indicate their level of understanding, with 100 mph designating complete understanding.
- Thumbs Up: Students respond to a whole-class question by putting thumbs up if they fully understand a concept, thumbs down if they do not understand, and thumbs to the side to indicate some area of confusion.
- Windshield: Students should respond "muddy, "buggy," or "clear" when the teacher asks them to describe their level of understanding. Previously, the teacher explained that "muddy" means the windshield is plastered with mud and the destination is not visible; this indicates little or no understanding. "Buggy" means that some debris is littering the windshield; this indicates partial understanding. A clear windshield indicates a high level of understanding.
- 12 words or less: In 12 words or less, have students summarize important aspects of a particular chunk of instruction or reading.
- Give One-Get One-Move On: Students are given paper and asked to list three to five ideas about the learning. Students draw a line after their last idea to separate their ideas from their classmates' lists. Students get up and interact with

one classmate at a time. Student gives an idea, gets an idea, and then moves on to another classmate.

- Flash Cards Learning Cell: Students develop questions and answers on their own. Working in pairs, the first student asks a question and the partner answers; then they switch roles. Each student can correct the other until a satisfactory answer is reached.
- One-Minute Paper: The teacher decides what the focus of the paper should be. Ask students "What was the most important thing you learned? What important question remains unanswered?" Set aside 5-10 minutes of the next class to discuss the results. This technique may also be used in the middle of a class.
- Circular Check: Students in groups are given a problem with a definite answer (good for math and science). The first student in each group completes the first step without contribution from others in the group and then passes it to the next student. The second student corrects any mistakes and completes the next step, again without input from the group. The problem gets passed to the next student and the process continues until the group has the correct answer.
- Misconception Check: Present students with common or predictable misconceptions about a designated concept, principle, or process. Ask them whether they agree or disagree and have them explain why. The misconception check can also be presented in the form of a multiple-choice or true-false quiz.
- Three-Minute Pause: The Three-Minute Pause provides a chance for students to stop, reflect on the concepts and ideas that have just been introduced, make connections to prior knowledge or experience, and seek clarification.
  - I changed my attitude about…
  - I became more aware of…
  - I was surprised about…
  - I felt…
  - I related to…
  - I empathized with…

- Idea Spinner: The teacher creates a spinner marked into four quadrants and labeled "Predict, Explain, Summarize, Evaluate." After new material is presented, the teacher spins the spinner and asks students to answer a question based on the location of the spinner.
- Idea Wave: Each student lists three to five ideas about the assigned topic. One volunteer begins the "idea wave" by sharing his idea. The student to the right of the volunteer shares one idea; the next student to the right shares one idea. The teacher directs the idea wave until several different ideas have been shared. At the end of the formal idea wave, a few volunteers who were not included may contribute.
- Hot Seat: The teacher places key reflection or probing questions on random seats throughout the room. When prompted, students check their seats and answer the questions. Students who do not have a hot-seat question are asked to agree or disagree with the response and explain their thinking.
- Green Light: Students have red, yellow, and green objects accessible (e.g., popsicle sticks, poker chips, cards). When prompted to reflect on a learning target or readiness for a task, they place the color on their desk that describes their comfort level or readiness (red: stuck or not ready; yellow: need support soon; green: ready to start).
- Whip Around: When a brief answer can show understanding, self-assessment, or readiness for a task, teachers ask students to respond to a standard prompt one at a time, in rapid succession around the room.
- Alphaboxes Summary (template in Appendix): Pick a few letters of the alphabet (for example, A, N, and L). Students must creatively take their summary and configure it to begin with the letters chosen.
- Letter Mix-Up: Similar to a word puzzle, provide about 20 random letters. Instruct students to use the letters to create a one- or two-word summary of their learning. You decide if they can use letters more than once.

- Jenga: On jenga blocks, write equations, key vocabulary terms, etc. As students remove blocks to avoid a spill, they have to solve problems, answer, or summarize content correctly.
- Foam Frisbee Toss: Add content on the top of a foam Frisbee (e.g., multiplication facts [8 x ____], vocabulary/content [Abraham Lincoln], rhyming words [say a word that rhymes with _____], etc.). Students toss the frisbee around, with the catcher filling in missing words, solving math problems to support fluency, defining key terms, and so on.
- What Else?: At the bottom of an assessment, the last question is: "What else do you know about this topic that wasn't asked?"
- Plickers is a classroom response app that teachers can use easily without having devices for every student. Students hold up a plicker QR code to signal their answer to a question posed by the teacher. The teacher scans the room, and the smart device picks up their answers and displays the students' answers visually.
- Socrative is a technology tool similar to Kahoot! and Quizziz. Educators can initiate formative assessments through quizzes, quick question polls, exit tickets, and space races by sending out a tailored class code.
- Blooms Cube: Cut out a cube (from an online cube template), and on each side of the cube write various levels of Blooms questions (questions range from *Knowledge* to *Evaluation*). After content delivery, provide teams of students with a cube. Students take turns tossing the cube and answering the question on the side that lands up (see Figure 5.6). If students gets stuck, they can phone a team member to help answer the question. A template is in Figure 5.6.
- From a deck of cards, provide students with a heart, club, diamond, or spade. Differentiate instruction by strategically deciding which student receives specific cards.
  - Hearts: Something from the heart. How did you feel? What did it mean to you?

Directions: Build your questioning cube by cutting out the template along the solid lines and folding along the dotted lines. Tape or glue the flaps.

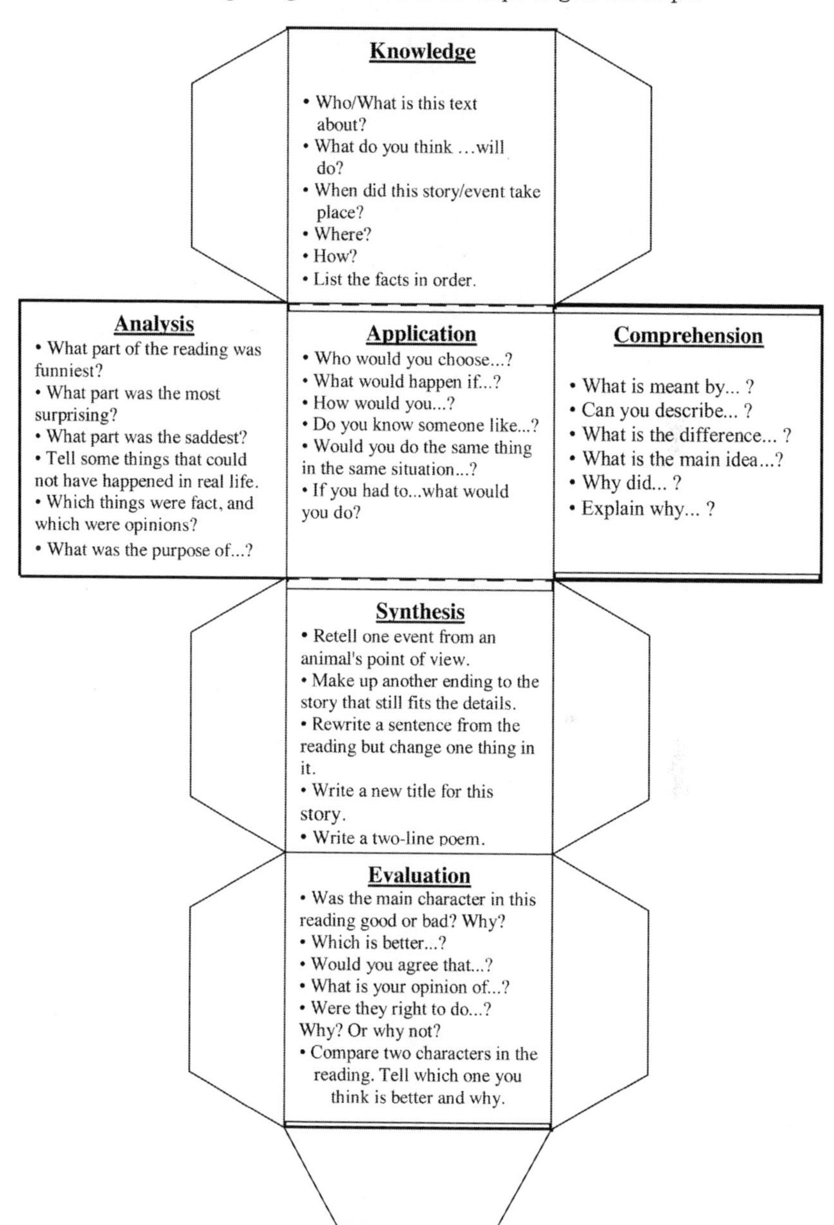

FIGURE 5.6 Blooms Cube

- Clubs: Things that grew—new ideas, new thoughts, a new point of view on the content.
- Diamonds: Gems that last forever. What are some of the gems of wisdom gathered from the content?
- Spades: Used to dig in the garden. What questions do you have about the content?

When we check all students' levels of understanding throughout each lesson (not just at the end of a lesson), it sets the tone that everyone's thinking is important and necessary, and we enhance the learning and engagement of all. Even better, in classroom with two dynamic teachers, co-teachers can use the data to differentiate and do something different for different students. Using some new assessment strategies in lessons can help us shake up learning and collect data from all students to adjust instruction effectively on the spot.

Multiple Ways to Assess Learning

Table 5.1 shares various products that students can use to demonstrate mastery of academic content. The multimedia category will keep expanding, as new technology tools and resources become available (see Table 5.1)What new tech tools can you add? Which assessment opportunities have you provided to students? What assessment strategies could be added to your classroom? The bottom three rows of Table 5.1 allow you to add ideas (both newly discovered assessment opportunities and assessment strategies absent from this list).

Special Education Teachers

In addition to using great assessment practices, special education teachers also progressively monitor and collect rich data aligned to each individual student's IEP goals. It is essential in co-taught classrooms that both teachers not only collect informal and formal data throughout, but also keep a log to document growth around IEP goals. I recommend creating one data sheet for all of the students with IEPs in the classroom. Print it out and place it on a joint class clipboard or in a data folder for teachers to pass back and forth at the beginning and end of class. Right in the moment, teachers

TABLE 5.1 Multiple Ways to Assess Learning

Written	*Verbal*	*Tactile*	*Visual*	*Multimedia*
Advertisement	Choral reading	Sculpture	Gallery walk	Flipgrid
Tweet	Game show	Mobile	Diagram	Autodraw
Cartoon/ Comic	Song	Mosaic	Map	Bookcreator
Learning center	Debate	Mask	Timeline	Storybird
Newspaper article	Skit/role play	Content shield	Poster	Aww App interactive whiteboard
Blog	News report	Costume	Photo gallery	MakeBeliefs Comix
Creative writing	Puppet show	Gameboard	Padlet/Lino	Pixton Comics
Magazine	Commercial	Mural	Photo essay	Google Chrome Music Lab
Travel log	Poem	Pantomime	Book cover	Canvas online posters
Greeting card	Oral report	Scavenger hunt using GooseChase	Collage/ Padlet	Lucidchart
Brochure	Audacity	Puzzle	Bulletin board	Picktochart
Journal	Guest speaker	Legos	Picture dictionary	Show Me iPad app
Infographic	Flipgrid	Foldable	Model	Little Bird Tales

can time-stamp students' progress on their IEP goals as students orally discuss concepts and share anecdotal data from the check-ins with other students. Ensure that students' IEP goals are standards-based, to support students in making gains in their respective grade curriculum simultaneously. As students complete assignments, the assignments can be tossed into a student or the class folder to support progress monitoring on IEP goals. Three essential documents to compile for the class data clipboard or class folder for students with disabilities: Accommodations (see Figure 5.7), IEP Goals/Objectives (see Figure 5.8), and Daily Dashboard (Anecdotal notes) (see Figure 5.9). Sample data templates are in Appendix.

Block 6 Accommodations	Classroom	Copy of Notes	Concise/Clarify Directions	Extended Time	Preferential Seating	Enlarged Text	Progress Reports	Calculator	Set of Books @ home	Frequent Prompts	Chunk Information	Read Aloud	Testing	Read Aloud	Chunking	Extended Time	Breaks	Small Group Testing	Clarify Directions
Bob		X						X				X					X		
Mark				X					X									X	
Allisa						X													
John			X				X			X		X		X					

FIGURE 5.7 Accommodations Planner

	Reading			Writing				Math				Functional
Student Names	Will correctly read 19 out of 20 words on the first attempt	Will fluently read unfamiliar fifth-grade reading passages of 300 or more words at a rate of 100 words per minute in all settings		Will use the keyword outline process to create a written composition	Will edit his writing for spelling, punctuation, and grammar errors							Student Specific Goals *may include functional skills*
Barney	4/3 ELA			3/28 S.S.								Improve organization skills for class work and homework through specific, repetitive instruction: 5/6
Fred	4/4 ELA				4/12 ELA							
Wilma												
Betty												

FIGURE 5.8 IEP Goal/Objectives Organizer

Student	Check-in	Homework	Class Practice	Exit Ticket	Other
Joe	Calm		Assist with ## 4-6	3/4	Called parent to share good news
Mary	Upset about test score			2/4	
Devon	Provided with a 3-min break		Needs more time	5/5	
T'Shara		Perfect		3/5	IEP meeting is on 5/6

FIGURE 5.9 Daily Dashboard

In Closing

Assessment is a key component of a highly effective differentiated classroom, and it doesn't have to be a bore for you or students. Have fun and offer novel ways to share learning of content standards and objectives. Use a variety of formative assessment strategies for students to demonstrate their "smarts" using various modalities and product options. Move beyond *just* paper-and-pencil assessments and provide a multitude of opportunities to use technology, show creative expression, and demonstrate higher-order thinking. When a dance instructor says, "Freestyle," no one gets sad—quite the opposite, everyone gets excited! Similarly, assessment in our classroom isn't punitive, a "go cha," or another stressor for students to add to their long list of reasons to despise school. Our adolescents are already overly stressed and anxious, and students often cite school as a significant stressor. Teen depression keeps rising each year, and adolescent teen suicide has increased by 70% (National Center for Health Statistics, 2014). We don't want school and a penalizing quiz to be added stressors or the reason a child says, "I can't go to school today." We want ALL students to get excited about proving their learning. When students excitedly share and demonstrate content knowledge and skills, it shows (yet again) that you are a great teacher and they have done some amazing learning. So, get "freestyle" with your assessment practices and watch students show off.

Top 7 Dance Moves

Which of these moves can you try tomorrow? Which moves can you share with your team?

1. As a school team, count the number of worksheets students receive either on paper or on a computer during a day. Another possibility is for a teacher to shadow a student's entire class schedule and count the number of times the student engages with a lower thinking level assessment (recall, remembering, etc.). Commit to reducing worksheets (or worksheets on a computer) and add one or two assessment learning opportunities from the list of assessment strategies.
2. Yearning to know more about John Hattie's Visible Thinking and high-impact strategies that make a difference for students? Visit Visiblelearning.org and select "Hattie Ranking." Consider which instructional practices you use, and which practices you could intentionally add to your daily instruction.
3. Review the instructional assessment practices for literacy and math. Which assessment strategy can you add to your daily classroom instruction to support higher levels of discussion and thinking?
4. Form an *Assessment Team* at your grade level and try one of the "outside-the-box" assessment strategies. To see novel assessment strategies such as the Mannequin Assessment (a/k/a tableau) visit the Teacher Toolkit at www.theteachertoolkit.com, select "courses," and browse more ways to "Check for Understanding."
5. Try one of the novel, outside-the-box assessment strategies to get students talking. Specifically, the Brown Bag Assessment can be used across the entire curriculum. There are many adaptations of this assessment strategy for various contents. Visit

Adlit.org and its "Brown Bag Exam" page to see the many strategies to move students up the Blooms' and Webb's higher-order thinking ladders.

6. Looking for more assessment practices to provide students with multiple ways to share their learning? Visit the Universal Design for Learning Goalbook free app toolkit with UDL strategies to ensure that students have multiple forms of action and expression (a/k/a "sharing what you learned.") The direct link: https://goalbookapp.com/toolkit/v/strategies.
7. Ready for extension on assessment practices? The next step is to categorize your daily assessments that you provide students. There are different types of assessments and each type has implications for student learning. Search YouTube for "William Dylan" and learn about "Assessment for Learning" vs. "Assessment of Learning." Which category do most of your assessments fall into? Note implications and next steps.

List your next dance steps for providing a variety of learning opportunities for students to demonstrate their learning.

____

____

____

____

____

Accountability Partner: ______________________________
Check-in Date: ______________________________

Good Luck and Dance Your Heart Out!

PART THREE

Making Your Mark

In Part Two we spiced up the rhythm in instructional practices. A common language on Specially Designed Instruction (SDI) was shared, as well as practical examples of what SDI is and what it looks like. There were opportunities to reflect, self-assess, and collect a few practical approaches to add "special" for our students with exceptionalities. Choice is a huge motivator, so adding choice at the beginning, middle, or end of a lesson can engage our diverse learners and support teachers in differentiating instruction on a consistent basis. Part Three continues the dancing journey of *Making a Mark* in the lives of students, preparing students for life beyond multiple-choice questions. Chapter 6 is dedicated to the practices of connecting social and emotional learning (SEL) with academic instruction. By embedding SEL daily across the entire school community, students generate the greatest transfer of skills beyond the classroom and into the world. Chapter 7, the concluding chapter, is centered on the benefits of self-care, both for us and for our students. Our self-care practices can rejuvenate and reinvigorate us so that we respond to student misbehavior with dignity and differentiation.

Hooks to Guide Part Three:

Chapter 6: Do we intentionally plan for and incorporate social-emotional learning every day in every class in our school community?

Chapter 7: In what ways do I practice self-care so that I can continually pour into myself and my students, especially when they present behavior challenges?

6

Waltz

The Social-Emotional Learning Connection

The history of ballroom dance is full of important moments when new styles revolutionize the dance culture. The waltz (from German *walzen*, "to revolve") is one of those dances; it is perhaps the most iconic ballroom dance there is. The waltz was first danced in Germany and Austria between the 13th and 18th centuries. Everyone has heard of the waltz, but only a few people know what it really is. Sound similar to social-emotional learning? We've heard of SEL, but what is it?

The waltz dance is characterized by a step, slide, and step in 3/4 time. The waltz is so influential that many have added their own variations. For example, there is the Viennese waltz (made popular by the Strauss family), International Standard waltz, American-Style waltz, the Scandinavian waltz, the Mexican waltz, the Valse Musette, the cross-step waltz (French Valse Boston), and the Cajun waltz, to name just a few. Like the iconic waltz movement, there are lots of great variations (frameworks) for social-emotional learning. For example, the Collaborative for Academic Social and Emotional Learning (CASEL) defines social and emotional learning as skills that allow us to navigate the world, to recognize our own feelings, and to work effectively with other people. CASEL outlines the "big five" skills that students need to develop: self-awareness, self-management, social awareness, relationship skills, and responsible decision-making. Nancy Fisher, Douglas Frey, and Dominique Smith share five tenets for SEL integrated throughout the school community: agency and identity, emotional regulation, cognitive regulation, social skills and relationships, and public spirit. Lastly, there is Transformative Education's SEL Integration Approach: Strong Relationships, Explicit Instruction, Thoughtful Modeling, Practice Opportunities, Teachable Moments, and Conducive Environments. No matter which version of SEL you espouse, one thing is for sure: this work is very important.

Social-emotional learning has become the recognized term for referring to the foundational skills, attitudes, and behaviors that facilitate the development of key intrapersonal and interpersonal skills that help promote school engagement and set the stage for later success as an adult. That's the whole goal of education, right? The SEL movement began in the 1980s and gained momentum with publication of Daniel Goleman's book, *Emotional Intelligence: Why It Can Matter More than IQ*. In that book, Goleman notes that IQ accounts for only about 20% of success in life; the remaining 80% is attributable to factors related to emotional intelligence, such as self-awareness, ability to manage emotions, empathy, social consciousness, self-restraint, and ability to nurture positive relationships. Almost every employment index site lists what they want employees to be/have: problem solvers, critical thinkers, emotional intelligence, creative, cognitive flexibility, people management, service orientation, and effective team members (*Future of Jobs Report*, World Economic Forum, 2018).

In many cases, schools only provide students with SEL opportunities through a specific program, such as an elective class period or afterschool option. However, what is really needed—though far less common—is for schools to amplify the principles in the SEL programs and introduce them into the fabric of the school community itself. All of the three SEL frameworks cited earlier are built on the belief that *all* learning is social and emotional. Thus, SEL must become a deliberate presence in our classrooms and entire school community. Instead of asking, "Which program should we use?," our question should be "How can we integrate the tenets of SEL into our everyday lessons?" When schools recognize SEL as an official component of the curriculum, teachers are allowed to operationalize it in their classrooms so that SEL is not a stand-alone lesson that only occurs once a week and gets little follow-up throughout. Whether using a commercial program or homegrown resources, teachers take advantage of the many opportunities academic learning presents for an integrated approach. Equity applied to SEL helps us understand that there are many variables that can affect our students' development of social-emotional learning. Thus, we start to understand that SEL will look different for different cultures and that different students will need different supports for this type of learning. Your "why" as a school community will drive your practices around SEL work. What drives your school? Is it compliance or conformity (sending kids to detention because they are not quite sitting down in rows or standing silently in a straight line)? Or is your school's "why" empowerment, liberation, social justice? If so, SEL will be much easier to integrate into your daily instructional practices. Your "why" will determine how you use SEL as a lever or tool for equity.

As with my four co-teaching models, I believe that if we keep the idea of SEL concrete and as simple as possible, we can integrate it more seamlessly. SEL won't feel like just another initiative or another program to add on top of everything else. All SEL work begins with relationships, building meaningful connections and partnerships with students (Chapter 1): the foundation for everything we do in effective teaching and learning.

SEL integration is not like a Blood Moon: it's not a once-every-now-and-then type of thing. It is recursive and ongoing, and the social and emotional resources should be practiced and reinforced in every class in the school community. Schools must continually monitor and analyze school climate data, and refine the work they do to foster students' social and emotional development. The SEL competencies are great, but we can't generically keep them as is; we need to be flexible based on the relationships we've developed with our students. Relationships with students and community are paramount to SEL.

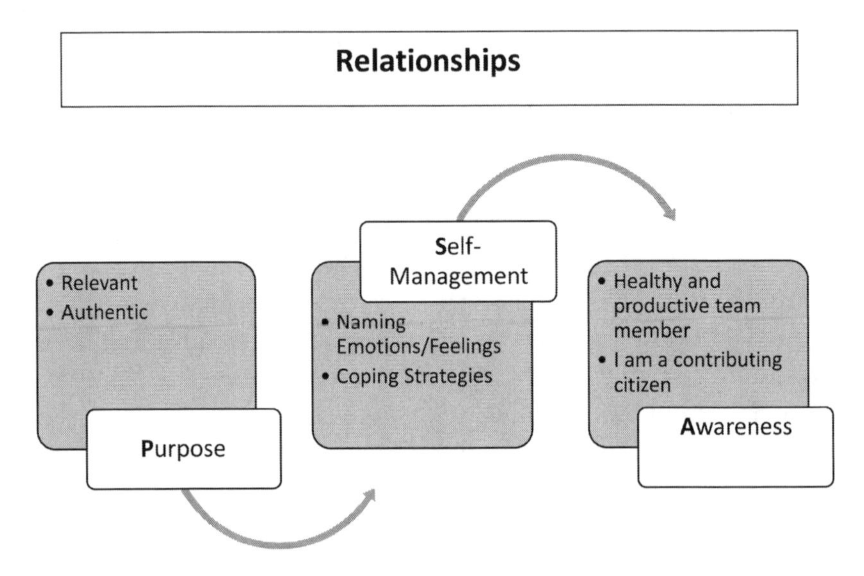

FIGURE 6.1 The P.S.A. for Social Emotional Learning

This is my **PSA for SEL**: Every day, every class, every school, ensure that students have opportunities to engage in **P**urpose, **S**elf-Management, and **A**wareness (see Figure 6.1). *Purpose*: At any given moment, a student should be able to answer the question, "Why is what you are learning important?" The P for *Purpose* is that "why." For example, "Why I am staying after school to work on multiplication facts rather than going home to take care of my siblings while Dad is at work?" or "Why am I learning about two-step equations when I need to go to work to earn money to help pay the rent?" If teachers deliberately connected these dots every day and provided relevant learning opportunities with content, perhaps we could start to engage students before we lose them. I cannot stress enough that many of our students with disabilities need the "why." *Self-management* (a/k/a *self-regulation)* is the skill that so many of our learners with exceptionalities need to learn and practice. Whether students are dealing with behavioral issues, trauma, feelings of helplessness, or stress, they need to be able to regulate their emotions. Self-management is the ability to name and regulate one's emotions to handle stress, control impulses, persevere in overcoming obstacles, express emotions appropriately, and return to a healthy state of response. *Awareness* includes teaching and learning opportunities for students to build social awareness skills (a/k/a playing well with others.) Social awareness skills include empathy, perspective-taking, respect for others, celebrating diversity, acknowledging bias, and taking actions to be anti-racist. Overall, social awareness consists of learning how to become a contributing member of society both in and out of the classroom. Our students need to feel empowered that they can make a big difference in the world, and we absolutely need them to. Unlike an elevator, there are no capacity restrictions on joining the "Good Human Club," and we want as many members as possible.

Purpose

As you plan and teach content, your goal is to ensure that curriculum is relevant to the world and our young people's lives. We want to guarantee that children from all backgrounds can see themselves in the curriculum daily. At any given time, can students answer three questions: "Why is this important?" "How does this connect to the real world?" and "How can I use this new knowledge/skill in the outside world?" We want students to say, "I find what I am learning relevant to the real world" and "I have opportunities for authentic connection with other students around the world." The bottom line is purpose, and relevance *is* the purpose and motivation for learning. Try this: On your way into your planning meeting, pick up a local newspaper and check what's happening in the world. For example, is there a way to connect the study of Harriet Tubman with a local figure who is fighting for civil rights? Perhaps students could write about Harriet Tubman and analyze what the world would be like if she didn't exist.

Relevance in Math

> There are two versions of math in the lives of many Americans: the strange and boring subject that they encountered in classrooms and an interesting set of ideas that is the math of the world, and is curiously different and surprisingly engaging. Our task is to introduce this

> second version to today's students, get them excited about math, and prepare them for the future.
>
> —Jo Boaler, Nomellini-Olivier Professor of Mathematics Education at Stanford University

If you haven't started to experience the Jo Boaler magic, visit the instructional strategy-infused math website www.youcubed.org, watch a few of her "films," and discuss how math should really be taught. One of my favorite videos (today) is the "Rethinking Giftedness" one. Much like a lot of her work, this video explores student mindset, stereotypes such as labeling a student in math as "smart" and "gifted," and the ramifications for students who receive these labels and those who don't.

It cannot be overstated: *Relevance is the purpose and motivation for learning*. Students should be able to connect our math curriculum to themselves, the real world, and authentic use of the skills learned. Contrary to popular belief, not every student wakes up excited about the Pythagorean theorem. It's no secret that a lot of students hate math. To them, math is just a bunch of random skills to memorize and regurgitate, and they see math class as totally disconnected from their lives. When students see no reason to learn, they don't. This is especially true for our learners with exceptionalities. However, math can be related to social and emotional learning just like any other subject: if students can connect the dots of why this standard is important and how they can use it outside of school, they will be motivated and invested to learn it and feel good about learning it. As math teachers, we have the opportunity to change this trajectory and get students excited about math, like we are. Adding and connecting relevance to our math instruction every day takes deliberate planning to analyze standards, find hooks, and make connections to the purpose so we get students talking and debating over mathematical phenomena.

Three-Act Task Approach

A great way to connect real-world problems to our mathematical standards is to use the "Three-Act Task" approach. As defined by

Dan Myer (2011) "a Three-Act Task is a whole group mathematics task consisting of three distinct parts: an engaging and perplexing Act One, an information and solution seeking Act Two, and a solution discussion and solution revealing Act Three."

Act One: The goal is to engage and perplex. Usually, a video or a picture that gets students excited about the math is used. Students are asked where the math is throughout: What do they notice and wonder? In Act One, students identify the main question, make estimations, and consider what they need to know in order to solve a problem.

Possible questions:

- What do you notice?
- What do you wonder?
- What questions do you have?
- What's your guess?
- What does a wrong answer look like?
- What is an answer that would be way too high? Too low?

Act One engages every student. Every student can share what they noticed; no background knowledge is necessary, and there is no right or wrong observation. Every student is on the same playing field, so they can enter this math learning opportunity with success and optimism. This is a great hook for students with disabilities because teachers can add and reinforce mathematical language as students discuss their findings throughout.

Act Two: The teacher reveals more information. The goal is for students to seek information and problem solve. Here students find the information needed to solve the problem. A second visual or video is provided to help give needed information. During Act Two, students need to gather tools, information, and resources to answer the question/solve the problem. The teacher asks, "What more information do you need to know to answer our question? and "How would you get it?"

Act Three: The goal is to reveal, discuss, and extend into the current math lesson and standards. The problem is resolved. Students share how they solved the problem, finding similarities among the examples provided in a guided discussion. The teacher pushes thinking through carefully selected student work based on the objective. It requires a higher-order conversation about sources of error. It states the objective of the day. Students come up with a title for their lesson. The teacher asks students questions such as "Why was our answer close but not exact?" "What did our model not include that it should have?" "What did our model include that it shouldn't have?"

The most famous example of the Three-Act Task approach is Dan Myer's "Nana's Chocolate Milk." In Act One, we find out that Nana likes her chocolate milk made with exact measurements of milk and chocolate powder mix: one cup of milk and four scoops of chocolate powder. However, in the video the child pours one cup of milk and does five scoops of powder mix (instead of four). Uh oh! The question posed to students is, "How can I fix this? How can I make it the right mix of chocolate and milk?" Invite student discussion and ask prompting questions. Some students may say, "Add more milk or take some milk away from the error cup." In Act Two, a few visual scaffolds are provided, such as a double number line for cups of milk and scoops of chocolate. Teacher follows up, "How many different solutions can you find?" and for those students who might have said, "Just pour some of the other cup into the first cup," provide a stimulating challenge by asking, "The glass won't hold two cups of liquid. How does that affect your solution?" In Act Three, the solution is given and students get to share their reflections and refinements. This is a fraction lesson, a review, a hook, or an extension that invites ALL students into learning complex math (especially our students with exceptionalities and students acquiring English as a second language). I won't spoil the ending and the task extension; to see that, google Dan Myer's Three Act, "Nana's Chocolate Milk." In this example, the teacher has added purpose to learning about fractions and students are able to connect math to the real world.

The following websites have dozens of Three-Act Task lessons for K-12 mathematics:

http://blog.mrmeyer.com
https://whenmathhappens.com/3-act-math
https://tapintoteenminds.com
http://www.estimation180.com/lessons.html
https://gfletchy.com/3-act-lessons
https://mikewiernicki.com/3-act-tasks
https://www.youcubed.org (Jo Boaler's site)
https://www.mathhooks.com
http://www.andrewbusch.us/math-tasks.html

Two additional resources that can support us with ensuring purpose and relevance with our math standards are MashUp Math and Mathalicious (doesn't that just make math sound deliciously tasty?). MashUp Math is free and Mathalicious is worth the 30-day free trial with a possible subscription as a department. Mash Up Math provides standards-based math videos with connections to the real world. Mathalicious sets the pattern for linking mathematics to real-world problems, engaging students in deep discussion and inquiry to find solutions. From subjects such as, "Do people with small feet pay too much for shoes? Do taller Olympic sprinters have an unfair advantage? How have video game consoles changed over time … and are we building the Matrix?" the lesson plans, videos, and resources will hook students instantly and get them talking about math.

Relevance in Literacy

> *"One child, one teacher, one book and one pen can change the world."*
>
> —*MalalaYousafzai*

If our curriculum doesn't provide students the opportunity at every grade level, in every unit, to read and write about things that matter—substance that can shape them as humans, their footprint in creating a better world—we are missing a huge piece of relevance in literacy instruction. After selecting text worthy enough to devote class time to, the goal beyond comprehension and analysis is for students to do something meaningful with the text. The text we choose should inspire students to debate ethical dilemmas, write about change, or investigate a historical topic. If the text we read doesn't inspire students, why are we reading it? We want students to read and write with a purpose. Students should believe that their writing is their voice to the world, guided by the question, "How can my voice create change?" Writing with authenticity is the opportunity to meaningfully share one's words with an audience for a purpose, whether it is blogging, spoken word, or a classroom socratic seminar. Our goal should always be to find authentic ways to engage our students in sharing their voice across the curriculum and with the world to make an impact globally. Whether it's writing to share recipes of how culture shapes tradition with a fellow student in Brazil or creating a multimedia digital scrapbook to present elements of family history and ancestry identity to a classroom across the state, the options for writing and sharing ideas authentically are endless. There are tons of fantastic global education collaboration websites (e.g., Epals.com, Tigweb.org, GlobalSchoolNet.org, and Globaledguide.org) that contain millions of opportunities to write for a purpose, share writing with other students, add more kindness to the world, and solve real-world problems. By searching grade-level and content standards, students can connect on meaningful projects and make their voices count!

How do we get our students excited about writing and effective at it? One of the most effective, evidence-based approaches for supporting our students with learning disabilities is the Self-Regulated Strategy Development (SRSD) model for writing strategies instruction (Table 6.1). SRSD was developed by Harris & Graham (1996), with the goal to support at-risk children and children with learning disabilities. However, SRSD has been shown to be effective for all students across disciplines, grade levels, and English-language learners. The research demonstrates the important role of strategy instruction for improving writing, and for boosting learners' planning, editing, and overall written product quality for learners with exceptionalities (De La Paz, 2007;

TABLE 6.1 Self-Regulated Strategy Development (SRSD) model

Stage	*Process*	*Purpose*
Stage One Develop background knowledge	Provide a pre-assessment to check for background knowledge. Develop necessary routines, vocabulary, and exemplars of success criteria. Students develop their writing goal to self-monitor throughout the process.	Elicit motivation around discussion about writing and why this type of writing is important in the real world/sharing your voice. Increase background knowledge.
Stage 2 Discuss it	Discuss the strategy, including benefits and expectations for success.	Provide the how and when to use this writing strategy routine. Self-regulation procedures are emphasized (e.g., goal setting, monitoring, positive self-talk, etc.).
Stage 3 Model it	Use explicit instruction to model the specific strategy ("I Do, We Do, You Do [Together], You DO [Alone]")	Teachers model the strategy. Teachers provide think-aloud and inner thought process for overcoming obstacles.
Stage 4 Memorize it	Provide or facilitate the development of guided organizers, checklists, and mnemonic devices to support internalization of the process.	Practice steps of the process. Students memorize the writing strategy routine.
Stage 5 Support it	Provide guided practices with immediate feedback and reinforcement.	Students practice writing with help (longest of all stages).
Stage 6 Independent	Student practices the strategy independently.	Students write independently.

De La Paz & Graham, 2002; Englert, 2009; Graham, 2006; Graham & Perin, 2007; Perin, 2007). Though the academic area of focus is writing (including sentence construction, planning and revising, and genre element knowledge) and self-regulation strategies for writing (including goal-setting, self-instructions, self-assessment and self-monitoring, and self-reinforcement), teachers have used SRSD for reading and mathematics with great success. The SRSD process consists of six recursive steps with embedded self-regulation procedures around specific writing frames and routines (see Table 6.1) Though there can be variations of the six steps, these steps are critical to supporting the SRSD process.

Self-Regulated Strategy Development (SRSD)

SRSD is designed for use with students with disabilities (including learning disabilities and behavioral disabilities), English-language learners, and any student at risk of academic failure. The academic area of focus is writing (including sentence construction, planning and revising, and genre element knowledge) and self-regulation strategies for writing (including goal setting, self-instructions, self-assessment and self-monitoring, and self-reinforcement).

> *Throughout the stages, teachers and students collaborate on the acquisition, implementation, evaluation, and modification of these strategies.*

For videos, lesson plans of SRSD, and explanations of the six stages, visit ThinkSRSD.com and Vanderbelt IRIS Center. Watch this video for a quick overview of the six stages: Six Steps of Writing Success

How is SRSD similar to or different from your writing instruction for students with disabilities? Perhaps you found that SRSD is more in depth than the stages of the writing process (brainstorming to publishing). Or perhaps the words "self-monitoring," "self-talk," and "writing strategy" routines popped out. Throughout the six stages, teachers and students collaborate on the acquisition, implementation, evaluation, and modification of writing strategies. Stage 1 provides all learners access into the writing task; every student can experience success as they set their personal writing goal. As teachers, we use this time to pre-assess knowledge on the type of writing and intentionally make connections on why writing is so important and how sharing your voice can inspire change in the world. Write for a purpose bigger than school uniform policies, perhaps why schools should go "green" and have solar panels and recycle bins. There are dozens of different writing routines and frames for the writing strategy instructions referred to in Stages 2-6. ThinkSRSD.com provides examples and free templates for writing strategy instruction. One of the most used examples of SRSD writing strategy instruction is "POW+TREE." This writing strategy helps students develop a systematic approach to an essay-writing task and self-monitor their progress as they become more independent (Harris, Graham, Mason, & Friedlander, 2008). Teachers have created visual anchor charts of a tree trunk, guided writing organizers with space to fill in the *TREE* section, and/or writing bookmarks to reinforce the process. POW + TREE is only one of many writing strategies available; visit ThinkSRSD.com's resources tab for more writing routines for various types of writing and grade levels.

P: Pick my ideas
O: Organize my notes
W: Write and say more
T: Topic sentence (Tell what you believe!)
R: Reasons 3 or more (Why do I believe this? Will my readers believe this?)
E: Explain Reasons (Say more about each reason)
E: Ending (Wrap it up)

Self-Management

Self-management is the ability to adjust your state of alertness and how you display your emotions through behavior in socially adaptive ways. When I explain it to five-year-olds, I say, "Self-management is being able to name and tame our emotions; we have to name it, in order to tame it." Throughout the process, students are taught how to use a variety of coping skills that will help them self-regulate and return to their best "selves," "learning ready" or "learning brain." Ultimately, teachers are helping students understand the psychological approach called H.A.L.T. Students should H.A.L.T. if they are Hungry, Angry, Lonely, or Tired. Each of these four physical or emotional conditions could cause anyone to react in a way that we could later regret. There are a variety of systematic and results-driven approaches that teachers use to successfully support students with self-management.

The Zones of Regulation

The Zones of Regulation is a systematic, cognitive behavioral approach used to teach self-regulation by categorizing the ways we feel and states of alertness we experience into four concrete zones, designated blue, green, yellow, and red. The Zones framework provides strategies to teach students to become more aware of controlling their emotions and impulses, manage their sensory needs, and improve their ability to solve problems. The best practice is to set up the Zones of Regulation across the entire school community for all students and include students with disabilities, rather than in just one classroom. In this way, every student hears consistent and reinforcing messaging around self-management skills throughout the entire day. From class to class, students utilize the same consistent language and routines to self-regulate. In this way students will have the opportunities, practice, and appropriate levels of support they require to become more responsible and independent over time. The eventual goal is to help students self-monitor their behavior without this intervention. The Zones are as follows:

BLUE Zone – Your body is running slow, such as when you are tired, sick, sad, or bored.

GREEN Zone – Like a green light, you are "good to go." Your body may feel happy, calm, and focused.

YELLOW Zone – This zone describes when you start to lose control, such as when you are frustrated, anxious, worried, silly, or surprised. Use caution when you are in this zone.

RED Zone – This zone is for extreme emotions such as anger, terror, and aggression. When you are in this zone, you are out of control, have trouble making good decisions, and must STOP!

Teachers should normalize all the zones: "It is OK to not be OK, *and* we have strategies to help us be healthy." We all have various feelings at different points in a day based on context; the goal is to learn how to self-regulate and use specific coping strategies to get back into the Green Zone. This process of learning is a journey, and at various times in the learning cycle students may need reinforcement and reminders. The top two websites to visit for resources with videos, books, lesson plans, and visual anchor charts are Zones of Regulation and Michelle Garcia Winner's Social Thinking.

Mood Meters

The Mood Meter is a part of the Yale Center of Emotional Intelligence RULER Program. The Mood Meter is a tool used to recognize and understand our own and other people's emotions. It's divided into four color quadrants—red, blue, green, and yellow—each representing a different set of feelings. Feelings are grouped together on the Mood Meter based on their pleasantness and energy level.

The four quadrants:

Red Feelings: High in energy and more unpleasant (e.g., angry, scared, anxious)
Blue Feelings: Low in energy and more unpleasant (e.g., sad, disappointed, lonely)
Green Feelings: Low in energy and more pleasant (e.g., calm, tranquil, and relaxed)
Yellow Feelings: High in energy and more pleasant (e.g., happy, excited, and curious)

To use a Mood Meter, encourage students to plot their feelings on the graph multiple times a day, such as before starting class, before/after a test, after recess, or during a disagreement. Facilitate discussions on various coping strategies and peer-assisted supports if students aren't feeling pleasant or are low in energy. The Teaching Channel has a great video in action of Mood Meters being used with younger students, titled *Building Emotional Literacy*. The Yale Center for Emotional Intelligence provides trainings on the RULER program and how to implement school-wide SEL practices.

Creative Self-Management Tools

Students can practice naming and talking through emotions they experience at various times during the school day using a

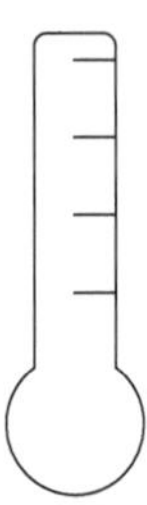

FIGURE 6.2 Self-regulation Thermometer

lot of creative self-regulation systems. Teachers could provide students with emoji check-ins. Using an array of emoji faces, teachers can ask students to choose an emoji that represents how they are feeling, why the emoji has changed (perhaps from recess to math), and what strategies they could use to return back to the desired emoji. Teachers have also provided their students with their own thermometer template (see Figure 6.2). On the thermometer, the emotions are listed bottom to top: calm (at the bottom); excited; agitated; and at the top "explosive." Beside each of the four emotions are the questions: How does it feel? What do I do? How do I look? What can other people do? The teacher provides a check-in and mini-conference at various times in the school day to check the pulse and energy of the classroom.

Another creative strategy teachers use to help students understand their feelings, what it looks like/sounds like as their emotions change, and when to stop and use a coping strategy is the Feelings Volcano. Students can create a literal volcano out of clay, draw a volcano, or use an empty cutout of a volcano. At the base of each student's volcano, students list what they look like and sound like when they feel good and ready to learn (calm and happy). Students continue this pattern of listing what they look like/feel like for various emotions, rising toward the volcano's peak of lava eruption. Some examples of various feelings are calm, unhappy, getting mad, frustrated, out-of-control explosion. At the top of the volcano is the explosion/tantrum/meltdown (possibly in response to a classmate saying something mean, or they couldn't play with a toy, or they got frustrated during reading, etc.). Students practice pausing and noticing their patterns so that before an explosion occurs, they can STOP before the explosion and employ a coping strategy, such as counting to 10, touching a Velcro spot, putting on headphones, getting a drink of water, or using bunny breaths (Gonoodle.com provides videos of breathing strategies to use when we get upset). Examples of looks like/sounds like behaviors moving up the volcano toward an explosion include: breathing change, flushing, sweating, shakiness; not listening, trying to walk away, biting, head down, poor eye contact; crying, cursing/growling, taking off clothes, closed body/fetal position; physical aggression, throwing things, breaking objects, running away, kicking/screaming, pushing response, etc. There are a variety of "Behavior Volcano" self-regulation templates and activities on Pinterest.

Because all students' processes change and stress in various ways, provide students with different ways to self-regulate. Keep an open dialogue with students; provide opportunities for them to share and write about what's on their minds and which coping strategies they find helpful. The National Educators for Restorative Practices site shares a variety of other Pulse Meters that can be used as tools to promote greater self-awareness and strengthen self-management, such as Sponge Bob faces, Yoda, Superhero status, and the like.

Coping Strategies

Normalize stress, anxiety, frustration, and other negative emotions with the overall idea that "It is OK to not be OK." Teachers need to explicitly teach students that there are various coping strategies to use when we feel our amygdalae getting out of control, and acknowledge that we all will use different techniques to self-regulate. It is not a one-size-fits-all approach: while closing my eyes will help *me* to focus, it may not do anything for you or the student dealing with trauma at home who is scarred to close the eyes. Our students need to learn how to use the strategy of their choice that will help them handle their emotions so that they can do their best learning. It is important to explicitly model how to use the coping strategies we offer to our students. If teachers don't model how to use a specific coping strategy, we shouldn't be surprised if we see a student throwing the stress ball across the classroom, ripping apart the feather, or laughing as they engage in box breaths, and so on.

For younger students, model and share just a few choices at a time; for older students, let them try out a few to see which coping technique will best support them with controlling and calming the amygdala. All students benefit from clear expectations on how to use their coping strategy. When teachers create a flexible classroom set-up where there are areas around the classroom that allow for personal use of various self-regulation techniques, students have time to discuss and reflect on their chosen strategy and how it helped them self-regulate various emotions.

Table 6.2 provides a variety of coping strategies students could choose from and use. Table 6.2 is not an exhaustive list of coping strategies, but it is a great starting place to provide students with choice to self-regulate based on their respective moods and emotions.

TABLE 6.2 Coping Strategies

Calming Techniques	*Distraction Techniques*	*Physical Techniques*
◆ Deep breathing with a pinwheel ◆ Deep breathing with bubbles ◆ Deep breathing with prompts ◆ Deep breathing shapes ◆ Deep breathing with a favorite toy ◆ Deep breathing with a feather ◆ Deep breathing while monitoring your pulse with your hand ◆ Explosion breaths ◆ Hands to shoulders ◆ Hoberman sphere ◆ Volcano breaths and check your air ◆ Focus on sounds ◆ Take a mindful yoga break ◆ Imagine your favorite place	◆ Write a story/poem about the issue or solving the problem ◆ Crossword/Sudoku/game ◆ Write about an act of kindness done to you, or one you want to share ◆ Creative thinking ◆ Create your own problem/question for content material ◆ Write about a fun event ◆ Laughter (watch 30 seconds of something funny) ◆ Sort something (blocks, straws, etc.) ◆ Learn something new ◆ Count backward from 100	◆ Squeeze something ◆ Use a stress ball ◆ Shred paper ◆ Pop bubble wrap ◆ Use a sand tray ◆ Climb steps ◆ Hold and toss a small stone ◆ Shuffle cards ◆ Make something ◆ Use a fidget spinner ◆ Walk ◆ Roll a golf ball under your feet ◆ Push against a wall ◆ Dance or pace in marked area of the classroom ◆ Punch a safe surface or air

(*Continued*)

TABLE 6.2 Coping Strategies *(Continued)*

Calming Techniques	*Distraction Techniques*	*Physical Techniques*
♦ Have a mindful snack break	♦ Repeat a mantra, "I am calm"	♦ Swing on a swing
♦ 54321 grounding technique	♦ Blow bubbles	♦ Chant or sing (flocabulary.com)
♦ Grounding self-talk about the present	♦ Sing a song	♦ Brain break (gonoodle.com)
♦ Think of your favorite things	♦ Squish some putty/clay	♦ Stretch
♦ Picture the people you care about	♦ Do gratitude journaling	♦ Yoga
♦ Say the alphabet slowly/backward	♦ Rock in a rocking chair	♦ Crinkle tissue paper
♦ Remember the words to a song you love	♦ Write a note to a friend giving advice on …	♦ Take a coloring break
♦ Run water over your hands	♦ Write a letter to your future self on strategies to use when frustrated/stressed	♦ Fold up like a pretzel
♦ Toss/squeeze a squishy ball		♦ Hop like a bunny
♦ Touch things around you — velcro strip, porcupine pen, etc.		
♦ Make a fist and then release it		
♦ Do progressive muscle relaxation		
♦ Do positive self-talk (provide visual stems examples/talk bubbles)		
♦ Take a drink of water		
♦ Count to 5 or 10		
♦ Block out sounds with noise-cancelling headphones		
♦ Watch a lava lamp or sand timer		
♦ Plow a miniature Zen sand garden		
♦ Shake a glitter/calming jar		
♦ Use your senses		
♦ Trace a pattern or use a therapeutic coloring book		

No student will ever regress in academic learning because a teacher provided routines around mindfulness, or stopped for two minutes to discuss mood, or provided time for a break to utilize a coping strategy when stressed, frustrated, or low. By incorporating social-emotional learning strategies such as self-management, we create better, expert learners, who understand their brain and how they learn so they can be healthy and present, and can react with kindness.

Awareness

Devoting valuable classroom time to building students' social awareness is a way to empower our students with life-long learning tools that will serve them long into adulthood. Today's employers say the capacity to collaborate to solve problems is going to be even more important for tomorrow's workers than content knowledge. Student collaboration can take many forms and we should vary the opportunities we provide for social skill engagement. Whether it's peer-to-peer teaching, connecting with children in other countries, or working together on websites and projects, all students benefit from shared challenges and successes. When we support students with learning how to explain, listen, and provide feedback, they practice higher-level skills such as evaluation and constructive critique.

Within the Classroom

When students connect positively with their peers, research shows they perform better in school. Peer relationships provide children with the opportunity to practice important collaborative skills (Trabasso & Bouchard, 2002). When asking students to interact with partners or small groups, it is not enough to simply tell students to turn and talk to a partner. Doing so may create a dynamic where one partner talks the majority of the time, where both partners talk at once, or where partners do not listen to each other's responses. It is imperative to establish behaviors for interactions, and to practice these behaviors often, so as to positively reinforce the desired college- and career-like team behaviors while students are interacting with their partners or in small groups. We do not make any assumptions: our students with disabilities, students acquiring English as a second language, and others, all need to be explicitly taught specific prosocial behaviors that will support healthy team dynamics. Some of these behaviors are:

1. **Eye contact:** Understand that there are various cultural norms on eye-contact. We want to model that making eye contact is one way to show respect to a speaker in school and in the workplace. We want to encourage students to make eye contact when their partners are speaking by modeling and by explaining that this is a sign of respect in our culture.
2. **Body language:** Body language such as leaning back with crossed arms demonstrates a disinterest in what someone is saying. In contrast, body language that features straight posture or leaning toward a partner demonstrates an interest in the partner is saying, and can make the speaker feel more comfortable and valued. We model body language that seeks to build bridges and connections with others.
3. **Volume:** Partner and small-group discussions can generate a lot of noise when many students are speaking at once. Participants can set specific parameters for—and model—appropriate volume when speaking with partners.
4. **Active Listening:** Another way to establish behaviors for listening during partner and group discussions is to assign active listening tasks at the beginning of each interaction and provide visual conversation stems. Doing so provides a focus for both what one partner is saying and what the other partner is listening for. When assigning an active listening task, we explicitly model language for how the listener will respond to the speaker's initial idea.

Explain that partners can listen actively in order to:

- Agree or disagree (e.g., I disagree with _____'s idea.)
- Restate an idea (e.g., So what you're saying is _____.)
- Collaborate with partners (e.g., What are your thoughts?)
- Ask for clarification (e.g., Can you explain what you mean by _____?)

Let's look at an instructional strategy that supports students in building effective social skills like productive communication and healthy team collaboration. As you read the strategy, consider two questions: What are the benefits of using a strategy like this for students with exceptionalities? How does this instructional strategy support social awareness (within the classroom)?

Save the Last Word for Me

Purpose: This discussion and literacy-based technique encourages meaningful classroom discussions by eliciting differing opinions and interpretations of text. Asking all students to think about their reading stimulates reflection and helps to develop active and thoughtful readers. This strategy ensures that every student participates and has something to share as the entire team simultaneously builds understanding.

Description:

1. Read
   Assign a worthy section of text (text that requires re-reading or is integral to a reading strategy lesson) and ask students to find three to five quotes from the text that they think are particularly interesting. The quotes may be something they agree or disagree with, something they find interesting, something they didn't know, something they would like to tell someone about, and so on.
2. Write
   Pass out sticky notes, slips of paper, or index cards to each student, one card for each quote they have found. On one side of the card, ask students to write down the statements from the text. On the other side, instruct

students to write why they chose that statement (feelings or comments about the statement).

3. Group
   Divide the class into groups of three to five students.
4. Share
   All students in the group share one of their quote cards. The first student, Participant A, reads one of their quotes to the group and shows where to locate it in the text. However, the student isn't allowed to make any comments about that quote until the other members of the group have given their reactions. Discussion rotates through the group, with each group member sharing why they think that quote was chosen. Specific prompts: What do you think it means? Why do you think these words/idea might be important? To whom?

   After several minutes, ask Participant A to read the back of their card (or to explain why they picked the quotation or idea), thus having "the last word" in the discussion of the statement.
5. Repeat
   This process continues until everyone in the group has shared at least one quote and had a chance to provide the last word in the discussion.

Differentiation:

Foster a debrief at the end of each cycle:

- What was a benefit of listening to others respond to your passage before you spoke? (social awareness)
- To what degree was it challenging to hold back your own thoughts while others spoke? (self-regulation and social awareness)
- What did you learn from others? (social awareness)

Using Images: This same process can be used with images instead of quotations. Give students a collection of posters, paintings, and photographs from the time period or book you will be studying and ask students to select three images that stand out to them.

Using Questions: Ask students to write down two or three "probing" questions the text raises for them. Students answer the questions on the back of their card. In small groups, students select one of their questions for the other students to discuss.

There are many benefits to using an instructional strategy like this to support analysis of a complex text. Every student has access to participate in text-based discussions. Perhaps a student didn't understand the text fully, but by the time every peer in the group commented, their understanding of the text will have authentically increased through collaboration. Students with disabilities benefit from a curriculum that provides opportunities for active engagement and text-based discourse (Vaughn et al., 2013). Students are all building higher-order thinking skills as they make inferences and connections. Even if students pick the same quote or sentence, each learner will pick that idea for a different reason. A big part of social awareness is understanding and valuing different perspectives. Provide visual conversation stems and model the conversation stems to support discussion. Utilize positive reinforcement when you hear students using the conversation stems during the *Save the Last Word for Me* protocol. To see *Save the Last Word for Me* in action with students and templates to support organization, visit the TeacherToolkit.com.

conversation card

Excuse me…

I'd like to add…

I disagree because…

I agree because …

I'm not sure what you mean...

I'm confused about...

According to page…

Can you share more about…?

I like how you …

Outside of the Classroom

When asked, "What did you learn today in school?" a student replied, "That politicians don't think young people care about politics like gun laws." Three days later this student led one of the biggest protest rallies with fellow classmates on gun reform. We want our students to have a sense of agency and determination, understanding that they truly can make a difference and get involved in solving issues around the world. Fifty years ago, much work was accomplished by individuals working alone, but not today. Much of all significant work is accomplished in teams, and in many cases these are global teams. When we engage our students in global issues and connect them with other students around the world, the benefits are phenomenal. Global collaboration promotes critical thinking and creativity, allowing transformation of the standards into engaging projects with real-world and authentic applications. Knowledge of other cultures around the world leads students to understanding and compassion. Our goal is to create students who take action or make a difference in resolving problems and changing the world for the better. The best place to start is with the UN's Sustainable Development Goals (SDGs). Start small by intentionally incorporating one or two of the 17 SDGs into your current standards. The SDGs allow us to help our students see interdisciplinary connections and become solution-driven, human-focused, globally relevant, and connected for change. One of my favorite websites, with lessons, stickers, videos, and posters, is The World's Largest Lesson Global Goals. Get Connected on Twitter: #TeachSDGs.

Incorporating SEL into Lesson Planning

Back to my P.S.A.: There is always a way to intentionally incorporate SEL into our instruction. Three guiding questions to use during planning are:

1. What social and emotional skills are necessary/applicable for success on the academic objective or standard?
2. How could a mini-lesson be included and modeled during the lesson?
3. What resources could be added to scaffold and support students in internalizing the skills?

Let's "SEL" a math standard and a literacy-based standard to model how practical it is to include SEL in academic planning. Both standards span multiple grade levels.

Math: Students make sense of problems and persevere in solving them.

1. SEL skills: Possess self-efficacy, work toward goals, control attention, manage personal stress, regulate emotions such as frustration, seek help when needed, exhibit positive motivation, hope, and optimism, display grit, determination, or perseverance.
2. Mini-Lesson: Growth mindset and/or effective effort strategies.
3. Provide students with a visual checklist to self-monitor steps in the process.

Literacy: Students engage effectively in a range of collaborative discussions with diverse partners on grade topics and texts.

1. SEL skills: respect others (e.g., listen carefully and accurately), understand other points of view and perspectives, identify social cues (verbal, physical) to determine how others feel, predict others' feelings and reactions, and manage and express emotions in relationships, respecting diverse viewpoints.
2. Mini-Lesson: Collaborative learning norms and expectations
3. Provide a visual anchor and table tents, and practice using conversation stems to foster productive and healthy teamwork.

In Closing

Educators are engaged in SEL whether we intend to be or not. The way we teach, how we teach, and what we choose to teach and not teach communicates our values loud and clear. In a time when the world seems to be moving at a fast and unpredictable pace, young people look to adults around them for wisdom about how to be an engaged, healthy, and inspired person. In his book, *Emotional Intelligence,* Daniel Goleman notes that IQ accounts for only about 20% of success in life; the remaining 80% is attributed to factors related to emotional intelligence, such as self-awareness, emotion management, empathy, social consciousness, self-restraint, and nurturing positive relationships. SEL is important work and we owe it to our students to prioritize it.

Fred Buckle, the handyman of Nonnatus House in a PBS show, *Call the Midwife*, said, "The waltz is all about protection. It's a dance that says, I have you in my arms, my dear. All is right with the world." We are the *Waltz* for many of our students, equipping them with social-emotional skills so they can be successful beyond our bricks and mortar and flourish as the contributing citizens we need them to be in our world.

Top 5 Dance Moves

Which of these moves can you try tomorrow? Which moves can you share with your team?

1. As a math team, watch Dan Myer's 2010 TED talk "Math Class needs a Make Over." Discuss ways that you can add more relevance to engage and connect students to the real world.
2. Review your district/school mission and vision for how to develop "The Whole Child." The Association for Supervision and Curriculum Development (ASCD) provides a Whole Child Network database with a free Whole Child School Improvement assessment tool, action planner, network guide, and lots more … for free. Visit ascd.org and on the home page sign up to be a part of the Whole Child Network hub of resources.
3. Still have a few folks who need convincing that SEL is super-important work worth prioritizing as first and foremost? Make the case for SEL by

(*Continued*)

visiting CASEL.org/impact to discover research, schools in action, videos from classrooms, and students sharing their growth as a result of social-Emotional Learning.

4. Teaching and integrating SEL is free. Looking to add components of specific SEL programs? The IES.ED.Gov What Works Clearinghouse (WWC) on "Behavior" can help. This site reviews the existing research on different programs, products, practices, and policies in education in order to support educators in making evidence-based decisions.
5. Create a Global Education PLC to ensure that students are building social and civic awareness. Vet one of the four global education databases (Epals.com, Tigweb.org, GlobalSchoolNet.org, and Globaledguide.org) and decide on a possible curriculum project to connect students with other students outside of their classroom. Bonus points for choosing a curriculum project that is multidisciplinary, connecting multiple subjects as well.

List your next dance steps for ensuring that SEL is a living, breathing component of everyday school opportunities for students.

____

____

____

____

____

Accountability Partner: ________________________

Check-in Date: ______________________________

Waltz like you own the place.

7

The Superhero's Dance

Take Care of You, So You Can Take Care of Them

> Not every superhero wears a cape, most are teachers. Legendary comic book writer Stan Lee defines a superhero as a person who does heroic deeds and can do them in a way that a normal person couldn't. Teachers are superheroes. Teachers, like superheroes accomplish extraordinary feats every day. Teachers sacrifice much of their own time for the benefit of their students, creating engaging lessons at 6 am, thinking up interesting inquiry-based projects through lunch, and planning for differentiation on a complex unit after school. It's been found that teachers make between 1200 and 1500 decisions a day.
>
> Phillip Jackson (1990).

Like air-traffic controllers who make dozens of decisions in a minute, teachers aren't always provided the credit for each "student" who lands successfully. Andrea Randall, writer of *In The Stillness* (2013), provides a great story on love and loss with many empowering quotes; one of my favorites is, "Heroes don't always wear capes, badges, or uniforms. Sometimes, they support those who do." As teachers, we inspire students to become professionals in every field, and every career field matters. Sometimes we see the results of our passion and commitment instantly; other times, that challenging student returns seven years later to tell us how we made an impact on their career choice. Teachers are role models, leaders, friends, motivators, and inspirers. They make students feel like they can fly and accomplish something they never thought they could do. Even over the summer, teachers are planning rich learning experiences In fact, as I finish up my book edits, many teachers are creating amazing remote learning experience for students … We never stop learning and becoming the best for our students.

Being superheroes, it only makes sense that our last dance of the book would provide the opportunity for you to put on your magical cape (literally and figuratively) and glide heroically like the superhero you are! The Superman dance to *Crank That* by Soulja Boy (2007) is the teacher's signature dance move. The Superman dance move was called the biggest dance fad since the Macarena, with an instructional YouTube video for the dance surpassing 27 million hits. The Superhero's dance move is distinct: arms in the air with pride for a job well done, an intentional chin up with pause to celebrate, and a glide to restore oneself the hard but life-saving work of teaching children. Though strong and magnificent as superheroes, teachers need to rejuvenate regularly. In fact, after solving humankind's problems, even Superman, one of the strongest superheroes, needs time to recharge. To recharge his powers, Superman flies toward the Earth's yellow sun and restores for a few moments through the photonucleic effect. Then he comes back and repeats all the superhero stuff again. This chapter is dedicated to recharging, so that you too, after winning, can come back and do all of the superhero stuff again and again.

We take care of our self, so we can be our best self for our students.

Take Care of You

Let's start this section on self-care with my rendition of Ze Frank's "Are You Human Test?"

"This is a human test, a test to see if you are human." Please nod your head *yes* if the following has ever happened to you.

- Have you ever misplaced your airline ticket multiple times from your point of check-in to the airline gate?

- Have you ever had so many passwords that you get locked out of one account at least once a week?
- Have you ever gone to the grocery store and forgotten the item you actually went into the grocery store for?
- Have you ever given a public talk to an audience, and believed they could tell how nervous you were?
- Have you ever been so tired that you poured water instead of milk into your cereal, coffee, or whatever? And still ate/drank it?
- Have you ever driven around a parking lot for 20 minutes to find a place to park?
- Have you ever had to take care of a sick loved one, worry about financial issues, or lost a family pet to death?

Good news. If you've experienced some of these things, you are human. You have experienced *stress*. We all feel stressed from time to time; it's a part of the emotional ups and downs of life. Stress has many sources. Tt can come from our environment, from our bodies, or our own thoughts and how we view the world around us. It is very natural to feel stressed around moments of excitement like a new baby or pressure such as tax time, but we are physiologically designed to deal with stress (both good and bad types) and react to it. When we feel under pressure, the nervous system instructs our bodies to release stress hormones such as adrenaline and cortisol. These hormones produce physiological changes to help us cope with the threat or danger we see or experience. This is called the "stress response" or the "fight-flight-freeze-forget" response. (Our teenagers tend to come up with a more creative "F" word for the "forget it" response.)

A few things start happening when we are in flight or fight mode. This is how I explain it to my middle-school students:

- In our brain, the amygdala, which is kind like our caveman brain, the limbic system located much deeper in our brain, the older part of our brain, turns on. Telling us to fight, flight, freeze, or forget it.
- When that part of the brain turns on, the blood energy flows there and shuts off our prefrontal cortex and the

rest of our outer cortexes. That's the part of the brain where we do our better thinking, where we think things through, find creative solutions to problems, see the big picture, and see things more accurately.

- When amygdala is on, other functions are off. My instinct is "How do I eliminate the threat?", not necessarily "What are the consequences?"
- When stressed out, it's hard to be loving, present, and rational. If we don't manage the stress, we tend not to be present in each opportunity, so we can become distracted and can miss out on big moments like this one…

On January 12, 2007, Joshua Bell, one of the world's most acclaimed violinists, set up in a DC metro subway station and played one of the most beautifully complex compositions in the world. Thousands of busy train riders rushing to their next destination missed this beautiful moment. Bell played six Bach pieces for about 45 minutes using his $3.5-million violin. Just two days earlier, in Boston, Bell's concert had sold out even though tickets were priced at more than $100 per ticket. In the subway, everyone was running to their "next place," and very few people were aware and stopped to capture this moment. In short, Joshua Bell played one of most magnificent violin pieces ever written and basically no one noticed. If we are not tuned in and present, we can miss something incredible, like walking past a musical savant playing a never-to-be-repeated performance.

Beautiful things happen when people learn to self-regulate emotions, enact self-care, and use stress-coping mechanisms to slow down and make informed, kind, and healthy decisions. At times, daily stress and anxiety from life in school and outside of school can become so high that we forget to pause, breathe, and practice self-care. The "Karma Repair Kit: Items 1-4" poem by Richard Brautigan provides a simple and practical process to slow down and consider what is needed to return to a state of inner peace:

1. Get enough food to eat, and eat it.
2. Find a place to sleep where it is quiet, and sleep there.

3. Reduce intellectual and emotional noise until you arrive at the silence of yourself, and listen to it.
4. ________

Steps 1 through 3 make perfect sense, right? Step 1: Eat a hearty meal, snack, something healthy or a favorite treat, to come back to a calm state. Step 2: Rest and pause to recenter your mind. Step 3: Take a break, step away from the situation, do something that can help you declutter frustration, so that when you are ready you can approach the situation with a fresh and hopeful outlook. Step 4 is left blank. Why? I believe it is because everyone might need something else, something additional, depending on the situation or their feelings, something specific to their psyche. What else do you need after a long day of teaching? Self-care is like a vending machine. Each row of the vending machine has different items, organized by category (chips vs. candy, etc.), and each item has a different price based on worth. Self-care is similar, depending on our energy or emotional need; for example, anxious, angry, stressed, sad—we may need different resources and actions steps to support us (see the 2A's and 2S's in Table 7.1). Table 7.1 provides examples of self-care. Any of the following strategies and resources can cross over categories to support multiple energy levels and emotional areas of need.

Don't wait until holiday season, parent conferences, or stressful moments to enact self-care. Have a plan and practices in place to utilize regularly. Make self-care a practice rather than a once-a-week occasion. When we are at our best, we can support our students with our very best self, especially when they make bad choices or engage in poor behavioral choices. The fact is that an escalated adult can't de-escalate an escalated child.

Taking Care of Students in the Twenty-First Century

The American Psychological Association produces a *Stress in America* report each year. In 2014, APA's survey reported that American teens say they experience stress in patterns similar to adults, and during the school year they report stress levels

TABLE 7.1 Ideas for Self-Care

Anxious	*Angry*	*Stressed*	*Sad*
Mindfulness pauses	Breathing practices (Belling breathing, Box breathing, etc.)	Dance Break	Practices of gratitude in the morning. Who can you say "Thank-You" to. Write a note of gratitude to let them know how much they matter to you and how you appreciate them.
Make a practical schedule and stick to it.	Smile or laugh – it relieves tension and can brighten your mood.	Prioritize items based on importance and due date. One item, one day at a time.	Develop healthful habits (exercise, nutritious food, lots of water, avoid skipping meals). Physical activity can life your mood.
Keep technology in its place. Don't check work related email outside of your working hours.	Try to see things in a different light/point of view.	Set reasonable standards.	Read positive things (spiritual, positive quotes, a good book).
Ask for help- can you delegate or share a task?	Sleep on it before making any major decisions.	Know your limitations and toss out perfectionism.	Laughing (Buzzfeed's list of the week's funniest tweets).
Reduce time you spend in stressful situations or with stressors.	Keep the big picture in mind. Ask yourself, "Will this problem be a big issue tomorrow or next week?"	Journaling: What stresses you and note your responses.	What excites and lights you up? Plan an activity to look forward to — maybe a special dinner with friends or family, tickets to a concert on a school night, or a vacation.

(*Continued*)

TABLE 7.1 Ideas for Self-Care *(Continued)*

Anxious	*Angry*	*Stressed*	*Sad*
Schedule down time and short breaks for things you love. Protect this time.	See the positive side of a situation: Lessons can be blessings in disguise.	Create a time block to relax and treat yourself each day.	Lake Coloring .com or App (free coloring and drawing experiences).
Kill your stress with kindness. What can you do to make someone else smile?	Assume positive intent.	Avoid harmful solutions to stress (caffeine, etc.).	Join and utilize a social support system (a mentor, friends, online communities that offer support)
Calm.com (free subscription for educators).	Try to forgive. It's good medicine.	Nourish bodies with fruits and vegetables regularly. Pinterest, Mindful Life and Eating Well share great recipes.	List things you enjoy people, things, and experiences. Calendar 1 of these daily.
Focused Breathing & Yoga Poses	Think of things that make you angry or mad. List the opposite of what makes you angry or mad.	Essential Oils (Rosemary supports focus & lavender to stay calm).	Increase positive self-talk and daily affirmations.
Build a community: Who are your people? People who understand your field and successfully employ self-care.	54321 Grounding Exercise (dozens of youtube videos can model this practice).	Practice self-compassion: Celebrate what's going well first. Teaching isn't hard because you are doing it wrong, it's hard because it is.	Talk to your doctor if it becomes overwhelming. Seeking professional help is not an admission of failure but a stance of being a strong superhero.

even higher than those reported by adults. Consider that, as teenagers' stress levels are rising, we are adding more tests, taking away their free time, reducing recess, and playing fewer and fewer games. Even things that used be to be relaxing and fun are now heavily competitive. There is more competition than ever, especially in the sports world. Doctors and surgeons are seeing more young athletes with body wear and tear that they used to see only in adults. Kids are experiencing serious stress.

Many of our students are also dealing with traumatic stress. The 2016 National Survey of Children's Health (NSCH) produced important statistics on just how widespread childhood trauma is. Just under half (45%) of children in the United States have experienced at least one adverse childhood experience (ACE). One in 10 children nationally have experienced three or more ACEs, placing them in a category of especially high risk. ACEs refer to three specific kinds of adversity children can face in the home environment: various forms of physical and emotional abuse, neglect, and household dysfunction. Specifically, these students may be dealing with a host of stressful conditions such as chronic poverty, addiction issues at home, systemic racism, food/sleep deprivation, chronic violence, homophobia, devasting economic situations, and fear of deportation/separation from their families, and many others.

ACEs

ACEs can affect the brain, development, and behavior. We all have normal alarm systems in our brain/body that let us know when we are under threat and mobilize us to respond for safety: to fight, flight (flee), or freeze the face of a threat. When youth experience continuous threats/trauma, the brain and body are put into a chronic state of fear, activating the "survival brain" for prolonged time periods. A youth's brain/body that develops within the context of trauma can be more easily triggered into "survival brain" by trauma reminders or "triggers" when there is no actual threat. When brains are triggered by threat or perception of threat, they release chemicals into the body to allows us to "survive" those states of stress. When chronically released in large doses, these chemicals become toxic to the body and create significant impairment in development. The website *ACES Too High* and the Harvard University Center on the Developing Child provides links to dozens of infographics, visual, and videos explaining how ACEs can affect the brain, development, and behavior.

Think about the classroom of students you support. How many would have an ACE score of at least One? Of Two? Of Three? How does this shift your approach in working with these vulnerable students? Our children are under tremendous stress and they aren't always and consistently receiving skills training to manage their difficult emotions/stress and learn self-management strategies to make healthy decisions. Stress doesn't excuse poor behavior, but it helps us, as teachers, to understand our children, and seek to **proactively** and **positively** support behavior change.

Proactively Support Student Behavior

Alongside building positive student relationships and an inclusive classroom (Chapter 1), there are two specific things we can add to our classroom to *proactively* support prosocial, college-like, and career-like behavior: classroom rules and procedures. As Benjamin Franklin put it best, "An ounce of prevention is worth a pound of treatment."

Classroom Rules

Rules with a relationship = respect; and rules without a relationship = rebellion. Table 7.2 provides a list of best practices to create rules that build connections, relationships, and respect.

A fun instructional strategy to review the classroom rules is the *Whip Around Circle*. Prepare a statement or question prompt that is aligned to the content, in this case, "classroom rules." Provide the prompt: "Think of one sentence and one word that

TABLE 7.2 Best Practices for Creating Rules

Do's	*Don'ts*
DO: ♦ Be Democratic (when students have a say, they are more accountable likely follow the rules). ♦ Stay away from negatives. ♦ State positive form of the rule ♦ Few in number (4-6) ♦ Pre-established consequences tied to following and not following class rules. ♦ Posted in a prominent place in the classroom ♦ Add visuals: Looks like/ Sounds like ♦ Practice a range of behaviors to exhibit rule criteria (got it, nope, and almost-but not there)	♦ Make any assumptions. ♦ Vagueness ("Treat Others Like You Want to be Treated" vs "Be respectful by listening when someone is speaking") ♦ Broad Expectations ("Be Responsible" vs. "Before leaving your seat, let a teacher know")

describe one of our rules." For academic content, the prompt could be adapted to, "Decide on one sentence and one word that sum up your learning for today."

1. Invite students to stand up and form a circle.
2. State and visually post the prompt, explaining that everyone should prepare one sentence and also a one-word response that summarizes their sentence; then allow a minute of private think time.
3. Position yourself in the circle so that you can reiterate big ideas and main points.
4. Ask for a volunteer to start off stating their response. The volunteer then chooses a direction to go (left or right), and participants continue to respond in turn around the circle.
5. After everyone's single sentence is shared, we travel the opposite way so everyone can share their one-word response. I allow repeats and duplicates in my circle (after all, repetition is good, right?). Another option is to let each student "pass" once if they wish.

Classroom Procedures

> "We don't rise to the level of our expectations; we fall to the level of our training."
>
> —Archilochus

Procedures are the six to nine processes in the class that are unique and occur daily (where to sharpen pencils, sit in the circle, transitions, etc.). Provide a rationale for each procedure and how it helps learning. Table 7.3 is a great three-step process for teaching procedures.

A fun instructional strategy for reviewing classroom procedures is Give One-Get One-Move On (GO-GO-MO). Students can describe various procedures and share the expectations with classmates in this structure. GO-GO-GO can be adapted for academic content across the curriculum. Below is an example of how you can use GO-GO-MO for academic instruction.

Preparation: Students fold a piece of paper into four boxes, and number each quadrant #1, #2, #3, and #4.

1. Students think of an important idea they have learned throughout the unit, about a character, vocabulary term, and so on.

TABLE 7.3 How to Teach a Procedure

Step 1: Teach Expectations	Establish specific criteria for procedures (looks like/sounds like). Explicitly Teach (I do, We Do, You Do [together], You Do [alone]). Practice Reteach as necessary. Assess learning on procedures.
Step 2: Monitor Behavior	Circulate in unpredictable patterns. Provide positive feedback. Use visual scans and collect data. Reteach and review.
Step 3: Provide Feedback	Give students (individually and as a class) clear information about the degree to which understand it and need refinement.

2. They write it down in Box #1 of their sheet of paper. .
3. They take their sheet and walk to another classmate to tell them their idea.
4. After they share their idea, the peer gives them an idea to write down in Box #2.
5. Students keep rotating around the room, giving an idea (Give One), getting an idea (Get One), and moving on (Move On) until all four boxes are full of ideas!

For classroom procedures, have students follow the same routine by sharing a classroom procedure they appreciate and explaining the routine correctly to a peer.

Positively Supporting Student Behavior

Here we need to share a few fundamental notes about behavior, people, and instruction. Behavior has a purpose (goal-oriented), behavior is a series of predictable actions and reactions, and behavior communicates a message (are we listening to the message?) Social beings want to be happy; they have a desire to belong and feel significant in the eyes of others. Behavior can change, just as poor behavior can be learned: good behavior can be taught. Behavior strategies are a part of our instructional responsibility. Our goal is to discipline with differentiation and dignity (Discipline, Differentiation, Dignity).

Sometimes, with our most challenging students, we punish them, kick the student out of class, suspend them from school, and label them "bad." What lesson is the child learning from this process? Zero-tolerance policy punishment solves no problem at all. The child's problem behavior usually continues and even escalates, and then eventually the child is deprived of learning again. Discipline, unlike punishment, provides guidance, focuses on learning, tries to resolve conflict, enhances communication, models respect, and aims to problem solve. Discipline teaches students responsibility and life skills, so that they can learn these valuable lessons in the schoolhouse before it becomes too late in the real world. Ultimately, our discipline approach should help our students become even better "good humans."

When we discipline with differentiation, we understand that we can't use a standardized, one-size-fits-all approach for every student demonstrating similar behaviors. Behavior is complex and situations matter. This means we need to aim to understand the function of why a child is misbehaving. The following are two examples of *not* understanding the function of a child's behavior.

1. A teacher provides a student who is acting out to avoid Read 180 with a time-out.
2. A student who longs for adult attention engages in problem behavior, and the teacher stops science class to provide a lengthy redirection to that student in front of peers.

What is wrong with these interventions? The function of the behavior doesn't match the intervention provided. The first student is trying to avoid reading, and we've just given them an easy pass to disengage. The second student is craving attention, and the easiest way is to get it could be self-preservation (e.g., I'm funny). In this situation, if the teacher has developed a relationship with the student, the teacher could have provided authentic positive attention right at the beginning of class, caught the student doing something admirable in front of their classmates, or delegated a leadership task that the student enjoys (before the pattern of misbehavior started).

The ABCs (Antecedent, Behavior, Consequences) can support us in analyzing the severity, frequency, and duration of various behavior patterns. The A for *antecedent* is, "What happened before the behavior?" For example, in situation 1, perhaps the student couldn't understand any of the text and hasn't internalized that great reading strategy you taught, or maybe the student just came from science class where they dealt with a bully, so concentrating on reading is not top of the list. The B is for *behavior*: "What was the student's response?" The C is for *consequence*: "What happened immediately following the behavior?" This urges us to consider what we did. Did we reward, reinforce, take away? I strongly urge educators not to take away anything from a student, such as points, recess, or anything else.

Psychologists often assess the function of a student's behavior using a Motivation Assessment Scale to target a behavioral motivation (sensory, escape, attention, and tangible); but for us as teachers, the 3 A's (Awareness, Attention-seeking, and Ability) can provide good clues to the function of a behavior the majority of the time. The 3 A's help teachers discipline with differentiation, understanding that each student's behavior has a different function and a different response might be needed.

Awareness

The student is not aware that the behavior is inappropriate or can offend others. These behaviors are exemplified by the student who consistently calls out, the student who taps the pen on the desk, the student who cuts off others when they are talking, the student who says whatever is on their mind, and so on. When you ask these students to stop, the majority respond, "I'm not doing anything!" Remember, raising hands to talk, walking in straight lines, and so on are behaviors we may want in school, but based on different cultures, students may not generally do these things at home. When a student engages in ongoing misbehavior because of lack of awareness, our goal is to increase awareness of the desired/replacement behavior (the appropriate, college/career-like behaviors).

Suggested interventions

1. Use videos clips or create social stories/comic strips for the desired behaviors we want to see. Have student analyze behaviors and make personal connections.
2. Use concrete and tactile behavior systems to reinforce desired behaviors (token boards).
3. Create and provide opportunities for students to self-monitor and track appropriate behaviors using a personalized self-monitoring checklist that targets desired behaviors (e.g., I raised my hand before I shared, I took a turn, etc.). Students who track their own behaviors

gain greater control over their behaviors. Intervention Central provides a free "Self-Check Behavior Checklist Maker" that you can create with the student. Two to three behaviors are more than enough for some students.

4. Provide students with a set of color-coded strategy cards and allow them to signal when they need help reaching the appropriate behavior, indicating "I need help with (this behavior): On part of it! On most of it! On all of it!"

The three questions that can help distinguish awareness from ability are:

A. Does the student perform the behavior in other settings?
B. Does the student understand the expectations of the settings?
C. Is it within the student's ability to control the target behavior?

Ability

Sometimes students misbehave because they are unable to or do not know how to exhibit the desired behavior. The intervention plan should include giving the student the necessary skills and knowledge (adaptations and modifications). This category can include students with disabilities and those who don't have a disability. How would you support the following student in this common case study?

Case Study One: A very active first-grade student is rarely able to focus on many tasks and follow directions; the student fidgets and can't sit still for long periods of time. A psychologist evaluates her and suggest that implementing effective behavioral interventions would be the best way to support the student. Because the student's misbehavior is pervasive across a range of activities, it is reasonable to assume that the student may lack the knowledge and skill to be able to focus and pay attention for long periods of time. What behavioral accommodations would you put in place to support this student with on-task attention, focus, and hyperactivity? What are your next steps?

Were you thinking Attention Deficit/Hyperactivity Disorder? Maybe it is and maybe it's not. Either way, the primary focus for supporting this student will be to use brain-based interventions.

Suggested Interventions

1. Normalize the need. Create space in the back of the classroom for a student to get up; create a flexible classroom design with a standing desk, bouncy bands for chairs, Velcro under the desk, porcupine pens; provide fidget tools, etc. Often, all students start off with a desire to use the tools, but the novelty fades and the student who needs the tools will keep using them.
2. Chunk instruction (break task into small parts, complete the first two … of ten).

   Sequence instructional tasks mixed with positive reinforcement after each task is completed.Time-on instructional activity supports (sandglass timers, visual timers, apps like time-keeper extensions) may be very useful for students trying to manage their attention behaviors.
3. Reduce time sitting. Cut worksheet problems up and put them around the classroom for students to get up and solve. Let students choose their positions for reading. Provide processing breaks regularly.
4. Provide first/then boards to visually support students with sequencing on timed tasks. Provide the desired task and time period. When the student successfully completes the first task or time of being on task, they are then reinforced positively with their preferred activity.

Attention Seeking

Attention-seeking misbehaviors are behaviors that a student engages in to satisfy his/her other (often unconscious) needs for attention. Excessive helplessness, tantrums, defiance, inappropriate jokes, tattling, and minor disruptions are examples of behaviors that may be attention-seeking. When a student is seeking attention through misbehavior, any intervention effort that involves giving the student attention when he/she is misbehaving is likely to reinforce the inappropriate behavior. The goal in supporting attention seeking behaviors is twofold:

1. Reframe attention-seeking
   a. Understand Me (attunement seeking):
      i. Consider and respond to my needs (hungry, sleepy, lonely).
      ii. Organize and validate my feelings.
      iii. Be curious about what's happening for me.
   b. Protect Me (attachment seeking):
      i. See my extreme distress and the different ways it is being expressed (often inappropriately).
      ii. Support me to regulate (I don't know how to calm down or can't get there).
      iii. Help me feel safe.
2. De-escalate the situation and positively attend to and reinforce the positive target behaviors.

How would you support the student in this common case study?

Case Study 2: Student yells out a curse word, and says, "This is boring." The teacher approaches the student and reprimands him for misbehaving. Because the student finds the negative teacher attention to be reinforcing, he continues to misbehave, and the teacher naturally responds by reprimanding the student more often! An escalating, predictable cycle is established, with the student repeatedly acting-out and the teacher reprimanding him.

What strategies can be used to break out of this cycle?

This is where "dignity" pairs with differentiation. Dignity can help us quickly de-escalate the situation and not join in a predictable and unhelpful back-and-forth confrontation. Conflict will happen, but combat doesn't have to. e; combat is optional." Our response in that moment can either heal or harm our students on their road to behavior change. The behavior isn't about us, so we don't have to be the "winner" of the battle; in fact, we want to stay out of power struggles and keep the rest of the class learning. Don't engage in a back-and-forth dance with the student who is seeking attention due to an unmet need. Although we've been talking about groovy dance moves in this book, the reality is that students are much better dancers than we are, and they have more at stake: their reputation among their peers.

Because we have built a relationship with the student who is misbehaving, we can use pep and positivity to acknowledge the student's feelings and diffuse the situation. In the moment, a diffuser—something simple like, "That's inappropriate language," "I'm sorry you're frustrated," "Let's talk later"—is enough. There is no need to engage the student further at the time of the exchange. When the rest of the class is sorted out and working independently, that's a good time to have a private teaching and learning moment regarding the inappropriate behavior with the student personally, not in front of an audience. In short, when it is convenient for the teacher (and the teacher is mentally calmed down), circle back during independent work time to offer redirection, consequences, and other assistance to the student.

De-Escalation Strategies

1. Calm is contagious, so use diffusers. In many cases, you can diffuse challenging situations with a simple one- or two-word response (e.g., "I'm sorry," "I understand," "Probably so," "Nevertheless," etc.). The diffuser serves as a mental distraction and provides an opportunity for the student to give up the negative behavior without knowing they have done so … and instruction continues for the rest of the class. Student challenge-> Diffuser-> Move on. Table 7.4 provides a list of diffusers.
2. Act calm even if you are not.
3. Remind the student they are not in trouble, instead saying, "We need to problem solve."
4. Give choice. "When you are ready, I would like a sincere apology, or you can write me a note about why your behavior was inappropriate and how you plan to fix it."
5. Ask, 'What would help you right now?"
6. Say, "I am here for you."

TABLE 7.4 List of Common Diffusers

Diffusers		
Perhaps	I see that	I feel you
Good point	I understand your point	Regardless
Thank you for your observation	Wait, it gets better	You'll find out shortly
That's interesting	Noted	Thanks
I'll keep that in mind	Maybe so	Oh snap
I understand where you are coming from	Hold that thought	So it is
Um okay	Maybe so	Interesting
In the meantime	I hear you	Acknowledged
Got it	We need to move on	Sorry you feel that way
Duly noted	That's another way to look at it	We'll talk later (after…)
Thanks for sharing	Thanks for letting me know	I empathize
I appreciate your thought process	That's right	Roger that

7. Plan to ignore minor behaviors.
8. Offer to change something that you are doing.
9. Let the student use one of their coping strategies and return to the whole class in five minutes.
10. Talk about something the student likes, add humor, and/or share a story when you deal with this type of behavior and/or consequence.
11. Let the student talk without interrupting.
12. Allow their perspective to be included in the conversation: "I see where you are coming from."

Lots of behaviors in one class period? Try a Group Behavior Contingency (GBC) approach. A *group contingency* is a classroom management system designed to proactively support appropriate classroom behavior. Groups or teams of students are rewarded for exhibiting appropriate or desirable classroom behaviors rather than being punished or reprimanded for exhibiting inappropriate or undesirable behaviors. A GBC provides a starting place, with the goal being that students will eventually no longer need it, and the motivation to display healthy, college- and career-like behaviors is intrinsic. The seven steps to a GBC are:

1. Choose the target behaviors. Pick one or two behaviors that will make a huge impact on teaching and learning, such as "Using kind words of encouragement," "Listening when others are speaking," "Transitioning in 60 seconds or less," etc.
2. Choose your groups. You could decide that the whole class is working toward the reward, or partners, or teams.
3. Determine how groups earn points.
4. Decide how you will award points.
5. Choose who awards the points.
6. Determine a schedule.
7. Select rewards. A reward doesn't have to be food; it could be a four-minute YouTube break, reduced practice problems, five-minute dance break, Pajama day, work with your headphones on, math outside, etc. Let students decide the reinforcer.

Examples of a GBC

Students vs. Teacher is a great example of a GBC. Students vs. Teacher is an effective and low-preparation behavior management strategy that motivates even the most reluctant of students. It works like this.

- Use your class rules as a foundation, or specifically target a certain behavior (e.g., being a good friend).
- Write the rule with an image (if possible) near the point tally as a visual cue.
- When the students are following the rules, they get a point.
- When the students are not following the rules, the teacher gets a point.

At the end of the designated time period, the winner earns some special privilege. When the teacher wins, the students do not earn the privilege. Tangible rewards such as PBIS (Positive Behavior Interventions and Supports) tokens or a 30-second dance party may work well. After some time, the sheer joy of winning might be enough for your children.

Tips:

- The first few times you play, make sure your students win! You will get immediate buy-in. If they access the reinforcement and experience success, they will be invested the next time you play.
- When the students get a point for following the rules, make sure to comment (loudly and cheesily) on what the person doing that is earned the point. This will help further reinforce this desired behavior (e.g., I love how Andrew is taking turns so nicely with Graciela). Get into it! If you aren't, they won't be!

Adaptations

Have two or more designated times to identify the winner (for example, halfway through the lesson and after the lesson). Offer incentives such as bonus points; for instance, earn double points if every group is exhibiting the desired behavior.

Disciplining with Differentiation and Dignity

Never…
In the history of calming down
Has anyone ever calmed down
By being told to calm down.

Disciplining with differentiation also acknowledges that some of our challenging students are responsive and prefer specific positive reinforcers to let them know they are headed in the right direction. A one-size-fits-all reinforcer for every student might not work. Consider providing students with a "Forced Choice Reinforcement" survey. This survey gives specific data on what types of reinforcement a student benefits from on their road to behavior change toward "college and career" behaviors. The survey doesn't take too long, and for elementary students there are pictorial adaptations. If you google "Forced Choice Reinforcement Survey," you'll find dozens of variations to use.

The teacher reads the following script:

> In order to identify possible classroom reinforcers, it is important to go directly to the source, namely, you the student. Here is a paragraph that provides instructions for completing a series of "controlled choice" survey items about individual reinforcement preferences. Please read the following paragraph carefully: "Let's suppose that you have worked hard on an assignment and you think that you have done a super job on it. In thinking about a reward for your effort, which one of the two things below would you most like to have happen? Please choose the one from each pair that you would like best and mark an "X" in the blank that comes in front of it. Remember, mark only one blank for each pair."

Walk the student through each reward choice and mark their selection. Next to each reward choice is a code (A: Adult Approval; CM: Competitive Approval; P: Peer Approval; I: Independent Rewards; CN: Consumable Rewards. At the end of the 40 choices, you score and tally the total, which gives you greater insight on how to provide specific and tailored reinforcement. Err on the side of caution with consumable rewards, though: consumable rewards are harder to withdraw, and aren't a great teaching reinforcer (how often do we get a piece of chocolate for taking out the trash in the real world?). Also, if it seems a student is leaning heavily on consumable rewards as their reinforcer, this is an indicator that the student is hungry—so feed them.

In Closing

Take care of you, so you can take care of your students. Student misbehavior can be frustrating, especially after a long day of unanticipated stressors like the copy machine breaking down, forgetting lunch, taking care of a sick parent, and so on. Teachers working with students with trauma can be victims of vicarious trauma (in short, teachers can pick up their students' emotional baggage). When we are emotionally healthy, we are in a much better place to be proactive and positive in supporting student behavior change. Practice self-care regularly. In fact, in those classes where you feel the most stressed, include mindful minutes for you and the students together. I've often greeted my students at the door, noticed that their energy was low and wacky and said, "We're going to swap out this warm-up and have five minutes of mindful journaling while this calming musical medley plays so that we can come back to our learning-ready brains." Mindfulness has helped me and my students on days we didn't think we could keep going. When I introduce mindfulness to students, I explain, "Mindfulness is a special strategy of being in the moment, paying attention to the here and now, pausing, breathing, so that you can respond to a situation with kindness and wisdom, responding in a way that won't leave you with regrets." The 3 R's of mindfulness are "Rest, Recognize, Return" to an anchor of breath or image such as a favorite place or safe place or sounds. Ultimately, mindfulness empowers them to be able to control their thoughts and actions; they are the leader of their destiny and consequences.

Mindfulness is a tool that can address a variety of student social and emotional behaviors: impatience or a lack of impulse control, a lack of focus on the lesson or their work, support needed for getting along with classmates, giving up when learning gets challenging or they don't understand a concept, and having experience with trauma or stress from home. Studies have found many benefits and positive outcomes of using mindfulness practices in the classroom. For example, studies of mindfulness programs in schools have found that regular practice—even just a few minutes per day—improves students' self-control and increases their classroom participation, respect for others, happiness, and self-acceptance levels (Hawn Foundation, 2011; Schwartz, 2014; Zoogman et al., 2015). Once you teach students how to become mindful (it takes practice and time), they can take this tool with them everywhere and use it all the time. Most importantly, mindfulness is a self-care tool we can use to celebrate the great days and mitigate the tough days.

Top 5 Dance Moves

Which of these moves can you try tomorrow? Which moves can you share with your team?

1. Self-care. Create a "bucket list" of self-care items to calendar into your day for a week. Assess the benefits and add more as necessary. Create a school *Teacher Care* support team that collects and provides self-care nuggets in staff lounges.
2. In need of more evidence-based practices for specific student misbehaviors? Top three behavioral intervention sites are:
   a. http://www.pbisworld.com: This website allows teachers to click on specific behaviors and locate resources and strategies at all intervention tiers (from unmotivated to impulsive). An bonus for Special Education teachers is the "data" tab with dozens of behavior progress-monitoring tools (including a forced-choice reinforcement survey).
   b. http://www.interventioncentral.org: In addition to templates, this website provides strategies, research, and resources for various student behaviors. This is the site with the Self-Check Behavior Checklist Maker, a free application that allows teachers to quickly create checklists that students can use to self-monitor their behavior in the classroom.
   c. https://charts.intensiveintervention.org/ (Tool Charts: Behavior Intervention Charts): This website provides behavioral strategies and sample resources to use with students who may require academic and/or behavioral support. Each strategy includes a description of the (a) purpose and overview;

(b) behavior(s) addressed; (c) implementation procedures and considerations; (d) sample scripts or formats; (e) potential intensification strategies; and (f) additional resources and fillable templates.

3. Building and refining character takes explicit instruction and intentional time. There are many opportunities throughout the course of a day to support student behavior by including lessons on "character": who am I, how does my behavior affect me and others, and how can I become an upstanding citizen. Students benefit from character education. Visit:
   a. *Teaching Tolerance* at tolerance.org for dozens of lessons around being our best self.
   b. Teaching for Change at teachingforchange.org provides a growing list of books at various grade levels that can be used to support literacy and character education.
   c. Scholastic at scholastic.com "Character Education: Scholastic Teachables" shares lesson plans, worksheets, activities, writing prompts on social skills, positive behavior traits, and self-esteem.
   d. StartEmpathy.org provides a Empathy Toolkit of more than 60 lessons to support children in developing a hard skill of empathy (in English, Spanish, French, and Korean).
4. Mindfulness practices. Looking to add mindful moments for you and your students to focus and learn how to respond with kindness and wisdom? Wondering if little ones can get it or if older students will buy it? Visit www.mindfulschools.org to find films, lesson videos, presentations, and guided audios for introducing mindfulness to your school and classroom.

(*Continued*)

5. Engaging instruction is good classroom management. When students are engaged, there are fewer problem behaviors. Putting it all together, from Chapters 1 through 6, what instructional moves could support higher student engagement? Invite a colleague into your classroom to observe teacher and student behavior. Ask the collaborating teacher to script teacher and student actions (non-objectively). The goal is to scan the room at the beginning, middle, and end of class. Use the engagement scan format: At (time), ____ out of ____ students were engaged on task. Debrief and analyze engagement data.

List your next dance steps for taking care of yourself and/or students.

____

____

____

____

____

Accountability Partner:______________________________

Check-in Date: ______________________________

Take a dance break to the THE KINKS, "Wish I Could Fly Like Superman" (1979)

And *dance like no one's watching!*

Conclusion

As teachers, we know Aristotle's quote on learning to be rambunctiously true: "The more we know, the more we know we don't know." Teaching is one of the most humbling professions there is, and it is by far the most rewarding. Becoming the best teacher is a lifelong pursuit, a never-ending journey of smiles, crying, giving up, starting again, success, and then repeating the cycle all over again. We want ALL of our students to be college and career ready, but we always have to remember the list of college- and career-ready skills that aren't readily posted: kindness, responsibility, perseverance, optimism, courage, respect, compassion, adaptability, honesty, trustworthiness, and loyalty, to name just a few. As equitable educators, we are invested in high academic outcomes for every learner, and we also know that by developing the whole child we prepare our students to be better versions of themselves. As I stated in chapter one, inclusion is more than a seat in the classroom, it includes presuming competence and assets over deficits, removing barriers to instruction to provide meaningful access, and holding the highest expectations for students with disabilities. They can reach the highest of goals, it may take a little longer, but they will reach the highest of goals.

It is my hope that I provided concrete, actionable practices and strategies that educators can do to help students with disabilities thrive. I implore you to celebrate and continue to use great instructional practices that make an impact for our students with disabilities, our students are truly exceptional. With grace, start with the most important step of creating classrooms in which every student feels like they are welcome and belong and can be successful, the other instructional stuff will fall into place. In the Dot, by Peter H. Reynolds, Vashti reminds us that everything a teacher says and does can make a huge impact in a child's trajectory (even if that action seems small). Teachers make a mark in this world, and help their student's make theirs too. Continue to make your mark in our students' lives. Keep Shaking up Special Education.

I'll conclude with Maya Angelou's quote, "Everything in the universe has rhythm. Everything dances." Teach and dance like our lives depend on it, because our students lives really do.

On behalf of every student,

Thank-You.

Appendix A

"Starting" Conversations

Choice Board

Directions: With your partner, select *three* squares that would make a *tic-tac-toe* win. Next, take one minute to independently jot down your thoughts to the statements in your selected boxes. Last, take turns discussing your answers as a team.

Describe a homework policy that you've seen that is effective *Create an image that illustrates your thinking*	Take Turns: Each person take turns listing responsibilities you'd like to have in your classroom *Brainstorm your list independently. Then, each partner takes a turn sharing one item from their list*	Each person share what your philosophy is on "classroom discipline" *Take one minute each to share your philosophy. Then, create a list of three positively stated rules you both agree on*
If I was fly on the wall in your classroom, which statement would best describe what I'd usually see and hear: a. **On task quiet:** students sitting in rows completing independent work b. **On task noise:** students working in cooperative groupings *Explain the benefits to each type of learning*	Think of successful strategies you've witnessed for meaningfully including a student with a disability in the general education classroom *List at least two strategies and brainstorm how you can incorporate these into your classroom*	Pick the statement that best describes the type of cooperative learning seen most often in your class. a. A doubles tennis game – two players working together b. A basketball game – multiple players each with a specific role c. Three-legged race – two people working together to accomplish a common goal *Cocreate a jingle/rap/poem that incorporates your belief on cooperative learning*

(Continued)

Describe what your typical test/quiz looks like *Take one minute to share. Then brainstorm the answer to the following question:* *If tomorrow, paper and pencil tests were eliminated – how would you assess student learning?*	What are your strengths as an educator? *Take turns listing adjectives that describe you. Then, pick a color that best describes your teaching style and explain why you chose the color*	Using the Playdoh create a sculpture that describes an area of challenge or a pet peeve *Discuss how have you overcome this in the classroom?*

"Continuing" Conversations for Advanced Teams Choice Board

Directions: With your partner, select *three* squares that would make a *tic-tac-toe* win. Next, take one minute to independently jot down your thoughts to the statements in your selected boxes. Last, take turns discussing your answers as a team.

Think of successful strategies you've witnessed for meaningfully including a student with a disability in the general education classroom *List at least two strategies and brainstorm how you can incorporate these into your classroom*	What are our biggest hopes for our work as a team this year? What are our biggest hopes for our students? *Think of a slogan used in advertising that could be used for your class* *For example. Because you're worth it – L'Oreal*	Reflect on the classroom management strategies that you implemented last year. What would you like to remain the same? What could you enhance? *Think of your most challenging student last year. What is one thing you could do differently if the student was to repeat your class this year?*
If I was fly on the wall in your classroom, which statement would best describe what I'd usually see and hear: c. **On task quiet:** students sitting in rows completing independent work d. **On task noise:** students working in cooperative groupings *Explain the benefits to each type of learning*	How can we create systems to ensure students complete accurate and quality homework? *Decide on at least one homework system to implement and add to your class syllabus*	Choose the statement that best describes the frequency of your cooperative learning activities? a. Never b. Sometimes c. Often d. Daily *Cocreate a jingle/rap/poem that incorporates your belief on cooperative learning*

(Continued)

When I teach my class, I would be mostly likely to: a. Include students' life experiences or preexisting knowledge when I introduce a concept b. Require students to learn by doing creative problem-solving exercises, lab activities, and projects c. Engage students in problems that are outside the realm of possibility to force them to think creatively	Describe the best differentiated lesson you prepared last year? What made it such a strong learning experience? *Use Wikki Stix to represent your thought process when creating the activity*	Describe what your typical test/quiz looks like *Then brainstorm the answer to the following question:* *If tomorrow, paper and pencil tests were eliminated – how would you assess student learning?*

B.A.S.E Co-teaching Planning Guide

Big Ideas (Essential Questions, Enduring Understandings, Content & Language Objectives, Key Vocabulary)			
Week One	Week Two	Week Three	Week Four
Transfer Task and/or Summative Assessment			

⇩

Analyzing Areas of Difficulty/Misconceptions

⇩

creating Specialized Strategies and Supports
Differentiation/scaffolding & Co-teaching Models that will support & engage all Learners

⇩

Evaluating
Analyze assessment data and strategies used

Adapted BASE Model for Co-planning, Hawbaker et al. 2014

Guided Lesson Planning for Co-teaching

<table>
<tr><td colspan="2">Teacher:
Teacher:</td><td colspan="3">Curriculum unit:
End of unit assessment:</td><td>Week of:</td></tr>
<tr><td colspan="2">Big idea/essential question(s):</td><td colspan="4">Reflection on teacher and student performance from last week:</td></tr>
<tr><td></td><td>Monday</td><td>Tuesday</td><td>Wednesday</td><td>Thursday</td><td>Friday</td></tr>
<tr><td><u>Stage One:</u> desired results
♦ Mastery Objective(s)</td><td>Mastery Objective:

Skill:</td><td>Mastery Objective:

Skill:</td><td>Mastery Objective:

Skill:</td><td>Mastery Objective:

Skill:</td><td>Mastery Objective:

Skill:</td></tr>
<tr><td><u>Stage Two:</u> assessment evidence
♦ Pre-assessment
♦ Formative
♦ Summative</td><td></td><td></td><td></td><td></td><td></td></tr>
<tr><td><u>Stage Three:</u> learning plan and co-teaching model (*)
♦ Sequence of your assessment, teaching, and learning tasks
♦ Specialized strategies for differentiation based on student interest and readiness; flexible grouping
♦ Academic vocabulary
♦ Extending learning beyond the lesson and classroom</td><td>Warm-Up (*)
Middle (*)
Closure (*)</td><td>Warm-Up (*)
Middle (*)
Closure (*)</td><td>Warm-Up (*)
Middle (*)
Closure (*)</td><td>Warm-Up (*)
Middle (*)
Closure (*)</td><td>Warm-Up (*)
Middle (*)
Closure (*)</td></tr>
<tr><td>Academic and behavioral adaptations</td><td></td><td></td><td></td><td></td><td></td></tr>
<tr><td>Assign responsibilities: materials and resources</td><td></td><td></td><td></td><td></td><td></td></tr>
<tr><td colspan="6"><u>Co-planning meeting agenda</u> = 70% Plan Instruction & Matching Co-teaching Model; 30% Assigning Responsibilities & Reflection
* Co-teaching structure: (O) One lead/One engage (S) Station teaching (P) Parallel teaching (A) Alternative teaching</td></tr>
</table>

One Lead/One Engage Co-teaching R.E.V. Up Guide

Benchmark/Objectives:

Essential questions:

Enduring Understandings:

Skills and Knowledge:

Student's IEP goals and accommodations:

One Lead/One Engage Co-teaching:

Lead	*Support*
Teacher:	*Teacher:*
	♦ *Based on content goals, I will collect data on:* ♦ *Based on our learners with IEPs, I will specialize instruction by:* ♦ *I plan to engage all learners and insert a processing break after/before:* ♦ *I will emphasize and clarify important ideas by:* ♦ *I may need to integrate technology tools to support:*

What does our student data show? How will we differentiate instruction to support student achievement?

Examples of One Lead/One Engage Co-teaching

ELA *Example 1*	*ELA* *Example 2*
Elementary	Secondary
Students are seated around one teacher in the group circle while the other teacher is behind the group. The lesson's goal is for students to recall three elements from *Emmanuel's Dream* by Laurie Thompson. As students state the three elements in order, the teacher seated behind the circle places a check and applicable annotations next to each student's name as they exhibit progress in skill areas. The teachers have created a one-page data sheet with a list of all the students and across the top of the page, each of the skills being stressed in this unit study. The co-teachers have a discussion on student progress and plan to do alternative teach tomorrow to support the students who are ready for extension.	Co-teachers of ELA 8 are concerned about a student who shuts down and refuses to engage when the class independently reads their unit novel. For a 15-minute period while one teacher leads large-group instruction, the other teacher completes an ABC analysis (antecedents, behaviors, and consequences). For example, when the teacher says take out your novel and begin to read silently (antecedent), the student slams her fist down and says, "I don't want to read (behavior)," and the teacher replies, "If you don't read today, you are going to be behind (consequence)." Using this approach, the teachers meet to determine the student's learning barriers, meet with the student, and differentiate the process to provide auditory options for the text.

Alternative Co-teaching R.E.V. Up Planning Guide

Objectives:

Essential questions:

Enduring understandings:

Skills and knowledge:

Student's IEP goals and accommodations:

Review of student data for groupings:

Lesson plan	Alternative teaching activity	Teacher A	Teacher B
Opening **(Warm-up, HW support, etc.)**	**Large group:** **Small alternative teach group (pre-teach, re-teach, extend):**		
	and/or		
Body **(Introduction of new material, guided practice, etc.)**	**Large group:** **Small alternative teach group (pre-teach, re-teach, extend):**		
	and/or		
Closure **(Independent, collaborative practice, exit ticket, etc.)**	**Large group:** **Small alternative teach group (pre-teach, re-teach, extend):**		

What does our student data show? How will we differentiate instruction to support student achievement?

Example ELA Lesson Plan for Alternative Co-teaching

Analyze How Inferences Create Meaning
Objective: Cite strong and thorough textual evidence to support analysis of what the text says explicitly as well as inferences drawn from the text, including determining where the text leaves matters uncertain.

Lesson plan	Alternative Co-teaching	Teacher A	Teacher B
Opening **10 minutes** **(Warm-up, HW support, etc.)**	**Large group:** *Teacher A* conducts and reviews the warm-up. A few students share their creative writing journal. **Small alternative teach group (pre-teach, re-teach, extend):** Teacher B has analyzed the upcoming lesson on inferences and realizes that specific students could benefit from a pre-teach to introduce key terms and a framework to effectively make an inference. Before the lesson, *Teacher B* selects specific students that could benefit from this additional support and emails co-teacher. As students rotate into class, Teacher B gathers these students at the side table. Students will be answering text dependent questions such as "What makes you think he is nervous? Did your inference about ___ change? & What consistencies do these ideas convey? Before students engage with their second reading, Teacher B provides a pre-teach mini-lesson on "inferences." Teacher B provides the five students with an iPad and has them view two-minutes of the LearnZillion video on how making inferences creates meaning and jot down *Aha!s* on post-its. After the video, the teacher provides a "Making Inference Formula Organizer: It Says, I Say, and So" to model how to use background knowledge and explicit language from the text to make an inference. Students read another section of the text and practice using the inference formula with teacher feedback. Students are transitioned back into the whole group. Teacher A transitions the class into a full lesson on "citing strong and thorough textual evidence to support analysis of what the text says explicitly as well as inferences drawn from the text."	Large group	Small group

Example Math Lesson Plan for Alternative Co-teaching

Equations

Objective: Explain each step in solving a simple equation as following from the equality of numbers asserted at the previous step, starting from the assumption that the original equation has a solution. Construct a viable argument to justify a solution method.

Lesson plan	Alternative teaching activity	Teacher A	Teacher B
Body **(Re-teach)**	**Large group:** Students are working in partners to transform an equation into a real-life word problem. They are using Storybird to visually share their real-life word problem. **Small alternative teach group (pre-teach, re-teach, extend):** As students are working in partners in the whole group. Teacher B calls a student that was absent the day before and five students who have similar errors in solving equations (data was collected and analyzed from the exit ticket the day before). With the small group, Teacher B walks through solving an equation using a self-monitoring equation bookmark that the learning specialist created: Don't Call Me After Midnight (DCMAM) *D*istribute *C*ombine LikeTerms *M*ove variable *A*dd or Subtract *M*ultiply or Divide Students are each provided a bookmark and they use the bookmark to follow each step modeled. Students practice twice with the teacher using this mnemonic and once independently. Teacher B provides feedback. Teacher B sends students back to their seats so they can create their real-life equation. Teacher A and B quickly conference and circulate to support all students.	Large group	Small alternative group

*Note: Teacher B is the Content Expert in this example.

Station Co-teaching R.E.V. Up Support Guide

Benchmark/Objectives:

Essential questions:

Enduring understandings:

Skills and knowledge:

Student's IEP goals and accommodations:

Review of student data for groupings:

Teacher	*Teacher*	*Student-led station (s)*
Objective(s): **Activity(ies):** **Material(s):** **Evaluation:** **Time at station:**	**Objective(s):** **Activity(ies):** **Material(s):** **Evaluation:** **Time at station:**	**Objective(s):** **Activity(ies):** **Material(s):** **Evaluation:** **Time at station:**

Sample Secondary Lesson Plan for Station Co-teaching

Lesson on Plot Diagram

Time frame: 1 hour

In this lesson, students will learn how to make a plot diagram. The plot diagram will be used as an organizational tool to map the events in a story. This mapping of plot structure allows readers and writers to visualize the key features of stories. The students will create a plot diagram in order to learn how the sequence of events in a story creates a plot structure.

CCSS.ELALiteracy.RL.6.3 (grade 6): Describe how a particular story's or drama's plot unfolds in a series of episodes as well as how the characters respond or change as the plot moves toward a resolution.

Formative assessment: Students will complete a brief informal pre-assessment to determine their level of understanding of a plot diagram and the terminology that accompanies it. Students will be drawing a plot structure and labeling the parts they can remember from previous learning experiences. The students will be shown an example of a plot structure with the correct labeling of all parts on the interactive Smart Board: exposition, rising action, climax, falling action, and resolution. The students will volunteer to come up to the Smart Board and drag and drop the terms into the correct places on the plot structure diagram. A "thumbs up, thumbs down" assessment will be used to evaluate their own work. This assessment will guide teacher groupings for the station activities so that teachers can differentiate the questions and tasks for the various groupings. Students will be asked questions by the teacher as they work with their small groups to create a plot structure from a story they all are familiar with. In doing so, the teacher will be able to observe their comprehension levels and ability to understand plot progression.

Summative assessment: The students' final product of a plot diagram will be assessed. The diagram will have to show correct progression of plot along with properly labeling the exposition, rising action, climax, falling action, and resolution.

Materials and supplies:

- Copies of plot structure diagram filled in with correct terminology.
- Blank copies of plot structure diagram.
- Copies of plot structure diagram example.
- ReadWriteThink.com plot structure diagram interactive.
- Flocabulary Video: Plot Elements
- "All Summer in a Day" text.
- Smart Board plot diagram interactive file created by teacher.
- Consensogram.

Lesson plan adapted from CAST Universal Design for Learning Lesson Builder @http://udlexchange.cast.org/.

Teacher: *10 minutes*	*Teacher:* *10 minutes*	*Independent Station(s)* *10 minutes*
Activity(ies): An example plot structure diagram will be reviewed with the students on the Smart Board. The teacher will choose a story read previously in the school year and complete a plot diagram for it so students can see the process done correctly. Students will also be provided a hard and digital copy of the example as well.	**Activity(ies):** An example plot structure diagram will be reviewed with the students. The teacher will choose a story read previously in the school year. The teacher will model how to complete a plot diagram so that students can see the process.	**Activity(ies):** The students will watch a short video from flocabulary.com on Teacher Tube titled "Plot Elements." This will give students a digital, visual, and audio/musical representation of the elements of plot. The dialogue of the song is provided in captions at the bottom of the screen.

Teacher: *10 minutes*	*Teacher:* *10 minutes*	*Independent Station(s)* *10 minutes*
Within their small groups, students will choose a story that they are all familiar with, from elementary school and create a plot diagram. To create the plot diagram students can use the digital interactive on the "Read, Write, Think" website or fill in a handout of a plot diagram. Teacher will ask questions to check for understanding and provide feedback. (Examples of possible stories: Little Red Riding Hood, Three Little Pigs, Goldie Locks and the Three Bears, The Very Hungry Caterpillar, etc.).	Within the small group students will work together with sentence strips to match elements of the plot with the details of another story. Teacher will ask questions to check for understanding and provide feedback.	Once the video is over, students will complete a short activity on elements of plot. Students will work together to match elements of the plot with details from a story they have previously read. *As a scaffold, provide an outline or student work product from the previously read story.

Whole group:
Teachers and students debrief the stations. Students will be given a supplementary short story titled, "All Summer in a Day," by Ray Bradbury. After teachers prepare students for the reading, students can choose which version of the text they would like to use for the first read. The text will be provided on audio, hard copy, and digitally. After the students read the short story, they will create a plot structure diagram correctly showing the sequence of significant events in the story. Each of the parts of the plot structure diagram should be included (exposition, rising action, climax, falling action, and resolution). Students will go back to their goals for the lesson and evaluate their ability to correctly fill in a plot structure diagram. As an exit ticket, students will place a dot on a consensogram displaying their understanding of a plot structure diagram. The categories will be: I can do this on my own and can explain how to do it, I can do this on my own or I can do this if I get help or see an example.

Sample Activities for Elementary Station Co-teaching

<table>
<tr><th>Teacher:

Guided reading lesson</th><th>Teacher:

Writing station</th><th>Student-led station(s)

Partner work: word workstation</th></tr>
<tr><td>Teacher uses data and strategically chooses a text for various student groupings and has students:
♦ Point and locate word features
♦ Find or match letters and words in book.
♦ Create sketches to represent the feature sounds or words in the story.
♦ Act out key ideas/events
♦ Use modeled word analysis and reading strategies
There are multiple ways to engage students in reading the text:
♦ Each student has a copy of the text (preferred).
♦ Text is projected for the group to see.
♦ Small groups of students engage with the text.</td><td>Teacher supports the various partner groupings in this station and collects data on the following activity:
In partners:
♦ One student dictates a sentence:
• I painted a picture of my dog.
• I like to learn about whales.
• The Earth is the third planet from the sun.
• My father bought me ice cream. My brother plays soccer with me.
• My mother reads me books at night.
♦ The other student writes the sentence in their notebook, scoops the sentence, and highlights the trick words.
♦ Switch roles allowing the other student to dictate and the other student to write.
Support: Provide visual pictures to support some sentences.</td><td>In partners, students:
♦ Take out their magnetic letters and magnetic letter board.
♦ Partner 1 reads the nonsense words below to their partner:
florp, flarp, stri, strid, slint, slernt, stend, stemp, sharf, shirf, che, chur, parst, charst, losrt, lerst, plebe, plube.
♦ Partner 2 listens to the nonsense words and builds the words with magnetic letters.
Challenge: Students must use and write trick words in a sentence.</td></tr>
</table>

Note: During co-planning time, co-teachers should use data to strategically group and partner students.
For more phonics activities for workstations visit http://www.education.com/activity/phonics.

Parallel Co-teaching R.E.V Up Guide

Benchmark/Objectives:

Essential questions:

Skills and knowledge:

Summative assessment/task:

Student's IEP goals and accommodations:

Review of student data for groupings:

Group A	*Group B*
Teacher:	**Teacher:**
Student names:	**Student names:**
Lesson sequence: **Materials:** **Evaluation:**	**Lesson sequence:** **Materials:** **Evaluation:**
What does our student data show? How will we differentiate instruction to support student achievement?	

Example of Parallel Co-teaching in Action

<table>
<tr><td colspan="2">During co-planning, Mr. Rick and Ms. Ross analyzed and sorted student's written summary responses for an open response question in social studies. Based on the data and the structure of the text, the teachers realize that some students had difficulty sequencing and organizing the many events. The co-teachers decide that about half of the class could benefit from additional scaffolds to support reading comprehension. Based on learners, the co-teachers use the parallel co-teaching model to fix up specific students' comprehension gaps in order to move students to the next "level of comprehension."</td></tr>
<tr><td colspan="2">As students enter the classroom, the teachers hand each student a blue or red color token which indicates the section of the classroom they should gather at (the teachers have practiced and reinforced this routine). Once students arrive at their designated space in the classroom, each teacher begins their targeted instruction.</td></tr>
<tr><td>Group A</td><td>Group B</td></tr>
<tr><td>Lesson sequence: (15 minutes)

Students create a three-component criteria for success rubric and peer edit each other's "Objective Summary Frame (who, what, where, when, why, one sentence summary)" for the informational text.
The teacher extends students learning by having them consider information that should be included and how they could increase their level of detail.
Students rewrite their written responses using the peer and teacher feedback.</td><td>Lesson sequence: (15 minutes)

The teacher facilitates student discussion on the text: students identify the seven key events in the story and write each event on a blank sentence strip. The teacher strategically uses text dependent questions to support students in re-reading the text, identifying the big ideas and describing how the seven main events shape the outcome of the text (for their "objective summary frame").
After each strip is visually displayed, the teacher has students complete their own personal sequence diagram connecting the seven events. The teacher instructs students to highlight the "who, what, where, when, why" using evidence from the text on their sequence diagram.
Students use their sequence diagram to rewrite their written responses.</td></tr>
<tr><td colspan="2">Whole group debrief:
A few students from both groups share their written responses with the entire class and the teachers provide feedback. Teachers engage students in the next phase of reading the text. Students re-read the text to develop their ability to interpret structure and author's craft.</td></tr>
</table>

Note: The objective of the lesson does not change; based on student data, students in group B are provided additional targeted scaffolds to support reading comprehension.

Co-teaching Practices: Successfully Navigating Conflict

What can cause conflict?	*Strategies for mediating conflict*
Differences in teaching styles	Complete and revisit the Co-teaching Choice Boards to reflect and review team progress and commitments
Differences in philosophical approaches to teaching and learning	♦ Develop a mindset, "It's all about our students"
Ethics and beliefs systems	♦ Anticipate possible barriers and create resolutions and potential solutions (use Collaborative Solutions Planner attached) ♦ Consider asking someone to mediate (a colleague trusted by both parties)
The feeling of insecurity	♦ Hear each other out fully and without emotion
Fear of something new or change	♦ Focus on student data and student need ♦ Trying saying "yes" before "no" ♦ Agree to always compromise
Issues of trust	♦ Use honesty and respect in your conversations ♦ Speak from the "I" POV vs "You" POV ♦ Clarify roles and expectations ♦ Focus on each other's areas of strength
The use of terms like "my students" and "your students"	♦ Agree to use Inclusive language and build a relationship where it is safe to make mistakes
Maximizing planning time	♦ Use an agenda to stay on task (focus on the solution and 1-2 action steps) ♦ Use an agreed upon lesson planner to share important lesson items and content matter with each other ♦ Divide responsibilities

Appendix B

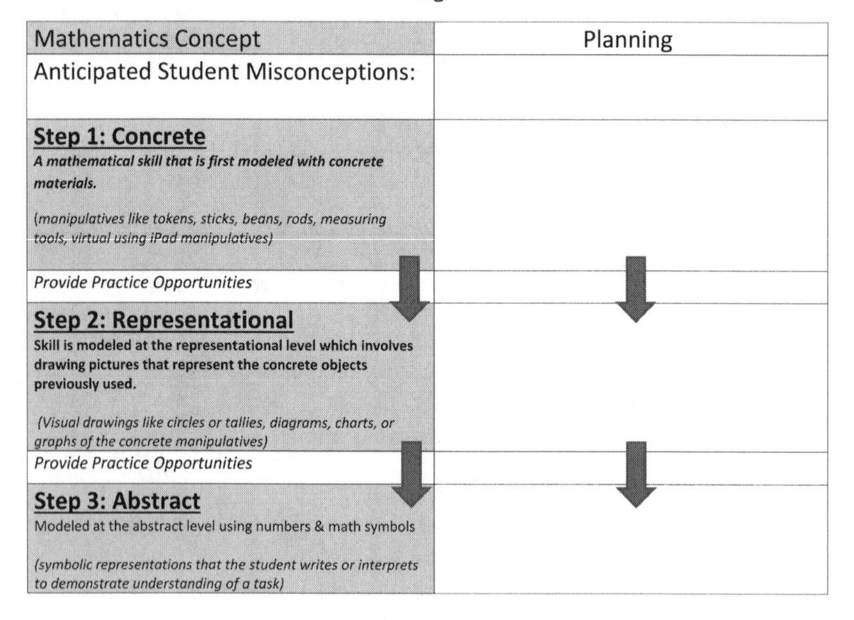

Concrete-Representational-Abstract (CRA)
Planning Sheet

Mathematics Concept	Planning
Anticipated Student Misconceptions:	
Step 1: Concrete ***A mathematical skill that is first modeled with concrete materials.*** *(manipulatives like tokens, sticks, beans, rods, measuring tools, virtual using iPad manipulatives)*	
Provide Practice Opportunities	
Step 2: Representational **Skill is modeled at the representational level which involves drawing pictures that represent the concrete objects previously used.** *(Visual drawings like circles or tallies, diagrams, charts, or graphs of the concrete manipulatives)*	
Provide Practice Opportunities	
Step 3: Abstract Modeled at the abstract level using numbers & math symbols *(symbolic representations that the student writes or interprets to demonstrate understanding of a task)*	

Specially Designed Instruction (SDI): Communication

Specially designed instruction is the instruction provided to a student with a disability who has an individualized education plan (IEP) to help him/her master IEP goals/objectives and ensure access to and progress in the general curriculum. Specially designed instruction goes beyond differentiated instruction and addresses the unique needs that exist because of a student's disability. Specially designed instruction should be implemented in addition to, not in place of, differentiated instruction.

Area of impact	*Specially designed instruction (SDI)* *What the "teacher does" through instructional practices*	*Accommodations or modifications* *What the student will use to access curriculum and make significant progress*
Nonverbal	◆ Scaffolded instruction: visual, written, verbal, physical, picture prompts, and cues ◆ Scaffolded instruction of visual cue cards (cued speech) ◆ System of least prompts ◆ Direct instruction of American Sign Language ◆ Multiple-modality strategies ◆ Explicit instruction use of body language ◆ Modeling of how to attend to speaker • Computer-assisted instruction	◆ Visual, written, tactual, verbal, physical, picture prompts, and cue – Hand under hand vs. hand over hand physical guidance/exploration ◆ American Sign Language ◆ Communication systems and switch-activated devices ◆ Augmentative and high-technology communication devices ◆ Dynamic screens ◆ Communication boards/books/cards ◆ Picture-based communication ◆ Establishing and maintaining eye contact ◆ Switch accessible and scan accessible ◆ Educational interpreter ◆ Other
Listening comprehension	◆ Modeling ◆ Chunking ◆ Written prompts ◆ Preview – teach – review ◆ Outline skills and listening guides ◆ Teach note taking/identification of relevant information ◆ Repeat what is heard (student) ◆ visual prompts/cues/aids ◆ Paraphrasing/summarizing ◆ Mnemonic strategies ◆ Guided practice of listening strategies ◆ Corrective feedback and frequent comprehension checks ◆ Highlighting key words	◆ Repeated directions ◆ Frequent comprehension checks ◆ Visual prompts ◆ Alternative note-taking ◆ Extended processing time and allow wait time (5–10 seconds) ◆ Paraphrasing, rephrasing, simplifying and summarizing ◆ Previewing questions ◆ Preferential seating ◆ Advanced organizer ◆ Focus, concrete statements (avoid abstract language) ◆ Digitized recorder ◆ Digitized/electronic formatted materials ◆ Highlighting key words ◆ Listening and note guides

(Continued)

Area of impact	*Specially designed instruction (SDI)* *What the "teacher does" through instructional practices*	*Accommodations or modifications* *What the student will use to access curriculum and make significant progress*
Expressive language/oral expression	◆ Scaffolded instruction in how to respond to verbal prompts ◆ Scaffolded instruction in how to respond to cue cards ◆ Modeling how to respond to visual prompts ◆ Guided repetitions ◆ Guided rehearsal, role play, use of scripts ◆ Time delay strategies ◆ Modeling ◆ Instruction in conversational skills (i.e., initiating, maintaining, ending) ◆ Word retrieval drills: categories, attributes, functions ◆ Questioning techniques ◆ Sentence Strips (sentence builders) ◆ Verbal, picture, visual, written prompts/cues	◆ Verbal prompts and cue cards ◆ Extended response time ◆ Allow written tests ◆ Recorded materials ◆ Preferential seating ◆ Directions in multiple forms (i.e., restate, rephrase, oral directions) ◆ Oral reading on volunteer basis or pre-preparation time ◆ Rehearsal, use of scripts ◆ Alternate means for demonstrating learning in place of oral reports (i.e., displays, projects, technology, written, etc.) ◆ Video self-modeling ◆ Questioning techniques ◆ Thesaurus to find words to write or say ◆ Assistive technology like Word prediction software (Read, Write, Gold) ◆ Structured outline or graphic organizer to plan written assignments or presentations ◆ Use demonstrations or video-recorded responses for classroom assignments

Voice	◆ Modeling ◆ Vocal strategies ◆ Social skills instruction ◆ Calming and relaxation strategies ◆ Instruction in self-monitoring strategies ◆ Visualization techniques ◆ Instruction in recognition of vocal abusive patterns ◆ Oral motor intervention ◆ Social stories ◆ Direct teaching of replacement behaviors	◆ Self-monitoring checklists ◆ Calming strategies cues ◆ Variety of questioning techniques ◆ Signal system for recognizing abusive vocal patterns ◆ Behavior management plan ◆ Limit amount of talking time ◆ Develop signal system so student will know when abusive patterns are being used ◆ Control environment to eliminate opportunities for vocal abuse ◆ Assistive technology or tape recorders
Fluency	◆ Instruction on maintaining eye contact ◆ Instruction using choral reading and speaking responses ◆ Instruction using reading responses ◆ Instruction of relaxation strategies ◆ Modeling ◆ Starter techniques ◆ Auditory cues ◆ Chunking of words or sentences ◆ Easy onset ◆ Prolongation ◆ Breathing techniques	◆ Extended response time ◆ Opportunity to speak first in oral group situations ◆ Individual instead of group presentations ◆ Relaxation strategies ◆ Self-monitoring ◆ Allow adequate response time ◆ Allow wait time ◆ Peer buddy ◆ Modeling ◆ Calming techniques ◆ Only call on student to answer questions when student volunteers

(Continued)

Area of impact	*Specially designed instruction (SDI)* *What the "teacher does" through instructional practices*	*Accommodations or modifications* *What the student will use to access curriculum and make significant progress*
	◆ Counseling techniques ◆ Role playing ◆ Tactile cues ◆ Self-monitoring techniques ◆ Visualization ◆ Timed repeating reading	◆ Chunking ◆ Assistive technology ◆ Assistance with speaking tasks
Receptive Language	◆ Scaffolded instruction to use visual, written, picture prompts, and cues ◆ Modeling ◆ System of least prompts ◆ Simultaneous prompting ◆ Time delay ◆ Instruction in how to respond to verbal cues ◆ Instruction of core vocabulary with cue cards ◆ Instruction in using visualization ◆ Instruction in using verbal rehearsal ◆ Cloze procedures ◆ Auditory bombardment of language targets ◆ Verbal repetition ◆ Instruction of mnemonic strategies ◆ Pre-teach critical information	◆ Preferential seating ◆ Repetition of directions ◆ Simple directions ◆ Gestures and visual cues ◆ Paraphrasing and rephrasing ◆ Visual prompts ◆ Concrete to abstract representations ◆ Picture schedule • Picture cues • Tactual cues • Object to picture schedule • Calendar/routine system • Sentence strips • Assistive technology; tape recorders • Self-cueing strategies • Gradually building complexity of task • Teacher wait time • Preferential seating

	◆ Instruction for understanding of humor and absurdities ◆ Explicitly teach elements of critical thinking ◆ Explicit instruction in how to make inferences and predictions ◆ Explicit instruction in how to draw conclusions and make generalizations ◆ Visualization ◆ Direct instruction ◆ Auditory bombardment of language targets ◆ Verbal repetition ◆ Mnemonic strategies	• State and restate directions (repeat directions) • Speak with slow rate of speech • Simplify and paraphrase directions • Use gestures and visual cues • Rephrase directions • Establish routine to obtain student attention • Use picture schedule and cues
Pragmatics	◆ Instruction using social scripting ◆ Instruction using social stories ◆ Instruction using written prompts ◆ Modeling and role-playing ◆ Instruction in how to respond to verbal prompting ◆ Guided responding ◆ Instruction in environmental prompting (i.e., personal space awareness) ◆ Chaining and shaping ◆ Video self-modeling ◆ Instruction in conversational turn-taking, initiating/terminating conversation, commenting, and asking questions ◆ Instruction in relevant emotion/feeling words	◆ Role-playing ◆ Monitoring and quick feedback ◆ Peer buddy/monitoring ◆ Environmental prompts (i.e., personal space awareness) ◆ Providing/addressing sensory issues ◆ Provide opportunities for: turn taking, initiating/terminating conversation, commenting, asking questions ◆ Assistive technology

(Continued)

Area of impact	*Specially designed instruction (SDI)* *What the "teacher does" through instructional practices*	*Accommodations or modifications* *What the student will use to access curriculum and make significant progress*
Articulation/ phonology	◆ Auditory discrimination training ◆ Modeling and mirror training ◆ Oral motor exercises ad prompts ◆ Visual and touch prompts/cues ◆ Repetitive drill/trials ◆ Time delay ◆ Minimal pair drills ◆ Auditory bombardment ◆ Guided rehearsal ◆ Phoneme placement cues and Elkonin boxes ◆ Tactile and visual prompts/cues ◆ Discrete phoneme production training ◆ Oral motor desensitization/stimulation ◆ Cued speech ◆ Vocal practice and rehearsal ◆ Phonemic awareness training ◆ Direct instruction ◆ Open and closed set training	◆ Use of assistive technology, FM system, speech to text/text to speech, and tape recorders ◆ Tactile, visual, and kinesthetic cues ◆ Extended response time ◆ Verbal cues for correct speech samples and sounds ◆ Modeling of correct speech patterns when student makes incorrect speech patterns ◆ Oral prompts and short statements (eliminate abstract language) ◆ Preferential seating ◆ Vocabulary cue cards and color-coded key words ◆ Step-by-step directions ◆ Allow adequate response time ◆ Educational interpreter ◆ Previewing questions ◆ Outline skills and paraphrasing ◆ Step-by-step directions (eliminate abstract language) ◆ Frequent comprehension checks ◆ Content-based vocabulary ◆ Personal directory ◆ Computer support ◆ Monitor and provide feedback (oral, signed, etc.)

Specially Designed Instruction (SDI): Vocational

Specially designed instruction is the instruction provided to a student with a disability who has an individualized education plan (IEP) to help him/her master IEP goals/objectives and ensure access to and progress in the general curriculum. Specially designed instruction goes beyond differentiated instruction and addresses the unique needs that exist because of a student's disability. Specially designed instruction should be implemented in addition to, not in place of, differentiated instruction.

Area of impact	*Specially designed instruction (SDI)* *What the "teacher does" through instructional practices*	*Accommodations and/or modifications* *What the student will use to access curriculum and make significant progress*
Task Completion/ On-Task Behavior	◆ Explicit instruction in how to use self-talk ◆ Modeling video self-modeling ◆ Differential reinforcement ◆ Instruction in how to use checklist to self-monitor/evaluate ◆ Explicit instruction in student task analysis ◆ Direct instruction in using graphic organizers ◆ System of least prompts ◆ Simultaneous prompting ◆ Explicit instruction in how to respond to cueing (verbal, nonverbal, visual, picture, photo, etc.) ◆ Guided practice in alternative note-taking ◆ Pre-teaching critical information and vocabulary ◆ Re-teaching through repetition and summarization of important points, particularly at the conclusion of the lecture or discussion ◆ Pre-teaching assignments ◆ Scaffolded instruction for taking breaks	◆ Chunking assignments ◆ Use of visual timers and pacing ◆ Dual set of materials for school and home ◆ Paraphrasing ◆ Extended time ◆ Rubrics and scoring guides ◆ Peer tutor ◆ Mentors ◆ Oral presentation of materials ◆ Redirection and corrective feedback ◆ Behavior contract ◆ Environmental adaptations ◆ Assistive technology ◆ Written prompts or directions ◆ Information broken down into steps or key components ◆ Important ideas written on the board or overhead transparencies with different colors for emphasis or coding ◆ Active involvement with the content through discussion, small group interaction, or problem-solving activities ◆ Repetition and summarization of important points, particularly at the conclusion of the lecture or discussion ◆ Structured organizers for note taking, such as a copy of overheads, outline of lecture, or graphic organizers ◆ Copies of notes taken by peer ◆ Recorded class lectures and discussion ◆ Time to meet with the instructor after class for clarification.

Task Completion/ On-Task Behavior	♦ Pre-teaching new vocabulary introduced prior to a lesson, a glossary of terms ♦ Overview of lessons or advance organizers ♦ Material presented in a logical/ sequential manner and with explicit cues to shift from one aspect to the next	♦ Work systems ♦ Graphic organizers ♦ Cue cards (i.e., definitions, examples, models, flow chart) ♦ Preview assignment ♦ Personal copy of rules and expectations ♦ Specific role and responsibility when working in a group ♦ Positive reinforcement for following class rules ♦ Adult or peer to seek assistance when the teacher is unavailable ♦ Seat away from distractions such as windows, air vents, doors, resource areas, and other individuals who may disrupt the student ♦ Quiet place to complete independent work ♦ Tasks that can be completed in short periods of time ♦ Structured opportunities to get up and move
Organization	♦ Modeling through use of video self-monitoring ♦ Differential reinforcement ♦ Scaffolded instruction in using verbal prompts and cues ♦ Scaffolded instruction in using visual prompts and cues direct instruction in organization systems ♦ Mnemonics ♦ Advance organizers	♦ Duplicates ♦ Extended time ♦ Shortened assignment ♦ Dual set of materials for school and home ♦ Step-by-step instructions ♦ Color/tactual coding of materials ♦ Assignment notebook ♦ Calendar ♦ Peer tutor/buddy ♦ Dividers and organizers ♦ Work systems ♦ Contracts with reinforcements

(Continued)

Area of impact	*Specially designed instruction (SDI)* *What the "teacher does" through instructional practices*	*Accommodations and/or modifications* *What the student will use to access curriculum and make significant progress*
Working independently	◆ Strategy instruction ◆ Instruction in using verbal prompts and cues ◆ Instruction in using visual prompts and cues ◆ Instruction using task analysis	◆ Shortened assignments ◆ Study carrel ◆ Work systems ◆ Assignments and tasks given in segments ◆ Redirection (verbal, nonverbal, physical, visual, etc.) ◆ Faded prompts ◆ Positive/corrective feedback ◆ Assignments divided into parts with corresponding due dates ◆ Individual responsibility checklist with checkpoints along the way ◆ Reward system to motivate assignment completion – let the student engage in an activity of choice following the completion of a required assignment ◆ Picture schedules ◆ Access to learning resources and instructional materials outside of class like: • Digital recorder • Digitized/electronic formatted materials • Highlighting key words • Listening guides

Specially Designed Instruction Planning Form

This form is intended to be used as a planning guide to assist in the determination of specially designed instruction and amount of services based on students' impact of disability.

Description of area of need and/or impact of disability	*Required service and goal*	*Specially designed instruction Teacher actions during service delivery*	*Amount of service time required to address the area of need*	*Data collection*
	Required service: Goal:			
	Required service: Goal:			

Appendix C

Choice Board Activity

Objective: ____________________ **Unit/Theme:** ____________________

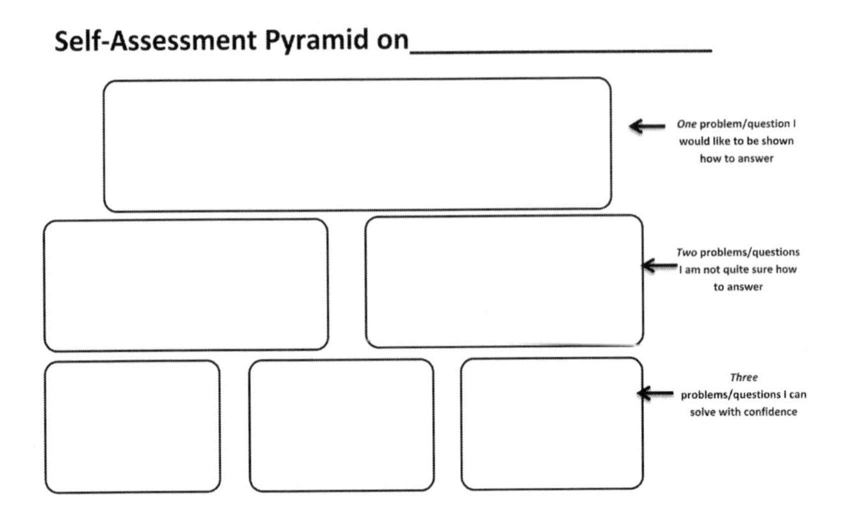
Self-Assessment Pyramid on______________________
One problem/question I would like to be shown how to answer
Two problems/questions I am not quite sure how to answer
Three problems/questions I can solve with confidence

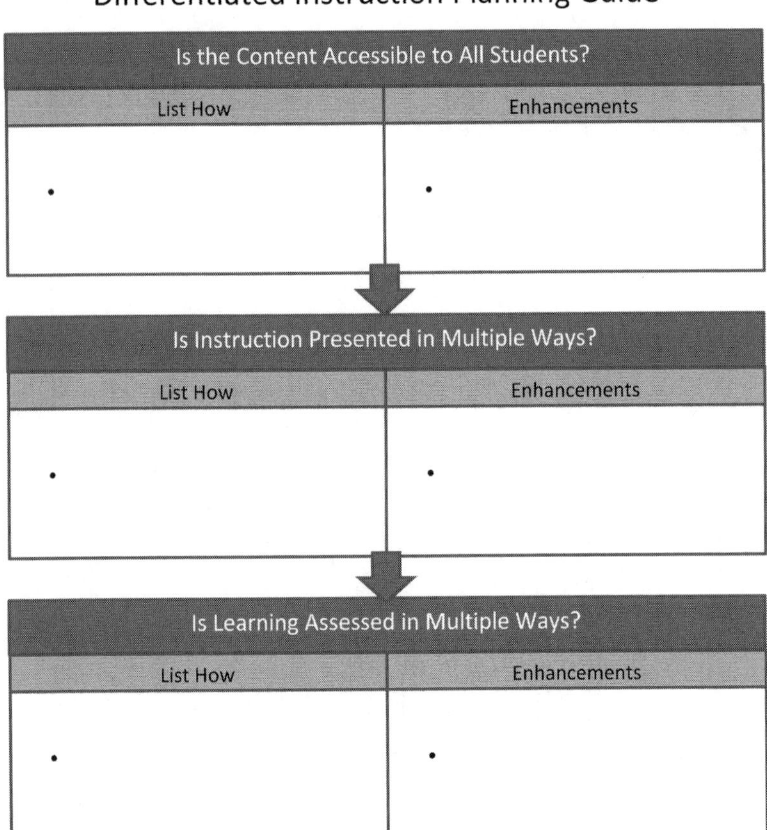
Differentiated Instruction Planning Guide
Is the Content Accessible to All Students?
List How
Enhancements
•
•
Is Instruction Presented in Multiple Ways?
List How
Enhancements
•
•
Is Learning Assessed in Multiple Ways?
List How
Enhancements
•
•

Appendix D

<table>
<tr><th colspan="2">QAR
Question-Answer Relationship</th></tr>
<tr><td colspan="2">In the book</td></tr>
<tr><td>Right there</td><td>Think and search questions</td></tr>
<tr><td>The answer is in one place in the text
♦ Reread
♦ Scan
♦ Look for key words

How old was Amelia when she became the youngest person ever to ski to the South Pole?</td><td>The answer is in several places in the text
♦ Skim
♦ Reread
♦ Summarize

What are the different conditions Amelia faced that made her journey challenging?</td></tr>
<tr><td colspan="2">In my head</td></tr>
<tr><td>Author and you</td><td>On my own</td></tr>
<tr><td>The answer is not directly in the text
♦ Reread
♦ Predict
♦ Think critically about what the author says

How would you adapt to traveling through Antarctica?</td><td>The answer is not in the text
♦ Think about what you already know
♦ Think about what you read before
♦ Make connections

What is the coldest temperature ever recorded in Antarctica?</td></tr>
</table>

Alpaboxes

Name of Reader(s): ______________________________

The Book: ______________________________

Directions:

A	B	C	D
E	F	G	H
I	J	K	L
M	N	O	P
Q	R	S	T
U	V	W	XYZ

Directions: Build your questioning cube by cutting out the template along the solid lines and folding along the dotted lines. Tape or glue the flaps. Provide 1 cube to a team of students.

Knowledge

- Who/What is this text about?
- What do you think …will do?
- When did this story/event take place?
- Where?
- How?
- List the facts in order.

Analysis

- What part of the reading was funniest?
- What part was the most exciting?
- What part was the saddest?
- Tell some things that could not have happened in real life.
- Which things were fact, and which were opinions?
- What was the purpose of...?

Application

- Who would you choose...?
- What would happen if...?
- How would you...?
- Do you know someone like...?
- Would you do the same thing in the same situation...?
- If you had to...what would you do?

Comprehension

- What is meant by... ?
- Can you describe... ?
- What is the difference... ?
- What is the main idea...?
- Why did... ?
- Explain why... ?

Synthesis

- Retell one event from an animal's point of view.
- How could we/you...?
- Make up another ending to the story that still fits the details.
- Rewrite a sentence from the reading but change one thing in it.
- Write a new title for this story.

Evaluation

- Was the main character in this reading good or bad? Why?
- Which is better...?
- Would you agree that...?
- What is your opinion of...?
- Were they right to do...? Why? Or why not?
- Compare two characters in the reading. Tell which one you think is better and why.

Accommodations	Classroom												Testing						

Data Collection Sheet

Block 7 Teacher: ____________________________

Week of ________ DataCollector(s):________________________

Student goals	*Date*	*Date*	*Date*	*Date*	*Date*
Mike Jones Be able to count change up to five dollars using various pennies, nickles, dimes, quarters, and dollars with 80% accuracy on three out of five opportunities					
Susie White Be able to identify a given coin's worth and count change up to three dollars using various pennies, nickels, dimes, quarters, and dollars with 80% accuracy on three opportunities					
Michael Lawerence To accurately use a visual calendar to locate specific information, given minimum indirect verbal prompting with 90% accuracy					
Meredith Stone Count out various bills up to $10 to cover four specified amounts with verbal prompts for three trials as documented quarterly to support her with her DRS program					
Samir El-Nakeeb Be able to count change up to two dollars using various pennies, nickels, dimes, quarters, and dollars with 80% accuracy on three opportunities					

(Continued)

Student goals	*Date*	*Date*	*Date*	*Date*	*Date*
Khalid Mounaji Correctly identify numbers 11 through 20 on four of five trials so that he may access public transportation to travel to a laundry facility					
Mehdi Mounaji Correctly identify numbers 1, 2, and 3 on four of five trials to facilitate Mehdi counting towels in hotel housekeeping					
Charlie Rodriguez Charlie will count money amounts up to five dollars with 100% accuracy on four out of five observed opportunities quarterly					
Nazish Shah Will correctly sort pennies from nickels, dimes, and quarters on four of five opportunities to prepare to use public transportation to a jobsite of her interest					
Dominique Turner Solve problems involving time and money, with 80% accuracy on three occasions quarterly, in preparation for working as a food preparation worker after graduation					
Alejandra Alvarez Identify the numbers from 1 to 5 with 80% accuracy for four out of five trials					

Key
+ Met objective
- Did not meet objective
P Prompt given

	Reading			*Writing*				*Math*				*Functional*
Student Names												*Student specific goals may include functional skills*

References

Archer, A.L., & Hughes, C.A. (2011). *Explicit instruction: Effective and efficient teaching*. Guilford Press.

Baker, S., Gersten, R., & Lee, D. (2002). A synthesis of empirical research on teaching mathematics to low-achieving students. *Elementary School Journal*, 103(1), 51–73. https://doi.org/10.1086/499715.

Beers, G.K., & Probst, R.E. (2016). *Reading nonfiction: Notice & note stances, signposts, and strategies*. Heinemann.

Beninghof, A.M. (2011). *Co-teaching that works: Structures and strategies for maximizing student learning*. Jossey-Bass.

Biancarosa, C., & Snow, C. E. (2006). Reading next—A vision for action and research in middle and high school literacy: A report to Carnegie Corporation of New York (2nd ed.). *Alliance for Excellent Education*. https://production carnegie.s3.amazonaws.com/filer_public/b7/5f/b75fba81-16cb-422d-ab59-373a6a07eb74/ccny_report_2004_reading.pdf

De La Paz, S. (2007). Managing cognitive demands for writing: Comparing the effects of instructional components in strategy instruction. *Reading & Writing Quarterly*, *23*(3), 249–266. https://doi.org/10.1080/10573560701277609

De La Paz, S., & Graham, S. (2002). Explicitly teaching strategies, skills, and knowledge: Writing instruction in middle school classrooms. *Journal of Educational Psychology*, *94*(4), 687–698. https://doi.org/10.1037/0022-0663.94.4.687

Dieker, L., & Hines, R.A. (2013). *Strategies for teaching content effectively in the inclusive secondary classroom* (13th ed.). Pearson Education.

Englert, C. S. (2009). Connecting the dots in a research program to develop, implement, and evaluate strategic literacy interventions for struggling readers and writers. *Learning Disabilities Research & Practice*, *24*(2), 104–120. https://doi.org/10.1111/j.1540-5826.2009.00284.x

Fitzell, S. (2010). *Co-teaching and collaboration in the classroom*. Cogent Catalyst Publications.

Friend, M.P. (2013). *Co-teach!: A handbook for creating and sustaining effective classroom partnerships in inclusive schools* (2d ed.). Marilyn Friend, Inc.

Fuchs, L. S., Fuchs, D., & Compton, D. (2010). Rethinking response to intervention at middle and high school. *School Psychology Review, 39(1),* 22–28. https://community.ksde.org/LinkClick.aspx?fileticket=UHHfJ7n2cgc%3D&tabid=6150&mid=15106

Gersten, R., Chard, D.J., Jayanthi, M., Baker, S.K., Morphy, P., & Flojo, J. (2009). Mathematics instruction for students with learning disabilities: A meta-analysis of instructional components. *Review of Educational Research*, 79(3), 1202–1242. https://doi.org/10.3102/0034654309334431

Graham, S. (2006). Strategy instruction and the teaching of writing: A meta-analysis. In MacArthur, C. A., Graham, S., & Fitzgerald, J. (Eds.), *Handbook of writing research* (pp. 187–207). The Guilford Press.

Harris, K. R., & Graham, S. (1996). Making the writing process work: Strategies for composition and self-regulation. Cambridge, MA: Brookline Books.

Graham, S., & Perin, D. (2007). *Writing next: Effective strategies to improve writing of adolescents in middle and high schools – A report to Carnegie Corporation of New York.* Alliance for Excellent Education. http://www.all4ed.org/files/WritingNext.pdf.

Grant, R. (1993). Strategic training for using text headings to improve students' processing of content. *Journal of Reading*, 36(6), 482–488. doi:10.2307/40016468.

Greene, R. (2016). Lost and Found: Helping Behaviorally Challenging Students (and, While You're At It, All the Others) (J-B Ed: Reach and Teach). San Francisco, CA: Jossey-Bass.

Hammond, Z. (2015). *Culturally responsive teaching and the brain: Promoting authentic engagement and rigor among culturally and linguistically diverse students*. Thousand Oaks, CA: Corwin.

Harris, K., Graham, S., Mason, L., & Friedlander, B. (2008). *Powerful writing strategies for all students*. Paul H. Brookes Publishing.

Hawbaker, B.W., Balong, M., Buckwalter, S., & Runyon, S. (2001). Building a strong base of support for all students through coplanning. *Teaching Exceptional Children* 33(4), 24–30. https://doi.org/10.1177/004005990103300404

Hawn Foundation, F. (2011). The MindUp curriculum: Brain-focused strategies for learning—and living. Scholastic Teaching Resources.

Hwang, H., & Duke, N. K. (2020). Content counts and motivation matters: Reading comprehension in third-grade students who are English learners. *AERA Open*, 6(1). https://doi.org/10.1177/2332858419899075

Jackson, P.W. (1990). *Life in classrooms*. Teachers College Press.

Legault, L., Green-Demers, I., & Pelletier, L. (2006). Why do high school students lack motivation in the classroom? Toward an understanding of academic motivation and the role of social support. *Journal of Educational Psychology*, 98(3), 567–582. https://doi.org/10.1037/0022-0663.98.3.567

Leinhardt, G., & Zigmond, N. (1988). The effects of self-questioning and story structure training on the reading comprehension of poor readers. *Learning Disabilities Research*, 4(1), 45–51.

Murawski, W. W., & Dieker, L. (2008). 50 ways to keep your co-teacher: Strategies for before, during, and after co-teaching. *TEACHING Exceptional Children*, 40(4), 40–48. https://doi.org/10.1177 004005990804000405

Myers. D (2011, May 11). The three acts of a mathematical story. [Blog post]. Retrieved from https://blog.mrmeyer.com/2011/the-three-acts-of-a-mathematical-story/

National Institute for Literacy. (2007). What content area teachers should know about adolescent literacy. Retrieved from http://lincs.ed.gov/publications/pdf/adolescent_literacy07.pdf

Neal, M. (2012, June). Conferencing Gloves. *Mandy Neal Teaching with Simplicity*. [Blog post]. Retrieved from https://www.teachingwithsimplicity.com

Perin, D. (2007). Best practices in teaching writing to adolescents. In S. Graham, C. MacArthur, & J. Fitzgerald (Eds.), *Best practices in writing* (pp. 242–264). The Guilford Press.

Pierson, R. (2013, May). *Rita Pierson: Every kid needs a champion* [Video file]. Retrieved from https://www.ted.com/talks/rita_pierson_every_kid_needs_a_champion?language=en

Recht, D. R., & Leslie, L. (1988). Effect of prior knowledge on good and poor readers' memory of text. *Journal of Educational Psychology*, 80(1), 16. https://doi.org/10.1037/0022-0663.80.1.16

Shanahan, T., & Shanahan, C. (2008). Teaching disciplinary literacy to adolescents: Rethinking content-area literacy. *Harvard Educational Review*, 78(1), 40–59. https://doi.org/10.17763/haer.78.1.v62444321p602101

Trabasso, T., & Bouchard, E. (2002). Teaching readers how to comprehend text strategically. In C. Collins & M. Pressley (Eds.), *Comprehension instruction: Research-based best practices* (pp. 176–200). The Guilford Press.

Vaughn, S., Swanson, E.A., Roberts, G., Wanzek, J., Stillman-Spisak, S.J., Solis, M., & Simmons, D. (2013). Improving reading comprehension and social studies knowledge in middle school. *Reading Research Quarterly*, 48(1), 77–93. https://doi.org/10.1002/rrq.039

Zoogman, S., Goldberg, S.B., & Hoyt, W.T. et al. (2015). Mindfulness interventions with youth: a meta-analysis. *Mindfulness*, 6, 290–302. https://doi.org/10.1007/s12671-013-0260-4

Further Reading

Brautigan, R. (1967). Karma Repair Kit: Items 1-4. The Communication Company.

Child and Adolescent Health Measurement Initiative. National Survey of Children's Health Data. 2016. Data Resource Center for Child and Adolescent Health supported by the U.S. Department of Health and Human Services, Health Resources and Services Administration (HRSA), Maternal and Child Health Bureau (MCHB). Retrieved 04/06/2020 from www.childhealthdata.org.

Comer, J. (1995). Lecture given at Education Service Center, Region IV. Houston, TX.

Deshler, D. D., & Schumaker, J. B. (1993). Strategy mastery by at-risk students: Not a simple matter. *The Elementary School Journal*, *94*(2), 153–167. https://doi.org/10.1086/461757

Englert, C., & Mariage, T. (1991). Making students partners in the comprehension process: Organizing the reading "posse". *Learning Disability Quarterly*, *14*(2), 123–138. https://doi.org/10.2307%2F1510519

Faggella-Luby, M., Schumaker, J.S., & Deshler, D.D. (2007). Embedded learning strategy instruction: Story-structure pedagogy in heterogeneous secondary literature classes. *Learning Disability Quarterly*, 30(2), 131–147. https://doi.org/10.2307/30035547

Flakes, S. (2019, January 28). *Create - don't deny - access to complex text.* MULTIBRIEFS. http://exclusive.multibriefs.com/content/create-dont-deny-access-to-complex-text/education

Flynn, L.J., Zheng, X., & Swanson, H. (2012). Instructing struggling older readers: A selective meta-analysis of intervention research. *Learning Disabilities Research & Practice.* 27(1), 21–32. https://doi.org/10.1111/j.1540-5826.2011.00347.x

Future of Jobs Report. (2018). World Economic Form. https://www.weforum.org/reports/the-future-of-jobs-report-2018.

Goleman, D., (2005) *Emotional intelligence: Why it can matter more than IQ* (10th anniversary ed.). Bantam Books.

Hattie, J. (2015). The applicability of visible learning to higher education. *Scholarship of Teaching and Learning in Psychology*, 1(1), 79–91. https://doi.org/10.1037/stl0000021.

Hattie, J. (2012). *Visible learning for teachers*. Routledge.

Heinemann, K.S. (2013). *Inclusion: The common core curriculum and the high stakes tests: Boosting the outcomes for struggling learners, grades 5–12*. Heinemann Press.

Jobs, Steve. (2005). Steve Jobs: Stanford commencement address, June 2005.

Kagan. M, Kagan. S. (2015). Cooperative Learning; Workbook edition. Kagan Cooperative Learning.

Kohn, A. (2006). *The homework myth: Why our kids get too much of a bad thing*. Da Capo Life Long.

Marzano, R.J. (2004). *Building background knowledge for academic achievement: Research on what works in schools.* Association for Supervision and Curriculum Development. http://www.ascd.org/ASCD/pdf/siteASCD/video/buildingacademic.pdf

McLaughlin, M. (2013). Read-alouds and recreational reading always! Round-robin reading never! *Reading Today*, 31(1), 2–3.

McLeskey, J., Barringer, D., Billingsley, B., Brownell, M., Jackson, D., Kennedy, M. … Ziegler, D. (2017). High-leverage practices in special education. *Council for exceptional children & CEEDAR center.* https://ceedar.education.ufl.edu/wp-content/uploads/2017/07/CEC-HLP-Web.pdf

Newman, L., Marder, C., & Wagner, M. (2003). Instruction of secondary school students with disabilities in general education academic classes. In M. Wagner, L. Newman, R. Cameto, P. Levine, and C. Marder

(Eds.), *Going to school: Instructional contexts, programs, and participation of secondary school students with disabilities*. Menlo Park, CA: SRI International. http://www.nlts2.org/reports/2003_12/index.html.

Pratt, L.A., & Brody, D.J. (2014) Depression in the U.S. household population, 2009–2012. NCHS data brief, no 172. National Center for Health Statistics. https://www.cdc.gov/nchs/data/databriefs/db172.pdf

Schwarz, K. (2014, January 17). Low-income schools see big benefits in teaching mindfulness. *KQED*. https://www.kqed.org/mindshift/33463/low-income-schools-see-big-benefits-in-teaching-mindfulness

Swanson, E., Hairrell, A., Kent, S., Ciullo, S., Wanzek, J.A., & Vaughn, S. (2014). A synthesis and meta-analysis of reading interventions using social studies content for students with learning disabilities. *Journal of Learning Disabilities*, 47(2), 178–195. https://doi.org/10.1177/0022219412451131

Tuckman, B.W. (1965). Developmental sequence in small groups. *Psychological Bulletin*, *63*(6), 384–399. https://doi.org/10.1037/h0022100

Vaughn, S., Roberts, G., Swanson, E., Wanzek, J., Fall, A., & Stillman-Spisak, S. (2015). Improving middle-school students' knowledge and comprehension in social studies: A replication. *Educational Psychology Review*, 27, 31–50. https://doi.org/10.1007/s10648-014-9274-2

Wexler, N. (2019). Elementary education has gone terribly wrong. *The Atlantic*, August 2019. https://www.theatlantic.com/magazine/archive/2019/08/the-radical-case-for-teaching-kids-stuff/592765/